Harry S. Truman and the Fair Deal

PROBLEMS IN
AMERICAN CIVILIZATION

Under the editorial direction of
the late Edwin C. Rozwenc
Amherst College

Harry S. Truman and the Fair Deal

Edited and with an introduction by

Alonzo L. Hamby
Ohio University

D. C. HEATH AND COMPANY
Lexington, Massachusetts Toronto

For
Marion and Bonnie, Bruce and Carol

International Standard Book Number: 0-669-87080-3

Library of Congress Catalog Card Number: 73-22759

CONTENTS

IV THE POLITICS OF CIVIL RIGHTS

V CIVIL LIBERTIES: THE POLITICS OF LOYALTY

INTRODUCTION

When Harry S. Truman unexpectedly assumed the presidency upon the death of Franklin D. Roosevelt in April 1945, he was diffident, modest, and, many observers believed, frightened of his new and awesome responsibilities. When he left the White House on January 20, 1953, he was a confident, some said cocky, chief executive, certain in his own mind of the essential rightness of his policies and the vindication of history. In the intervening years, Truman and his advisers had shaped some of the most important developments in American foreign policy. They also had dealt with enormous problems at home: the maintenance of a peacetime prosperity within the safe middle course between a runaway inflation and a reversion to the Great Depression of the 1930s, the preservation and extension of the New Deal liberal tradition, the increasing demands of blacks for equality in American society, the crisis of civil liberties which accompanied the emergence of McCarthyism. Their handling of these problems was at least as important as foreign policy in determining their political fortunes and the contours of postwar American life. The pivotal event of the Truman presidency, the election of 1948, was decided almost wholly on issues of domestic reform, and its outcome confirmed that the United States, rather than reverting to "normalcy," would proceed along the path marked out by the New Deal.

Domestic issues alone would make the Truman years a period of great importance. The objective of this book is to examine Truman's handling of those issues. Part I surveys Truman's prepresidential career; Part II contains three conflicting interpretations of the administration's Fair Deal program; Part III examines three distinct phases of the administration's chronological development; Part IV contains different viewpoints on Truman's handling of civil rights problems; and Part V covers Truman's approach to civil liberties. The president's own viewpoint is represented by selections from the medium of communication in which he was most effective, the partisan political speech. The other selections represent the attitudes of contemporaries engaged in the political fights of the immediate postwar era and of historians, some of them barely old enough to remember when Truman was still president, but nonetheless almost as deeply and emotionally involved in the great issues of the period as were its partisan politicians.

Truman's pre–White House career, as Richard Kirkendall demonstrates, embodied in microcosm the modern experience of the Democratic party. Born into a family of Southern Democrats, he moved politically from the country to the city; a white Anglo-Saxon Protestant, he became one of the key figures in an Irish Catholic urban machine; a farmer and small businessman before going into politics, he adopted the welfare liberalism of the New Deal. By the time he became president, he had achieved a degree of identification with every important group in the party, from blacks to Southern segregationists. Practicing what might be called a politics of inclusion, he hoped to keep all these diverse interests within the Democratic fold. Was it a desirable goal to keep seemingly irreconcilable interests inside the party? Or did Truman's attitude contribute to the perpetuation of an unsatisfactory political stalemate?

Richard E. Neustadt, expressing in large measure the administration's own image of itself, argues that Truman's course was consistently in the direction of reform, but that the political situation was too complex and difficult to allow for change on the scale of the New Deal. Nevertheless, he believes, the "legislative balance sheet" was impressive. Truman defended the New Deal against the assaults of reactionary congressmen, obtained passage of laws which built upon and consolidated important New Deal measures, and defined important reform issues for the future. Most conservatives of the time would have agreed with this analysis, but where Neustadt pointed with pride, they viewed with alarm.

While Truman was in office, he absorbed vehement criticism from right-wing Republicans convinced that he was attempting to inflict an alien social-economic system upon America. The intellectual and political leader of this group, Robert A. Taft, was more willing than many of his followers to support limited reforms in such areas as federal aid to education, medical care for the indigent, and public housing. Still, Taft agreed with the essentials of the right-wing attack: Truman's Fair Deal amounted to socialism; socialism of any kind, even the British variety, was ultimately incompatible with political liberty; thus, the Fair Deal, if enacted, would inevitably lead to a totalitarianism as suffocating as that practiced in the Soviet Union. The legislative failure of the Fair Deal's most innovative programs may indicate that many Americans were persuaded by the conservative critique.

A decade and a half after Truman had left the presidency, a very different kind of criticism had developed among young revisionist historians, usually thinking of themselves as radicals and deeply affected by the traumas of the sixties—the Vietnam war, the discovery of poverty, the black revolution. Disillusioned with the "conventional liberalism" of their era—Lyndon Johnson's Great Society—they perceived its precursor, the Fair Deal, as even worse. Barton J. Bernstein's excellent summary of the revisionist viewpoint demonstrates how far the pendulum of criticism had swung. Where Taft had condemned the Fair Deal as socialistic, Bernstein and other New Left historians condemn it for not being socialistic enough. Bernstein depicts Truman's personal qualities of leadership as weak, but he also formulates a critique of Fair Deal liberalism itself. Both the Fair Dealers and the liberals outside the administration, he asserts, were shallow in their analyses of American society and excessively moderate in their programs. As he sees it, they uncritically celebrated pluralistic capitalism, made only token advances in civil rights, and overlooked the problem of poverty.

All historians would agree on at least one proposition—Truman faced difficult problems from the very beginning of his presidency. Upon taking office, he had to establish his authority, meet the military and diplomatic challenges attending the end of World War II, and manage a complex reconversion to a peacetime economy. Of all these massive tasks, "reconversion" was probably the hardest; underneath that abstract term lay a morass of specific difficulties—the menace of depression and unemployment, the threat of inflation, critical labor disputes, consumer shortages—all of them vitally affecting the comfort and welfare of the average citizen. Moreover, intimately connected with reconversion was the effort to revive the

New Deal, a project begun by Roosevelt and taken up by Truman. Mary H. Blewett traces the failure of this endeavor. FDR, she observes, had fared badly when he had adopted adversary tactics in dealing with Congress; it was thus natural for Truman to attempt conciliation, but in the end it was equally futile. Fundamentally, she believes, the president was overwhelmed by deeply rooted political-economic situations which could not be overcome by mere changes in tactics, and the Republican victory in the 1946 congressional elections amounted to a popular repudiation of his first year and a half in office.

After 1946, most political analysts discounted Truman's chances for 1948. The president's prospects seemed even dimmer when he faced revolts from both extremes of the Democratic party, Henry A. Wallace leading a new Progressive party of liberals and radicals disenchanted with the Cold War, J. Strom Thurmond heading the ticket of a States' Rights ("Dixiecrat") party in revolt against Truman's advocacy of civil rights legislation. The president nevertheless engaged in one of the most exhaustive campaigns in American history. Storming across the country, he slugged away at the Republican Congress and at his aloof and confident opponent, Governor Thomas E. Dewey of New York, put across a style which identified him with the "ordinary American," and raised issue after issue designed to remind the voters of bad times under the Republicans. Truman's very narrow victory, as Irwin Ross shows, confounded the "experts" and revealed the durability of the electoral coalition which Franklin D. Roosevelt had created. Yet, although he is sympathetic to Truman, Ross regards the outcome as something less than an unmitigated good. He suggests that a Dewey presidency might have been moderate and constructive; almost certainly, it would have spared the nation the partisan bitterness which led to McCarthyism.

Although the Fair Deal descended from Roosevelt's New Deal and had much in common with it, Alonzo L. Hamby asserts that there were important distinctions between the two. The New Deal had developed in response to an economic depression in which many doubted the survival of capitalism; the Fair Deal took shape during an era of inflationary prosperity. During the thirties, the major international menace had been fascism; in the Truman era, it was communism. Consequently, the Fair Deal was the political manifestation of a new "vital center" liberalism which equated communism with fascism and affirmed the potential of democratic capitalism for expansion and abundance. Successful in encouraging economic growth, the Fair Deal was ultimately unable to devise a political strategy powerful enough to overcome the rise of McCarthyism and the impact of the Korean War.

Where Hamby emphasizes the differences between the Fair Deal and predecessor reform movements, Richard O. Davies examines the Fair Deal from an angle which leads him into a critique of the long-held liberal conviction that social problems could be ameliorated by providing the poor with good living conditions. The Truman administration accepted this belief and in 1949 obtained passage of what seemed to be path-breaking legislation. In practice, public housing was vitiated by inadequate funding, poor administration, and local obstruction, but, Davies believes, the failure of the projects that were actually constructed demonstrates the futility of attacking symptoms rather than causes of social problems.

One area in which the Fair Deal advanced the cause of reform was the Negro drive for civil rights. Despite his Southern background and his rejection of social integration, Truman was a stronger advocate of civil rights than any president who preceded him. He appears to have genuinely believed in fair play and equal opportunity for the Negro, and he was keenly aware that his political interests demanded an appeal to the Northern black vote. He failed to get congressional passage of a broad civil rights program, including a Fair Employment Practices Committee, but he used his executive authority to order the desegregation of the armed forces, and his Justice Department intervened in important civil rights cases before the Supreme Court with *amicus curiae* arguments which attacked the entire legal structure of segregation. Many blacks felt at the time that, as Roy Wilkins put it, Truman had created "a new climate of opinion." Richard M. Dalfiume, arguing that the actual and symbolic importance of military integration was enormous, tends to agree. William C. Berman, writing from a revisionist standpoint, is more skeptical. Admitting that blacks made some progress, he finds it very limited, and he criticizes Truman's motives as crassly political.

If the Truman years represent an era of progress, however limited, in civil rights, they represent an era of retrogression in civil liberties. That the administration bore some responsibility for this

development is undeniable. In 1947, it established ill-conceived procedures to remove disloyal individuals from the federal bureaucracy.
Historians are nearly unanimous in agreeing that this loyalty program
did more harm than good. It subjected many individuals to malicious
accusations without giving them the safeguards, such as the right to
cross-examine their accusers or even be fully informed of the charges
against them, necessary to defend their reputations. The result was
the creation of an atmosphere of conformity and Big Brotherism
throughout the government. The administration also prosecuted the
leaders of the U.S. Communist party for conspiracy to advocate the
violent overthrow of the government, although this amounted in
reality to little more than the advocacy of Communist dogma.

There is some evidence that the administration saw these moves
primarily as political necessities rather than desirable policies, and
while its right hand abused civil liberties its left hand frequently
defended them. In 1950, shortly after the beginning of the Korean
War, Congress responded to popular hysteria about Communist
subversion by passing the McCarran Internal Security Act. Truman
vetoed the bill, denouncing it as unconstitutional sedition legislation; his disapproval was quickly overridden, but later Supreme
Court decisions vindicated his position. In 1951, he attempted to
appoint a blue-ribbon commission to evaluate the loyalty program
and the entire internal security problem, only to have the effort
blocked by right-wing congressmen. Unlike many Democratic politicians, he was not intimidated by the rise of McCarthyism, and, as
his speech to the American Legion indicates, he spoke out strongly
against unfounded accusation and character assassination. Yet
much of what he criticized in the Legion speech could be found
within the administration's own loyalty program.

Given such an ambivalent record, it is not surprising that historians
have disagreed on Truman and civil liberties. Athan Theoharis, a
leading revisionist, argues that Truman was responsible not only for
the loyalty program and the Communist prosecutions but for
McCarthyism in general because he pursued an anti-Soviet foreign
policy and employed anti-Communist rhetoric which created a
popular obsession with subversion. Alan Harper, on the other hand,
believes that, while the administration made mistakes which deserve
criticism, its room for maneuver was very limited, and it was largely
the victim of situations over which it possessed little or no control.

Beneath the historical debate on specific issues lies the question of just how much room Truman actually had for domestic accomplishment within the political environment surrounding his presidency. What could reasonably have been expected of any administration? Liberal-minded academicians tend to assume that almost any social reform is a good thing, that hence a president may be evaluated largely on the basis of the quantity of liberal-oriented change he achieves. But even if the assumption is granted, it must be subjected to the qualification that the American political system is not as receptive to liberal reform during some periods as it is during others. If it took the depression to make possible the New Deal, what could one reasonably expect during a period of inflationary prosperity? Truman's defenders argue that given such conditions, it was an achievement to preserve the heritage of the New Deal, make modest additions to it, and give an initial impetus to the civil rights movement.

If the pro-Truman historians are correct—and the revisionists dispute them—perhaps then the system was at fault. Scholars have gathered abundant evidence to show that the framers of the American constitution sought to diffuse power, protect vested interests, and frustrate rapid change and activist government. But perhaps it is unrealistic to expect any system to solve all our problems without creating new ones, and possibly it is doubly unrealistic to assume that the Truman administration should have anticipated the central concerns of the sixties and seventies and disposed of them for us. On these propositions, as well as on the more specific issues discussed in this book, the reader is ultimately left to his own judgment.

Conflict of Opinion

Was the Fair Deal within the American political tradition?

> It is said that Harry Truman is no Socialist. That makes little difference if all his policies lead to socialism. We are in danger of complete government control. . . . The only way to avoid a creeping socialism is to elect a Republican Congress in 1950 and a Republican president in 1952. . . . The issue is, in fact, the issue between continued progress under liberty and a socialized state.
>
> ROBERT A. TAFT

> We know that the little fellow is the backbone of this country, and we are dedicated to the principle that the government should promote the welfare of all the people. . . .
>
> People who have an opportunity to work and earn, and who have an assured income in their old age, are free. They are free of the fear of poverty. They are free of public or private charity. They can live happier, more useful lives. That's real freedom . . . that's not something to be slandered by trumped-up slogans.
>
> HARRY S. TRUMAN

Was Truman a sincere reformer and was the Fair Deal a successful reform movement?

> . . . Truman had satisfied the needs of his party in 1944. He had been born and raised in its Southern wing, had received his education in the realities of politics as a member of a Democratic city machine, and had been converted to the New Deal as he attempted to move on to the national political stage in 1934. As he had developed, he had not switched from one type of Democrat to another; he had added one to another, layer by layer, as he moved along.
>
> RICHARD S. KIRKENDALL

> As a consolidator, as a builder on foundations, Truman left an impressive legislative record; the greater part achieved, of course, in less than two years' time and by a single Congress. Moreover as protector, as defender, wielder of the veto against encroachments on the liberal preserve, Truman left a record of considerable success—an aspect of the Fair Deal not to be discounted.
>
> RICHARD E. NEUSTADT

> Even had all of the Fair Deal been enacted, liberal reform would have left many millions beyond the benefits of government. The very poor, the marginal men, those neglected but acknowledged by the New Deal, went ultimately unnoticed by the Fair Deal.
>
> BARTON J. BERNSTEIN

Did Truman and the Fair Deal advance the cause of civil rights?

You spoke, Sir, when you knew that many powerful influences in your own party (and in the party of the opposition) would not heed you. You reiterated your beliefs and restated your demands for legislation when political expediency dictated a compromise course. This is sheer personal courage. . . .

As you leave the White House you carry with you the gratitude and affectionate regard of millions of your Negro fellow citizens who, in less than a decade of your leadership, inspiration and determination, have seen the old order change right before their eyes.

ROY WILKINS to HARRY S. TRUMAN

. . . Centrist politician that he was, Truman moved only because he had no choice: Negro votes and the demands of the Cold War, not simple humanitarianism—though there may have been some of that—produced whatever token gains Negroes were to make in the years Truman inhabited the White House.

WILLIAM C. BERMAN

Was the Truman administration antilibertarian in its management of internal security issues?

Real Americanism means that we will protect freedom of speech—we will defend the right of people to say what they think, regardless of how much we may disagree with them. . . .

We want to protect the country against disloyalty—of course we do. We have been punishing people for disloyal acts, and we are going to keep on punishing the guilty whenever we have a case against them. But we don't want to destroy our whole system of justice in the process.

HARRY S. TRUMAN

. . . Truman, unwittingly and admittedly unintentionally, had contributed to the development of this intolerant, hysteric climate. . . .

The nature of Truman's rhetoric and his administration's various foreign policy–internal security decisions during the 1945–1949 period had served to shift the focus of the national debate to national security questions and to legitimate a conservative anticommunism. From an earlier concern over economic security and domestic issues, by 1950 the political debate centered on international developments and national security arguments; an appeal to anticommunism, without clearly defining what this denoted, had become the norm in post-1950 politics.

ATHAN G. THEOHARIS

I HARRY S. TRUMAN: POLITICIAN

Richard S. Kirkendall
TRUMAN'S PATH TO POWER

How do men reach the presidency? In this brief examination of Truman's prepresidential career, Richard S. Kirkendall argues that the Missourian reached the White House not through years of planning or scheming but through the development of a gregarious and pragmatic personality which enabled him to adapt successfully to different political situations and to win friends throughout the Democratic party.

For the biographer of a politician, the most important concept is "power," the ability to affect the behavior of others by rewarding or punishing them, if necessary. This concept supplies this type of scholar with the focus for his study; it suggests his major questions.

Obviously, Harry Truman became for a time a man of power. His power had limits; he could not bring Congress to endorse many of his major proposals on domestic affairs; he could not maintain his party in control of the national government. Nevertheless, he did possess very great power; enough to drop two atomic bombs upon Japan, to send a large amount of economic aid to southern and western Europe, to bring the United States into its first peacetime alliance, to send American troops to the defense of South Korea, and to remove a popular general from command.

How did Truman become a man of power? This is the question I wish to explore here. In handling this question, I need to employ two other concepts of major importance for the biographer. The first is "personality," the individual's patterns of motivations, inner needs, attitudes, and behavior. The second is "situation," the factors and forces external to the individual that affect him significantly and that he in turn may shape.

To understand Truman's path to power, one must understand, in addition to Franklin Roosevelt's health, Truman's personality and the situation within the Democratic party.

Truman's situation was influenced heavily by what Franklin Roosevelt had done to that party. He had helped to make it more complex

From *Social Science* 43 (April, 1968): 67–73. Copyright © 1968 by the Social Science Publishing Company, Inc. Reprinted by permission of the Social Science Publishing Company.

and more powerful. He had accomplished this by adding a New Deal wing to the structure. The old party, a rather small organization since 1894, had been the party of the South and a few Northern urban machines; the new one also contained the urban masses, including the Negroes. In its ranks were the descendants of slaves as well as slaveholders. The new Democracy replaced the Republican party as the nation's majority party.

By 1944, a major feature of the Democratic party was intense internal conflict over policy and control. This conflict had been developing for nearly a decade as a large segment of the Southern wing had grown increasingly unhappy with much of the New Deal. These Southerners had great power in Congress and by cooperation with Republicans there they were able to frustrate Roosevelt on many domestic issues in the late 1930s and early 1940s. As the end of the war approached, the battle grew hotter. Roosevelt and his advisers and supporters began to think of the postwar world and made plans for a revival of the New Deal. Conservative Southern Democrats and their allies sought ways to reduce, or at least check, the enlargement of the New Deal.

In 1944, a focal point of conflict between the contending factions was the nomination of the party's vice-presidential candidate. The ardent New Dealers wished to stick with the incumbent Henry Wallace, who was a leading proponent of the New Deal revival. To Wallace's opponents, James Byrnes of South Carolina seemed a highly desirable substitute. The party did discard the idealistic intellectual who had been serving since 1940 as the vice-president but did not substitute the prominent and experienced Southern politician. Instead, the Democrats turned to a gregarious and pragmatic senator from a border state whose personality seemed to fit the needs of the situation within the party.

Harry Truman had not always been the gregarious person he was in 1944. He had been rather withdrawn as a boy. His thick glasses had hampered his efforts to join in the activities that other boys in Independence enjoyed. He had drawn close to his mother and had turned to books and the piano. The women of the neighborhood had admired him more than the boys did. While not unhappy, the early years of his life were far from satisfying. In spite of his great appetite for books, he failed to graduate at the top of his high school class. He hoped to become a soldier, but his poor eyesight prevented him from going to West Point. This ambition indicates that he wished to become something very different from what he was as a boy. Truman became highly gregarious as an adult. During World War I, he served successfully as a captain of an artillery battery and was very popular with his men, although their background was not like his. He was a Baptist and Mason from rural Missouri; they were Irish Catholics from Kansas City. After the war, he owned and operated a men's store in the city, and the store became for him much more than a place in which he could make money. It became a gathering place for his friends and a base from which he moved about the city visiting with other men and encouraging them to come to the store. Obviously, he had become a very different person from what he had been as a boy.

A decade on a farm just before the war had been a period of personality change for Truman. This period had been preceded by a half decade of uncertainty as to what he should do with his life. After high school, he had moved to Kansas City and worked at several jobs. Then he moved to his grandfather's farm in Grandview. His new responsibilities forced him to move outdoors and draw closer to his father, who worked beside him. The farm provided the young man with a rich opportunity to prove himself, for it was large and capable of benefiting from the latest developments in science and technology. Truman's bookish habits encouraged him to inform himself of these developments and to apply them. Grandview also provided a social situation with less rigorous competition than he had faced in Independence, for most ambitious and talented young men were looking elsewhere for their opportunities. (The boy who had led Truman's high school class, Charlie Ross, had moved on to state university and a highly successful career in journalism.) The farm also provided chances to become active in various male organizations, for this was not an isolated farm. The young farmer became an active member of the National Guard, the Masons, the Democratic party, and other groups.

Truman's new personality provided a foundation for his political career. Politics now became attractive to him, for such a career provided great opportunities for association with people. He became attractive to politicians, for he now seemed popular with people who could vote. Had he remained as he had been as a boy, he would not have moved along a path to power. Soon after his new personality emerged, he found such a path and took his first strides on it.

Truman had been born and raised a Southern Democrat. His ancestors had migrated to Missouri from Kentucky and had had Confederate sympathies during the Civil War. Like his father, he had become active in the Democratic party in Independence and rural Jackson County. "Missouri is far enough south to adopt the plan of white votes only in a Democratic primary," one of Truman's associates and supporters wrote in 1922. The public institutions, such as the schools, with which Truman was familiar in his home area, were segregated institutions.

Truman did not remain merely a Southern Democrat, however. He received much of his early political education as a member of an urban Democratic machine. While living on the farm, he joined Kansas City's Pendergast organization, which was trying to spread its influence into rural Jackson County. In 1922, the machine threw its weight behind him in the race for eastern district judge of the county court because the leaders of the organization recognized that he was popular outside the city and thus might help the machine grow stronger. During the next twelve years as a county official, he did help the machine gain strength, for he accepted one of the basic rules of machine politics and appointed its members to county offices that he controlled. In 1934, Pendergast, influenced again by confidence in Truman's popularity outside the city, asked him to run for the United States Senate and provided essential support in his successful campaigns.

Thus by the 1930s, Truman had ties with both of the major wings of the old Democracy. He had much support in rural Missouri, which looked at many questions as Southern Democrats did. He was also a loyal member of a powerful city machine. He accepted the point of view of the urban Democracy on many issues, including the importance of organization in politics. He believed that a politician needed support from the Pendergast organization in order to succeed in politics in Jackson County and Missouri.

In 1934, Truman added a new dimension to his point of view. He became a New Deal Democrat. Earlier he had participated in efforts to use government for economic purposes, especially to build roads, and to make the executive branch more efficient. He had supervised welfare agencies and promoted regional planning. Yet, though these parts of his career provided bases for acceptance of the New Deal, he had been closer to the old-deal groups like the American Legion, the Daughters of the American Revolution, and the Chamber of Commerce than to New Deal groups like labor unions and social workers. A change of some significance did take place in him in 1934. He campaigned for the Senate as a militant New Dealer, endorsing what had been done and promising to support further developments.

The change reflected Truman's tendency to accept rather than rebel against the major realities of politics. The New Deal was one of those realities in 1934. It was very popular and was helping Democrats throughout the country to achieve surprising victories. Democrats like Kansas City's Jim Reed were destroying their political careers by opposing Franklin Roosevelt's domestic programs. Truman helped rather than harmed his career by endorsing them.

As a senator, Truman fulfilled his promises to support the New Deal. He reached the Senate in time to vote for some of the most important parts of that movement, including social security and the Wagner Labor Relations Act. He supported the president in the "court fight" of 1937 while many other Democrats deserted him. And the senator devoted much of his attention to investigating the malpractices of financial and industrial leaders and to strengthening federal regulations of transportation facilities.

At the same time that Truman supported the New Deal, he attempted to strengthen and protect the Pendergast machine. He worked as he had earlier to obtain patronage for it and achieved one especially important success. Encouraged by Truman, Harry Hopkins appointed a Pendergast lieutenant as head of the Works Progress Administration (the WPA) in Missouri and thus gave the organization a large amount of influence upon the operations of the relief program in the state. Truman also defended the organization against the rising tide of criticism that eventually overwhelmed it. For example, he protested against the reappointment of one of its foes, Maurice Milligan, as district attorney in western Missouri.

Truman also developed good relations with Southern Democrats in Washington. He participated frequently in the social hours held by Vice-President John Nance Garner, "striking a blow for liberty" with this Texan even though he was becoming increasingly unhappy with Roosevelt. Truman even gave some encouragement to Garner's

A QUESTION OF DISCRETION

FIGURE 1. As this 1948 cartoon demonstrates, Truman's enemies never forgot his early association with the corrupt Pendergast machine. (*Reprinted courtesy of the Chicago Tribune*)

efforts to prevent Roosevelt from obtaining the nomination from his party for a third term. Truman also supported Pat Harrison of Mississippi for Senate majority leader against the administration's choice, Alben Barkley.

Harrison predicted in the late 1930s that, because of Truman's personality, big things lay ahead in his political career. He was revealing his gregarious, pragmatic traits in the very complicated situation within the Democratic party. Had he had intense, inflexible commitments to the doctrines of one wing of the party, he could not have functioned within it as he was. He seemed to place a higher value upon developing and maintaining good relations with the members of that party than upon promoting the point of view of one of its factions.

To move higher in American politics, Truman needed to become a national figure. World War II provided him with an opportunity to become more prominent. In taking advantage of that opportunity, he provided another demonstration of his ability to work with diverse groups and to avoid the kind of commitment to one of them that would cut him off from the others.

Truman became a prominent figure as head of a senatorial investigation committee that became known as the "Truman Committee." It dealt with the economic side of the war and helped to make him popular with a multitude of groups, especially the critics of big business and big government. His investigations and reports frequently criticized their contributions to the war effort. At the same time, his concentration upon the war programs enabled him to avoid identification with any one of the contending factions of the party. While he explored the construction of army camps, airplanes, and the like, other figures who were rising toward the top of the party, such as Henry Wallace, were taking stands on the issues that divided the party and the nation. Everyone wanted to win the war, and Truman's work clearly contributed toward that goal. Not everyone wanted to revive the New Deal.

As a consequence of the ways in which he had functioned on the national stage, Truman was acceptable to all of the major factions in the Democratic party in 1944. The leading promoter of his nomination as vice-president, Robert Hannegan, represented the urban machine faction. Hannegan had been a major figure in the Democratic organization in St. Louis, had helped Truman obtain reelection in 1940, and had become chairman of the Democratic National Committee just as the maneuvering for the Democratic national convention was getting under way in a serious fashion. He played an important part in convincing Roosevelt that the controversial Wallace would hurt the ticket while Truman would not.

Although the big push behind Truman's nomination came from

the urban-machine faction of the party, he would not have received the nomination if he had not been acceptable to the other parts of the complex Democratic party. Just as the Pendergast machine had supported him because he seemed popular outside of Kansas City, Hannegan and others supported him in 1944 because he seemed capable of appealing successfully to all parts of the party. The Southern faction accepted him, although its members preferred other candidates. These politicians consoled themselves with talk of Truman's Southern background and assurances that he was a much more desirable candidate than Wallace. New Dealers also accepted Truman, despite their preference for Wallace. They stressed Truman's voting record in the Senate with its consistent support for the New Deal and his obvious superiority to Byrnes from their point of view.

Wallace and Byrnes were far apart on the increasingly prominent civil rights issue, and Truman's handling of it provides a major explanation of his acceptability to the rival factions. In his earliest years in politics, he had not needed Negro support, for he had represented an area in which few Negroes lived. In 1924, when running for reelection as eastern district judge in Jackson County, he had failed to receive the endorsement of the Kansas City chapter of the National Association for the Advancement of Colored People (the NAACP) because the organization was not satisfied with his responses to a questionnaire concerning antilynching legislation, enforcement of the Thirteenth, Fourteenth, and Fifteenth Amendments, equal educational facilities, political and industrial equality, residential segregation, the Jackson County Home for Delinquent Boys, and the Ku Klux Klan. Seeking only the support of Jackson Countians outside of Kansas City, he was not subjected to significant pressure to depart from the Southern point of view that had affected his thinking for years.

In all of his elections after 1924, however, Truman needed and obtained support from Negro voters and their leaders in Missouri's urban centers. In those years, he gave more encouragement to the civil rights movement than he had in 1924. One episode is particularly revealing. Early in 1938, the Missouri senator cooperated with the NAACP in its efforts to get Congress to pass antilynching legislation. He voted unsuccessfully to bring the filibuster to an end. Samuel Lubell has told a tale about Truman's role in this episode that has the ring of truth, considering Truman's Southern background and also Lubell's contacts with Southern politicians. According to Lubell, when the antilynching bill came before Congress, Truman explained to a leader of the opposition that he sympathized with him because of the roles that his family had played during the Civil War, but the Missourian indicated that he would be forced to vote against the South because of the importance of the Negro vote in St. Louis and Kansas City.

Perhaps all that was involved in Truman's explanation to this Southern politician was Truman's yearning to make and keep friends and his refusal to allow doctrines to stand in the way of friendship. His performance revealed his ability to bridge gaps between people and work with diverse groups.

A Negro journalist writing in the summer of 1944 noted this quality in Truman: "You must understand that a true 'democratic' party is a party of minorities. Democracy means conciliation and agreement," Truman explained to the newsman. The latter pointed out that the party had gone to some lengths in its national convention to conciliate the South. "Why shouldn't we conciliate the South? Why shouldn't we conciliate the colored voter as well?" Truman asked. "Both are parts of the party." And he went on to declare that the Democratic party was "a balance between the liberal social planning and traditional reaction." The conversation enabled the journalist to understand why Truman "was at once acceptable to the southern bourbons and the northern progressives and union leaders as well." As he described the Democratic nominee to the readers of the Afro-American chain of papers: "There is some non-verbal quality about him that makes it possible for him to be at home on a cotton planter's verandah where the colored people are all 'boys' or 'gals' who bow and scrape. He is also at home with educated colored people and sincere progressive democrats. He understands both sides and leans heavily on the side of progress for people without regard to race."

Thus Truman became a man of great power when Franklin Roosevelt died in 1945 because Truman had satisfied the needs of his party in 1944. He had been born and raised in its Southern wing, had received his education in the realities of American politics as a member of a Democratic city machine, and had been converted to the New Deal as he attempted to move on to the national political stage in 1934. As he had developed, he had not switched from one type of Democrat to another; he had added one to another, layer by layer, as he moved along. By 1944, in other words, he contained all three types, just as his party did, and thereby became an ideal choice for his party, seemingly capable of holding the parts together.

How had he been able to accomplish this? The answer, I would suggest, lay in his personality—his pragmatic, gregarious patterns of thought and behavior. His commitments were to people, not to doctrines. He enjoyed the company of other men, developed friendships with many different groups of them, and did not worry too much about the different ideologies that they represented. His personality enabled him to bridge the gaps in his party.

My question has been, "How did Truman become a man of power?" I assume that the answers to this question could help us deal with another: "How did Truman use power?" In other words, I assume that a man brings to a position of power certain characteristics that were developed by his earlier experiences and that influence his behavior in office.

Implied in this discussion of Truman's path to power is the answer to another question: "Why did Truman seek power?" My hypothesis is that he did not. This is, of course, an exaggeration, stated so as to highlight my belief that power drives did not dominate him. Power came to him largely as a by-product of a pursuit of another interest: his interest in developing satisfying relations with other human beings. He devoted much of his attention to the capture and use of the power institutions of his society chiefly because he found in politics his best opportunities to develop satisfying relations with other men. As Richard Neustadt has suggested, Franklin Roosevelt was "hungry for the Presidency's power as his birthright," while Truman "felt no such hunger and laid claim to no such birthright." This should remind us that an accident, Roosevelt's death, played a very important role in Truman's rise. In brief, as many historical facts indicate, he did not plan his path to power.

II THE NATURE AND ACCOMPLISHMENT OF THE FAIR DEAL: THE LIBERAL-CONSERVATIVE-NEW LEFT DEBATE

Richard E. Neustadt

CONGRESS AND THE FAIR DEAL:
A LEGISLATIVE BALANCE SHEET

Richard E. Neustadt served on the White House staff under Truman before moving into academic life and winning recognition as one of the foremost authorities on the American presidency. Although written twenty years ago, this essay is still the best survey of the political history of the Truman years. Despite a superficial appearance of legislative failure, Neustadt asserts, Truman was more successful than most observers realized.

On September 6, 1945, three weeks after V-J Day, Harry S. Truman sent to Congress a twenty-one point program of domestic legislation—his first comprehensive venture in home affairs since Franklin Roosevelt's death five months before. This marked the beginning of a long series of presidential proposals for congressional action in the fields of economic development and social welfare; proposals which streamed out of the White House for nearly seven years, from the first session of the Seventy-ninth Congress through the second session of the Eighty-second; a legislative program which became each year more comprehensive, more organized, more definite, receiving after 1948, the distinction of a label: the Fair Deal.

Looking back upon this enterprise, this Fair Deal program and its fortunes in those years, no less an observer than Elmer Davis has ventured the following verdict:

> *All in all, in domestic affairs, Mr. Truman was an unsuccessful President. [He] presented . . . a liberal program which was coherent and logical as the New Deal had never been. Congress, not being liberal, refused to take it; yet every year he persisted in offering it all to them again and they still wouldn't take it. . . . Truman kept asking for all of it and getting none of it.*

This retrospective vision of the president who never changed his pace and of the Congress never altering in opposition is no doubt widely shared these days. No doubt, there is an element of reality

From *Public Policy* 5 (1954), ed. Carl Friedrich and John Kenneth Galbraith, 351–381. Copyright © 1954 by the President and Fellows of Harvard College. Reprinted by permission. (Footnotes edited.)

behind it. Certainly, President Truman held out for more than he could reasonably hope to gain; certainly his four Congresses persisted in frustrating many of his aims.

Yet in its bold relief and simple black and white, this vision of the Truman record misses much light and shadow in a very complex situation. And by virtue of its very sharpness and simplicity, it becomes a stumbling block to understanding and appraisal. Students of postwar politics and of the presidency, and Congress, have need to start their march through Truman's years with a more elaborate guide to the terrain than this quick characterization can supply.

It is much too soon, of course, for the definitive appraisal of the Fair Deal legislative program, its fundamental emphasis and purposes, its ultimate success or failure. But it is not too soon to go behind neat generalizations and draw a balance on the record as it stood when Truman left the White House. What was attempted, what accomplished, what lost? And more important still, what seem now, at this reading, to have been the underlying motivations, the determinative circumstances? These are the questions to which this essay is addressed.

A General Note on Congress—1945 to 1952

Before turning to the Fair Deal, as such, something need be said by way of background about the work load and the composition of the four Congresses which Truman faced as president.

These were the Congresses of postwar reconstruction and Cold War and Korea. For seven successive years their sessions tackled and put through an extraordinary series of administration measures in the fields of international cooperation, collective security and national defense; a series which for scope and scale and continuity has no precedent in our history.

On no previous occasion has American foreign policy required— much less received—comparable congressional participation for such a span of time. Rarely before, save at the onset of our greatest wars, has the Congress broken so much new and unfamiliar ground; rarely, if ever, has momentum been so long sustained.

One thinks of Franklin Roosevelt's first four years, and the legislative breakthrough into broad new areas of federal action here at home. We look back on that as a revolution—a stunning departure from the traditional limitations of predepression years. So, too, were these postwar programs revolutionary—shattering all manner of shibboleths and precedents, in the international sphere untouchable right up to World War II. And what stands out historically is a record of immense accomplishment, in legislative terms, both for the administration that framed the measures and for the Congresses that put them through.

The record becomes still more impressive when one recalls that President Truman never did command a "safe" working majority of the rank and file in either house of Congress. His "honeymoon" did not outlast the war. There was no bloc of "Truman men," sufficient for his purposes, on which he could rely to follow through, without cavil, whatever leads he gave. Rather, the thing was done through that extraordinary phenomenon, postwar "bipartisanship," a carefully conceived and executed coalition launched by Roosevelt, husbanded by Truman, actively furthered by effective leadership in the congressional power centers of both parties.

This enterprise was in its way as distinctive an achievement, for both president and Congress, as the roster of enactments which it helped to frame and legislate. Of course, the idyl of bipartisanship did not last forever. But even in 1952, the "internationalist" alignment, though reduced in strength by mass Republican defections —and some Democratic backsliding as well—remained a strong bifactional, if not bipartisan, reality, producing—in support of foreign policy—majorities, however bare, which could not have been mustered for a moment behind most Fair Deal domestic programs.

This raises a crucial point: the internationalist coalition, which supported Truman's foreign policy, existed, cheek by jowl, with a "conservative" coalition, which opposed administration policies at home. What's more, the two most vital elements in the conservative alignment, were also chief participants in the internationalist bloc— the "moderates" of both parties; the Vandenberg Midwest Republicans and the Russell Southern Democrats.

These were the swing groups, joining the "Fair Dealers" to beat off the "extremists" of both parties in their raids on foreign programs; joining the extremists in opposition to most of the Fair Dealers' pet proposals at home. Internationalism combined with conservatism was the formula which kept two coalitions going, side by side, through issue after issue, Congress after Congress.

A great deal happened after 1949 to sap the strength of the internationalist coalition. On the personality side, of course, came Vandenberg's illness and death, Connally's advancing age, Acheson's unpopularity. Deeper down were the accumulating frustrations of twenty Democratic years, capped with "Communism, Corruption, Korea"—and China; mercilessly exploited by congressional Republicans made desperate after 1948 and cured, thereby, of any faith in "high level" politics, or the "me-too" approach. In addition, after 1950, after Korea, came a development which threatened the whole basis of compatibility between internationalism and conservatism: the full cost of our commitments in the world—in dollars and in human terms as well—took on a new and frightening dimension. Conservatism and internationalism began to come unstuck, to war with one another. And if the Democratic "moderates"—taken as a whole—did not react as sharply or as soon as the Republicans who buried Vandenberg, this may be taken, partly, as a tribute to party loyalties and hopes for 1952.

Taking Truman's four Congresses together, in all these terms of work load and alignment, three further observations are in order. First, had no more been attempted or accomplished, by way of major, controversial, forward measures, than the great landmarks in the international and mobilization fields alone, we would still have to grant, in retrospect, that these were busy and productive years of legislation for the Congress—outstanding years, by prewar standards.

Moreover, whatever else might have been tried, on the domestic front, there was no time, from 1945 to 1952, when Truman's administration—given its foreign policy and the international situation from year to year—could afford to trade a major objective in the foreign field for some advantage in the domestic. Consistently, it was, and had to be, the other way around.

Finally, considering the integral relationships between the "internationalist" coalition which supported Truman and the conservative coalition which opposed him, every major venture in home affairs was bound to complicate the progress, endanger the timetable of those all-important measures in his foreign policy. From his first days in office, when he reaffirmed Roosevelt's arrangements for Republican participation in the San Francisco Conference, Truman acknowledged his dependence, in the foreign field, on elements of the anti-New Deal coalition—an enterprise which, always potent after 1937, had spent the wartime "truce" maturing its relations, building its lines and thwarting FDR on secondary issues.

Why, then, did Truman press a host of "hot" Fair Deal domestic issues, sure to arouse the wrath of this entrenched conservative alignment? To this question there is no single, easy answer, but rather a whole series, arising out of motivations and responses which varied with circumstance, over the years. To get at these we need now turn to straight, historical review, beginning with the first Truman "inventory" of legislative needs in home affairs—the twenty-one point program of 1945.

To Reaffirm the Roosevelt Purpose: 1945–1946

The original "twenty-one point" program went to Congress by special message on September 6, 1945. Then, within a ten-week span, the president sent Congress six more special messages, each adding a major new proposal to the September list. In January 1946, Truman again presented a "twenty-one point" program, in a radio appeal to the country, reiterated three weeks later in his annual message to the Congress. This second listing was somewhat different from the first. Most of September's minor points had been removed from the enumeration to make room, among the twenty-one, for measures recommended in October and November. And in the annual message there was discussion of additional proposals—over and above the list of twenty-one—which had not previously been mentioned at all.

In summarizing the domestic program which Truman set forth after V-J Day, it makes no sense at all to attach significance to order or to timing of particular proposals in this confusing sequence. Obviously some things were ready, came to mind, or got approval earlier than others. Obviously, also, these were the days of scatter-shot approach, when everything was put on record fast, in a sort of laundry-listing of postwar requirements with little indication of priority or emphasis.

What counts, here, is that between September 1945 and January 1946, Truman staked out for himself and his administration, a sweeping legislative program in the fields of social welfare and economic development, embracing, in essential outline if not in all details, the whole range of measures we now identify with the Fair Deal.

Nearly everything was there, though later formulations were to alter some specifics. Among September's numbered "points" were full employment legislation, expanded unemployment compensation, the permanent FEPC, an increased minimum wage, comprehensive housing legislation, a National Science Foundation, grants for hospital construction, permanent farm price supports, and—less specifically—protection and assistance for small business and expanded public works for resource conservation and development.

To these, the "points" of January's message added a comprehensive health program—including health insurance—nationalization of atomic energy and development of the St. Lawrence project. In addition, the message stressed, though it did not number, a "thoroughgoing reconsideration of our social security laws"; financial aid "to assist the states in assuring more nearly equal opportunities for . . . education"; an emergency veterans housing program "now under preparation"; and various kind words for statehood or self-government in the territories and insular possessions and the District of Columbia. Finally, of course, there were appropriate exhortations about extending price and rent controls.

This was the program Truman threw at Congress, the moment the war was won. Roosevelt had supplanted "Dr. New Deal" with "Dr. Win-the-War." Why then did Truman hurry so to call the old physician in again?

Look back two years, to January 1944, and part of the answer becomes plain. Remember Roosevelt's "Economic Bill of Rights," with which he opened that election year, the year of hoped-for victory in Europe and feared postwar depression here at home:

> *The right to a useful and remunerative job. . . .*
> *The right to earn enough. . . .*
> *The right of every farmer to . . . a decent living.*
> *The right of every businessman . . . to trade in . . . freedom from unfair competition. . . .*
> *The right of every family to a decent home.*
> *The right to adequate medical care. . . .*
> *The right to adequate protection from . . . fears of old age, sickness, accident and unemployment.*
> *The right to a good education.*
> *All these rights spell security. And after the war is won, we must be prepared to move forward in the implementation of these rights. . . .*

Truman was thus reasserting Roosevelt's stated purpose; not in so many words, not necessarily in Roosevelt's way, or with his means, or his specifics—or his men—but consciously and definitely this was for Truman an affirmation of fidelity to the cause and the direction of liberal democracy; rekindling the social outlook of the New Deal, if not, precisely, of the New Dealers.

The legislative program of 1945 was a reminder to the Democratic party, to the Congress, to the country, that there was continuity between the new national leadership and the old—and not merely in war policy, but in peace policy as well; not only overseas, but here at home.

Beyond this, the new president had a very personal stake in his September message: reaffirmation of his own philosophy, his own commitments, his own social outlook; denial of the complacent understandings, the comfortable assertions that now, with "That Man" gone, the White House would be "reasonable," "sound," and "safe." Harry Truman wanted, as he used to say, to separate the "men" from the "boys" among his summertime supporters. V-J Day brought him his first real chance to think or act in terms of home affairs, and he lost no time in straightening out the record on who he was and what he stood for.

Some of the New Dealers may not have been convinced; conservatives, however, were quick to understand that here, at least on paper, was a mortal challenge. Editors glowered; so did congressmen. And one of the president's "soundest" advisors, who ornamented the administration in that capacity from first to last, fought to the point of threatened resignation against sending that "socialistic" message to the Congress.

Here, then, is explanation for the character and overall direction of Truman's program. But what of its specific scope and range? Granting all this, why was so much territory covered all at once; why so many points; why, in fields like health and housing, go "all out" in a single bite?

Most commentators have seen these things simply as errors in tactics and judgment, charging them off to personal idiosyncrasy, or inexperience. Other presidents, it is said, would never have concocted so diverse a program, or asked, indiscriminately, for everything at once. But something more was operating here than just the human factor, however significant that may have been. We have no means of knowing what Roosevelt would have done, after the war. But we do know that he had made the "Economic Bill of Rights" an issue in the 1944 campaign—with Truman as his running mate. And in one of his last major campaign addresses, Roosevelt came out strongly, if in general terms, for most of the controversial measures Truman, a year later, urged on Congress.

We also know that in the postwar period, a Democratic president was bound to face a fundamentally different situation, a different set of popular alignments and demands than Roosevelt dealt with in the thirties. Then, the New Deal pioneered, releasing a flood of ideas and impulses for reform that had been dammed up since Wilson's time. And every effort in those years, each new program, every experiment, set into motion a widening circle of needs and expectations for governmental action—and of organized interest groups to defend the gains and voice the new requirements.

The first Roosevelt administration broke into virgin territory; the Truman administration had to deal with the demand for its consolidation and development. Clearly, Roosevelt was aware of this in 1944. Clearly, Truman's sweeping program in 1945 was conceived as a response. And not alone in 1945; from first to last, the Fair Deal legislative program sought to express the vastly heightened expectations of those groups of Americans on which the liberal cause depended for support.

For all these reasons, then, the Seventy-ninth Congress found itself encumbered with a great, diverse collection of proposals from the president. And what did Congress do? Not very much. This was the Congress elected with the Roosevelt-Truman ticket in 1944. But even before Roosevelt's death, it had shown little disposition to follow the White House lead in home affairs. At the very start of the first session, the conservative coalition got the bit between its teeth and almost overturned Henry Wallace's appointment as secretary of commerce. From then on, the coalition remained a power to be reckoned with, its temper not improved by Truman's exhortations, its influence culminating, finally, in emasculation of the price control extender, during the summer of 1946.

From the confusions, irritations and forebodings of defeat, which marked the whole course of its second session, the Seventy-ninth Congress did produce a number of the major measures Truman had proposed—most notably the Employment Act, the Atomic Energy Act, the Hospital Construction Act and the Veterans Emergency

Housing Act. The Congress was not ungenerous in authorizing and appropriating funds for reclamation, flood control, power and soil conservation; these also raised some landmarks on the Fair Deal road. But for the rest, at least in terms of final action, Congress stood still, or even "backslid" here and there—as with the Russell Amendment eliminating the wartime FEPC.

Perhaps, if experience over the months had not dispelled the specter of postwar unemployment, much more might have been done with Truman's program of September, 1945. But as it was, this turned out to be the least of worries for most Congressmen and their constituents back home. Not job shortages, but strikes, not pay envelopes but price regulations bothered both. The country, like the Congress, far from rallying to presidential visions of a better future, reacted negatively against the irritations of the present, and punished Truman's party with its worst congressional defeat in eighteen years.

To Pillory the Opposition: 1947–1948

To gauge the impact of the 1946 election on the attitude and outlook of the Truman administration, one merely has to contrast the president's address to the incoming Eightieth Congress, with his wide-ranging message and radio appeal of the preceding year.

The change in tone was very marked. In the annual messages of 1947 domestic affairs were relatively played down; domestic recommendations limited to a few specifics and some gently phrased, general remarks. In his State of the Union message, Truman gave more emphasis to budget balancing (e.g., no tax relief) than to any "welfare" measure, save the comprehensive housing program— which had Senator Taft among its sponsors. He also did "urge" action on the balance of his 1945 health program, but not under the heading of "major policies requiring the attention of the Congress." And while brief mention was made of social security, minimum wages and resource development, it is clear from the context that these, too, were relegated to some secondary category.

This was the comparatively mild and qualified domestic program which the president presented to a supremely confident opposition Congress, where he was generally regarded—on both sides of the aisle—as an historical curiosity, a holdover, a mere chair warmer by

accident of constitution, for two more years. The view was widely
shared. Inside the administration, many, perhaps most, of Truman's
advisers were persuaded, if not that all was over, at least that the
postwar reaffirmation of the liberal cause had been a crashing failure at the polls—out of fashion with the public, out of date for
officeholders.

The counsels of caution and conservatism within the president's
own entourage, muffled somewhat since the fall of 1945, were now
heard everywhere, voiced by almost everybody. Whatever Truman's
own views may have been, the course of his administration through
much of 1947 seemed to display real hesitancy, real indecisiveness
about further assertion of the cause he had so vigorously espoused
a year before.

It is true that as the spring wore on, the White House sent up
certain special messages along reminiscent lines. In May, another
health message repeated the proposals of 1945—but the tone was
mild and the issue, then, by no means so inflammable as it was to
become in later years. In June, the president vigorously protested
inadequacies in the rent control extender and called again for a
comprehensive housing program—but this included specific endorsement for Senator Taft's own bill.

Lump these reminders in with the rest, and Truman's domestic
program in the spring of 1947 still remains a very conciliatory version
of what had gone before. Under the initial impact of defeat, the
administration, clearly, had fallen way back to regroup. And with
the Truman Doctrine to be implemented that same spring, by that
same opposition Congress, it is no wonder there was hesitation and
divided counsel about where to take a stand and when, if ever, to
resume the forward march.

Yet, scarcely a year later, Harry Truman was back at the old
stand, once again, raising old banners, rubbing salt in old wounds,
firing broadsides at Congress more aggressively than ever. What
happened here? Wherefore the change from the conciliatory tone of
1947 to the uncompromising challenge of 1948? Obviously, somewhere along the line, the president became convinced that his
initial impulse had been correct, that he was right in 1945—that the
New Deal tradition, brought up-to-date, remained good policy—and
good politics—despite the setback of 1946. In this decision, Truman's
temperament, his social outlook, all sorts of subjective factors, no

doubt played a part. But also, in the course of 1947 there appeared some perfectly objective indications that a renewed offensive would be not merely "natural" but rational.

Twice, in the early summer of 1947, Truman vetoed tax reductions voted by the Congress. Both times he charged that the reductions were inequitable and ill-timed; that they relieved only upper-income groups, and would add new burdens of inflation for the rest to bear. Both times there was some stirring of approval and response around the country—both times his veto was sustained.

In point of fact, these vetoes were no new departure. They had been foreshadowed from the first by warnings in the annual messages. But the actuality of veto, and the words in which expressed, did convey a fresh impression: the vision of a sturdy president—courageous even in the face of lower taxes—defending the "national" interest and the "poor," against a heartless (Republican) Congress mindful only of the "rich." This was a new note—and it did not go badly.

Four days after his tax veto, Truman vetoed the Taft-Hartley Act. To the general public, the measure was chiefly notable, then and since, because it did something about work stoppages in "national emergency" disputes—an issue the president himself had recognized in prior messages to Congress. But to the spokesmen for organized labor the act was shot full of unwarrantable interferences with basic union rights which had been guaranteed, by law, for half a generation.

And when Truman struck out against these interferences—in the strongest language he had yet addressed to the Eightieth Congress—he evoked a warm response from a part of the public whose apathy, in 1946, had prominently helped defeat his party and his postwar cause. The quick congressional override of Truman's veto merely heightened this response from those who felt themselves despoiled—and further dramatized, for them, the vision of the presidential "tribune" standing up against the onslaughts of a rapacious (Republican) Congress.

Here, in the summer of 1947, were some straws in the wind. Their meaning was confirmed for the administration, even enlarged upon, at the special session in the fall.

When Truman called the Congress back to Washington, the principal emergency was international—with the economies of Western Europe verging on collapse. But in his address to the special session,

Truman asked not only for interim aid abroad—pending completion of the European Recovery Program—but also for a ten-point program against inflation, billed as an equal emergency at home. And the tenth point of this domestic plan was nothing less than selective restoration of price and wage controls.

This was the first occasion when Truman made an all-out public effort to revive and dramatize an issue which had failed him in 1946, capitalizing on a measure which—as everybody knew—was still anathema to the majority in Congress. This was the first occasion, too, since the election of 1946, when the president presumed to give so controversial a domestic issue equal billing with an essential aspect of his foreign policy.

The program for the 1947 special session was, no doubt, a trial run, in a sense. Had the result been very bad, the president might perhaps have stayed his hand in 1948. In the event, however, the majority in Congress found it expedient to enact something called an "anti-inflation" bill, a most limited measure but indicating that times—and prices—had changed since 1946. Moreover, despite the patent irritations which the price issue aroused, interim aid for Europe went through Congress without a hitch, and just before adjournment, the European Recovery Program was sent up and well received.

By January 1948, the president had obviously read the signs and portents of the half year before, and put out of mind the memory of defeat in 1946, with all the cautious counsels it provoked. Truman's address to the new session was confident and sharp, evoking all the liberal issues half-suppressed a year before. His presentation was much more coherent than it had been in 1945 or 1946, the language tighter, the focus sharper, the follow-up firmer. But nothing was omitted from the original post-war program and in a number of respects Truman went beyond any earlier commitments.

This was the message which set forth goals for the decade ahead. This was the message which proposed a new, "anti-inflationary" tax program: credits for low-income groups to offset the cost of living, with revenues to be recouped by increased levies on corporate profits.

The "tribune" of six months before, who had risen to protect the people against the acts of Congress, now sought their protection in demands on Congress for actions it could not, or would not, take. If the record of Congress could be turned against the opposition, then the president would make that record, not on performance, but on nonperformance, not on the opposition's issues but on his issues—those liberal measures which, perhaps, had not gone out of fashion after all.

And as Truman began, so he continued through the spring, with "a message a week," to keep Congress off balance and the spotlight on. In this series there was but one great new formulation—the civil rights message of February 1948. The legislative program it set forth incorporated most of the proposals of the President's Committee on Civil Rights, which had reported in December 1947.[1] The resulting explosion is still echoing in Congress and the Democratic party.

Of all Truman's proposals through eight years in office, these were, perhaps, the most controversial. That they loosed a lasting political storm, everyone knows; that they had special political significance in early 1948—appearing just as Henry Wallace made his break to the Progressive party—is certainly no secret. But there was much more than politics in this. The Civil Rights Committee had originally been established out of genuine concern lest there be repeated in the postwar years, the rioting and retrogression which followed World War I. Congressional indifference had been made manifest in 1946—hence the turn to prominent outsiders. Once having set these people to their task, on problems so potentially explosive, it is hardly credible that Truman could have ignored their report, no matter what the politics of his own situation.

Nothing else, half so dramatic, was unveiled by the president in 1948. But all the older measures were furbished up and trotted out anew. And as the months wore on, Truman's tone to Congress grew steadily more vigorous. He began by lambasting in January, and ended by lampooning in July.

His last address to the Eightieth Congress was the nearest thing to an outright campaign speech that he—or probably any other president—ever made before the assembled houses. Opening the

---

[1] The committee was created December 5, 1946, by Executive Order 9808. The main recommendations adopted by the president included a permanent commission on civil rights, a "compulsory" FEPC, antilynching and poll tax laws, strengthening of civil rights statutes and of government enforcement machinery. Also included in the presidential program were certain earlier administration proposals of a somewhat different nature: statehood for Hawaii and Alaska, self-government for Puerto Rico, Guam and Samoa, and home rule for the District of Columbia.

postconvention special session, he first demanded action to stop
inflation and start more houses—the ostensible purposes for which
Congress had been recalled. He then proceeded to list nine other
measures which he thought the Congress might be able to enact
without delaying the two primary items. Finally he listed every other
major proposal advanced since 1945, commenting: ". . . If this
Congress finds time to act on any of them now, the country will
greatly benefit. Certainly, the next Congress should take them up
immediately."

Of course, that hapless session accomplished precisely nothing,
in any of these categories. And Truman proceeded to pillory the
Eightieth Congress at every whistle stop across the country, working
his way to victory in the presidential election of 1948.

Toward a Liberal Majority: 1949–1950

The legislative program Harry Truman presented in 1949, to the new
Congress which had shared his victory, reflected all the Fair Deal
commitments of the 1948 campaign. "Certainly, the next Congress
should take them up immediately," he had proclaimed to the Republicans in July. And he could do no less in January than spread them
out—all of them—before his brand-new Democratic majorities.

All interest groups and sponsoring politicians understood the
"law of honeymoon"; none was prepared to stand aside, leaving a
pet proposal for some later, less naturally advantageous date. All
civil rights groups, and most politicians North and South, knew very
well that only the extra leverage of an early log jam would suffice,
in time, to shut off debate. All trade union spokesmen were agreed
that there could be no compromise on Taft-Hartley "repeal" and no
delay on any part of it. And so it went, group after group, issue after
issue.

Both president and Congress were thus prisoners, in a sense, of
the election and the way it had been won. It was one thing to throw
a host of highly controversial measures at an opposition Congress
which could—and did—reject most of them out of hand. It was quite
another thing to throw the same load on a relatively receptive Congress, prepared to make a try at action on them all. Action is much
harder than inaction; action on this scale, of this variety, an almost
intolerable burden on the complex machinery of the legislative

process—and on a president's capacity to focus attention, to rally support.

Despite this handicap, the Eighty-first Congress, be it said, turned out more New Deal–Fair Deal measures than any of its predecessors after 1938, or its successors either; becoming, on its record, the most liberal Congress in the last fifteen years.

This was the Congress that enacted the comprehensive housing program, providing generously for slum clearance, urban redevelopment and public housing; the Congress that put through the major revision of social security, doubling insurance and assistance benefits and greatly—though not universally—extending coverage. This was the Congress that reformed the Displaced Persons Act, increased the minimum wage, doubled the hospital construction program, authorized the National Science Foundation and the rural telephone program, suspended the "sliding scale" on price supports, extended the soil conservation program, provided new grants for planning state and local public works and plugged the long-standing merger loophole in the Clayton Act. And it was principally this Congress that financed Truman's last expansions of flood control, rural electrification, reclamation, public power and transmission lines.

But this record of domestic accomplishment was obscured for commentators, public and administration by a series of failures on the most dramatic and most dramatized of 1948's great expectations. In the first session of the Eighty-first Congress—the last full session before Korea—aid to education, health insurance, FEPC and Taft-Hartley repeal were taken up, debated, fought over and either stalled or killed outright somewhere along the line.

General aid to education—that is, maintenance and operation funds for state school systems—had won Senate approval in 1948, in a form that represented careful compromise among religious interests and between the richer and the poorer states. Reintroduced in 1949, the same measure speedily received Senate approval once again. But as the year wore on, these compromises started to unravel; various groups and individuals took second looks, had second thoughts. The whole basis of agreement fell apart before the Senate bill had cleared the House committee. There the bill remained, unreported at the session's end, eight months after Senate passage. There the second session found it—and left it.

The story on health is similar in some respects. The interest groups supporting Truman's health program and its congressional sponsors did not seriously hope for early victory on compulsory health insurance. But they—and the administration—saw this issue as a stick with which to beat the Congress into passing other major aspects of the program—increased hospital construction and research, aid to medical education and grants to local public health units; all obvious and necessary preliminaries to effective operation of any general insurance scheme. In the Senate, all four of these secondary measures were approved by early fall of 1949. Hospital construction and research grants—both expansions of existing programs—also fared well in the House. But the medical education and local health bills never got to the House floor. They were smothered to death in committee by a resurgent opposition—medical and other—which seized the stick of health insurance and used it to inflict increasing punishment, not only on these bills, their sponsors and supporters, but on the whole administration and the Democratic party.

In the case of civil rights, Truman's program was not merely stalled but buried during 1949. At the session's start, the interest groups—supported by the leadership in Congress and administration—would stand for nothing but a test on the most controversial measure of them all: compulsory FEPC. The measure's proponents were perfectly aware they could not gain compulsion from the House, nor cloture from the Senate, without a major showing of Republican support. This was not forthcoming; the test proved that at any rate. It also helped Democrats, Southern as well as Northern, discharge some pressing obligations toward constituents. But the long filibuster of 1949 was all the Senate could endure. None of its leaders was prepared to face another bloodletting in 1950.

The Congressional failure on Taft-Hartley repeal was just as conclusive as that on civil rights and much more surprising to administration, press and public. In 1949, the struggle in both houses was intense, but save for the injunction in emergency disputes—the one feature opponents of repeal could press home to the general public— the advocates of a new law probably would have had their way. The interest groups could not, or would not give on this; the administration could not, or would not impel them—so everything was lost; lost in 1949 and left, then, to await a new test in a new Congress. A decisive beating in the first session might be compromised in the second, but hardly reversed. And trade union leadership was in no mood for compromise.

Nor was the president. His response to each of these defeats in 1949—and other, lesser scars sustained that year—was a renewed recommendation in 1950. His January messages to the second session of the Eighty-first Congress included virtually all proposals still outstanding, that he had listed to the first session in his moment of honeymoon a year before.

Clearly, there was little hope, in 1950, for much of what he asked. Yet the Eighty-first Congress, as Truman was to say that spring, had "already reversed" its predecessor's backward "trend." And if the "trend" now ran the Fair Deal's way, perhaps what this Congress withheld, would be forthcoming from the next—the Eighty-second Congress to be elected in November.

Not since 1934 had the Democratic party increased its majorities in a midterm election; breaking into new terrain in North and West. Yet that, and nothing less, was surely Truman's goal for 1950. "I hope," remarked the president, "that by next January, some of the obstructionists will be removed." And not content with pressing, once again, all the remaining issues of 1948, he urged on Congress three further measures each of which, if it appealed at all, would tap new sources of support, beyond the groups and areas where Democratic power was presumably entrenched.

One of these measures involved a new departure for the president on farm legislation. His 1950 State of the Union message was the occasion for Truman's first formal use of the magic words connoting "Brannan Plan."[2] There he first attached the adjective "mandatory" to price supports, first urged "a system of production payments," first declared, "as a matter of national policy," that "safeguards must be maintained against slumps in farm prices," in order to support "farm income at fair levels."

---

[2] In May 1949, the secretary of agriculture, Charles Brannan, set before the Congressional Agriculture Committees, a complicated series of proposals, and suggestions—which, to his chagrin, an alert opposition promptly labeled "The (Socialistic) Brannan Plan." The complex and controversial specifics Brannan then advanced were intended to make price supports more nearly serve the purpose of maintaining high-level farm income under conditions of increasing total production and consumption, with subsidies ("production payments") to bridge the gap between an adequate return to the producer and an inviting price to the consumer on perishable commodities.

To the uninitiate these words may look very little different from their counterparts in prior presidential messages. But in the language of farm bureaucrats and organizations, these were magic words indeed, fighting words, emphasizing finally and officially, a sharp turn in Truman's agriculture policy—a turn which had begun in 1948, progressively distinguishing Democratic from Republican farm programs, and bringing the administration now to ground where the Republicans in Congress—not to speak of many Democrats—could not or would not follow.[3]

By the time Truman spoke in January 1950, the more far-reaching measures his words implied had already been rebuffed at the preceding session of the Congress—and the "Brannan Plan" had already become a scare word, rivaling "socialized medicine" in the campaign arsenal the Republicans were readying. Yet by his endorsement Truman seemed to say that scare word or no, here was an issue to cement for Democrats the farm support which he had gained so providentially in 1948.

The second new measure to be proposed in the State of the Union message for 1950, concerned the housing shortage "for middle-income groups, especially in large metropolitan areas." The Housing Act of 1949 had granted more aids for private home financing which swelled the flood of relatively high-priced houses. The act also had promised more public housing, with subsidized rentals for people in the lowest income brackets. Between these two types of housing was a gap, affecting mainly urban and suburban "middle" groups of white-collar and blue-collar families; swing groups politically, as time would show. For them, in 1950, the president proposed "new legislation authorizing a vigorous program to help cooperatives and other non-profit groups build housing which these families could afford."

The third of 1950's new proposals was billed as a mere promissory note in the State of the Union message. "I hope," said Truman, "to transmit to the Congress a series of proposals to . . . assist small

---

[3] The Agriculture Act of 1948, the so-called Hope-Aiken Bill, passed by the Republican Eightieth Congress, had emphasized "flexibility," its mechanism the "sliding scale," its underlying philosophy not maintenance of high income, but prevention of excessive loss. Brannan's proposals represented a sharply different philosophy about the purposes of federal action, let alone specifics. But the first session of the Eighty-first Congress went with him only a small part of the way. His more striking innovations were side-tracked during 1949.

business and to encourage the growth of new enterprises." As such, this was no more concrete than the benign expressions in many earlier messages and party platforms. But in the spring of 1950, the president kept his promise and put meat on these old bones with a comprehensive small business program far more elaborate than anything advanced since the emergency legislation of the early thirties. The immediate reaction, in Congress and out, was very favorable. A leading spokesman for "big" business called the Truman message "tempered, reasoned, non-political." Small business groups expressed great interest; even some bankers had kind words to say.

The president's small business program went to Congress as he entrained for the Far West, on his "nonpolitical" tour of May 1950. The Fair Deal's prospects were then enticing numbers of administration stalwarts to leave their safe House seats and campaign for the Senate. Many signs encouraged them. The country was prosperous, recession ending; the presidential program popular, to all appearances, attracting interest in useful quarters and stirring overt opposition only where most expected and least feared. Foreign policy was costly but not noticeably burdensome, defense pared down, the budget coming into balance.

Yet on the other side were signs of change, foretastes of things to come, making 1950 a very special year, a year of sharp transition, in retrospect a great divide. The preceding winter saw the last of Chinese Nationalist resistance on the Asian mainland. In January Alger Hiss was convicted in his second trial—and Secretary Acheson quoted from the Scriptures. In February, Senator McCarthy first shared with the public his discovery of communism's menace here at home. In May, Senator Kefauver's committee began televised crime hearings, exposing criminal connections of political machines in some of the nation's largest cities—where, as it happened, the Democratic party had been long in control.

And on the twenty-fifth of June, the North Korean Communists invaded the Republic of Korea.

Korea: The Great Divide

In legislative terms, the initial impact of Korea on the Fair Deal is symbolized by the collapse of Truman's small business program. Senate hearings had just got under way when the fighting began.

They terminated quickly in the first days of July. The Senate committee which had started down this track enthusiastically, turned off to tackle the Defense Production Act—controls for the new, part-way war economy.

All along the line, Fair Deal proposals were permanently shelved or set aside, as Congress worked on measures for defense. And on one of these measures, price controls, which had long been identified with the Fair Deal, not the president but Congress forced the issue—never again was Truman able to resurrect it as his own.

This calls for a short digression. In July 1950, the president did not raise the price control issue, because he feared it might delay congressional response on other needed measures of control; fearing, moreover, lest opinion overseas might take his call for direct controls as indicating all-out preparation for the general war Korean intervention was intended to avert, not foster.

But Congress proceeded, on its initiative, to include discretionary price and wage controls among the economic powers in the Defense Production Act. The measure became law September 8, 1950. For a variety of reasons, no general application of direct controls was attempted until nearly five months later. Meanwhile the Chinese attack of November 27 set off new buying waves, with consequent sharp price increases. And by the time a general freeze was instituted, January 26, 1951, this sequence of events had thoroughly shaken confidence in the administration's leadership on the inflation issue.

The fact that Truman subsequently fought for strengthened control legislation, while his congressional opponents shot holes in it at every opportunity, seems not to have restored the president's position in the public mind, nor recreated for the Democrats that popular response the issue had accorded them in 1948. The Republicans, if anyone, drew strength from popular discomfort with high prices, in subsequent elections.

Apart from price controls, the conflict in Korea drew congressional —and national—attention away from the traditional Fair Deal issues. As election time approached, in 1950, there was no backdrop of recent, relevant congressional debate to liven up these issues, stressing their affirmative appeal. Instead, the opposition had a field day with the negative refrain of "socialism"—or worse—invoking specters of the "Brannan Plan," "socialized medicine," and Alger

Hiss, to unnerve a public preoccupied with sacrifices in a far-off peninsula, nervous over rumors about "Chinese volunteers."

In the first week of November, the electorate—far from increasing Democratic power—reduced to a bare minimum the Democratic party's lead in both houses of Congress, abruptly closing the careers of some very senior senators and some very staunch administration congressmen. And in the last week of November the full-scale Chinese intervention in Korea turned virtual victory into disastrous retreat, confronting the administration and the country with a "new" war, a most uncertain future, and endless possibilities of worse to come.

Mobilization and Reluctant Retreat: 1951–1952

On December 15, 1950, the president proclaimed a National Emergency. Three weeks later, in January 1951, the Eighty-second Congress assembled to hear, in virtual silence, what Truman had to say.

His State of the Union message was somewhat reminiscent, in its tight organization and sharp phrasing, of the fighting address of 1948. But in tone and content it was, by far, the most conciliatory annual message since 1947.

The entire address was devoted to events abroad and mobilization at home. Its ten-point legislative program was couched in emergency terms. Among the ten points only one Fair Deal item remained in its entirety—aid for medical education, now billed as a means of "increasing the supply of doctors . . . critically needed for defense. . . ." Two other pillars of the Fair Deal program were included in qualified form. General aid to education was requested, "to meet . . . most urgent needs . . . ," with the proviso that "some of our plans will have to be deferred. . . ." And while there was no specific mention of Taft-Hartley, or its repeal, the president did ask "improvement of our labor laws to help provide stable . . . relations and . . . steady production in this emergency."

Aside from a bland and wholly unspecific reference to "improvements in our agriculture laws," an opening for subsequent proposals never made, these were the only references to Fair Deal measures in the presidential list of "subjects on which legislation will be needed. . . ." They were almost the only references in the entire message; but not quite. After his ten-point enumeration, Truman re-

ernment must give priority to activities that are
..ered "power development" as an example. Then he
..any of the things we would normally do . . . must be cur-
..ed or postponed . . ."; the door was finally closing, but—the
Congress should give continuing attention ". . . to measures . . .
for the long pull." There followed four brief and unelaborated but
unmistakable references to increased unemployment and old age
insurance, disability and health insurance, and civil rights.

As in 1947, so in 1951, the president was shifting emphasis, rele-
gating most welfare measures to some secondary order of priority,
without quite ceasing to be their advocate. It was too subtle a performance for the press; the distinctions much too fine for headlines
or wide public notice—though not, perhaps, for congressmen to
grasp. Yet in its way, this message represented Truman's recognition of the fundamental change in his circumstances and the nation's;
his nearest approach to Roosevelt's sharp, dramatic switch, a
decade earlier, from "Dr. New Deal" to "Dr. Win-the-War."

And unlike 1947, this mild beginning, in January 1951, heralded a
more conciliatory tone, an increased interest in negotiation, on some
of the Fair Deal's most striking programs. As the year wore on,
Truman gradually changed tactics on at least three fronts, seeking
different ground from that staked out in pre-Korean years.

The first of these shifts came in the field of health. There the administration was hopelessly on the defensive by 1951. The vocal
presence of an aroused and potent medical opposition, victorious in
trials of strength at 1950's elections, sufficed to make most congressmen suspect and fear a taint of "socialized medicine" in any Truman health measure, however limited its purpose or narrow its
scope. The president had barely raised the health insurance issue
in January 1951, but its mere invocation was now enough to halt all
legislation in the field. So far had the opposition come, from its days
on the defensive, back in 1949.

Finally, Truman voiced his recognition of the situation: "I am not
clinging to any particular plan," he told an audience in June. This was
followed, six months later, by appointment of the President's Commission on the Health Needs of the Nation, charged with surveying,
from the ground up, all problems and proposals in the field.[4] In

---

[4] The commission, chaired by Dr. Paul Magnuson, was established December 29,

January 1952, addressing the second session of the Eighty-second Congress, the president remarked of health insurance, "So far as I know it is still the best way. If there are . . . better answers I hope this Commission will find them."

A second change in tactics during 1951 came on the issue of Taft-Hartley. Senator Taft's triumphant reelection, the preceding autumn, had symbolized how futile were the hopes of 1949 for a renewal, in a "better" Congress, of that year's stalled attack. In Truman's January messages of 1951 there was no mention of "repeal." The following October, his first address at a trade-union affair, that year, was notable for subdued treatment of the issue. "We want a law . . . that will be fair . . . ," he said, "and . . . we will have that kind of law, in the long run . . ." and that was all. Two months later, the president enlarged upon this theme, telling the Congress, "We need . . . to improve our labor law . . . even the sponsors . . . admit it needs to be changed. . . ." The issue of "repeal" was dormant, so Truman seemed to say. Amendment, even perhaps piecemeal amendment—anathema in 1949—now measured the ambitions of his administration.

The president's third shift in emphasis came on his agriculture program. Since the Korean outbreak, farm prices had soared, along with the demand for food and fiber. There was little in the current situation to promote wide interest in Brannan's innovations, or counteract the socialistic specters that his "plan" invoked. In January 1951, the president had no specific comment on the ideas he had endorsed a year before. By January 1952, Truman was prepared with some specifics, but on much narrower ground. That year, his State of the Union message asked—and Congress shortly granted—renewed suspension of the "sliding scale" on price supports, which otherwise would have become effective at the end of 1952. For the rest, he simply remarked that there was "need to find . . . a less costly method for supporting perishable commodities than the law now provides"—a plug for "production payments," surely, but in a fashion that softpedalled the far-reaching overtones of 1950.

1951, and given a free hand. It reported, a year later, December 18, 1952, recommending, among many other things, various forms of public subsidy for private health insurance plans to meet the high cost of medical care—the problem to which Truman's governmental health insurance proposal had been addressed.

The year of 1951 turned out to be a hard and unrewarding time for the administration; a year marked by MacArthur's firing, by strenuous debates on foreign policy and on controls, by blighted hopes for quick truce in Korea, by snowballing complaints of government corruption—and by prolonged congressional indifference to the welfare measures on the trimmed-down Truman list.

The State of the Union message in January 1952 was less incisive than its predecessor—so was the emergency—but hardly less moderate in its approach on home affairs. Besides the new departures on health insurance, labor laws and farm legislation, the president appealed again for aid to education and the supplementary health bills of a year before. Again he mentioned power needs. Again he raised, briefly and generally, the issues of civil rights. Otherwise, in only two respects did he go beyond specifics urged in 1951—asking cost-of-living increases for social security recipients and readjustment benefits for Korean veterans.

These two requests were granted rather promptly, giving Truman his last minor successes. But in the spring of 1952, the second session of the Eighty-second Congress was interested less in legislating than investigating; less concerned with pending measures than with administration struggles over corruption—and the steel dispute; preoccupied above all else with the coming presidential nominations and the campaign to follow in the fall. The session's main contribution to the Fair Deal program was not positive, but negative, rousing one last Truman proposal in opposition to the McCarran Act; creating one more Fair Deal issue, liberalization of the immigration laws.

In this fashion, Truman's last Congress slowed to a close. And in Chicago, that July, appeared a final summary of Fair Deal business left undone—the Democratic platform of 1952.

What Truman had played down, in his last annual messages, the platform now set forth in some detail. It called for action on the civil rights program, avoiding retrogression by a hair; pledged still more improvement in the social insurance laws; promised more resource conservation and development, including public power; urged federal help for schools, this time stressing construction along with "general" aid; called for a firm stand on public housing and revived the "middle income" issue of two years before; spoke feelingly of protection and assistance for small business, hinting at specifics unmentioned since Korea; adopted Truman's formula on health, with kind words for the President's Commission; followed him also on farm price supports, on immigration and on a host of lesser issues, long the stock-in-trade of Democratic documents.

At one point only did the platform diverge sharply from the president's more recent formulations. On Taft-Hartley it abandoned his new stand, reverting to the cliché of "repeal." The Democratic candidate was put to some trouble by this change, but it cannot be said to have much mattered to the voters.

It had been seven years since Harry Truman, reaffirming Roosevelt's purpose, first charted the Fair Deal in his twenty-one point program of 1945. Now it received its last expression in his party's platform for 1952. This remains the final statement. In January 1953, Truman and his party yielded office to the first Republican administration in twenty years.

A Fair Deal Balance Sheet

Set the platform of 1952 alongside the program of 1945, allow for changing circumstances and particulars, then run a quick calculation on the Fair Deal legislative program. What did Truman gain in seven years from his four Congresses? What came of all the trials and tribulations recorded in this essay?

In the first place, it is clear that Truman managed to obtain from Congress means for modernizing, bringing up to date, a number of outstanding New Deal landmarks in social welfare and economic development, among them: social security, minimum wages, public health and housing; farm price supports, rural electrification, soil conservation, reclamation, flood control and public power. Not all of these were strictly New Deal innovations, but all gained either life or impetus from Roosevelt in the thirties. And in the new circumstances of the postwar forties they were renewed, elaborated, enlarged upon, by legislative action urged in Truman's Fair Deal program; even their underlying rationale nailed down in law by the Employment Act of 1946.

This is significant, and not alone by virtue of particulars attained. A generation earlier, the very spirit of Wilsonian New Freedom had been buried deep in the debris of reaction following world war. Not so with the New Deal.

As a consolidator, as a builder on foundations, Truman left an impressive legislative record; the greater part achieved, of course, in less than two years' time, and by a single Congress. Moreover as protector, as defender, wielder of the veto against encroachments on the liberal preserve, Truman left a record of considerable success—an aspect of the Fair Deal not to be discounted. He could not always hold his ground, sustained some major losses, but in the process managed to inflict much punishment on his opponents.

The greater Truman vetoes pretty well define what might be called the legislative program of the conservative coalition in his time. On many of these measures he made his veto stick, as with the offshore oil bills in 1946 and 1952, or natural gas and basing points in 1950. On certain others—like the Gearhardt Resolution in 1948—what one Congress enacted over his veto, the next retracted at his demand.[5] And on a few—especially the two already noted—Congress overrode him, and the ground once lost was not made up in Truman's time: the Taft-Hartley Act in 1947 and the McCarran Act in 1952.[6]

Besides these, Truman asked of Congress four main things which were denied him: aid to education, health insurance, civil rights and —for want of better shorthand—"Brannan Plan." On the outstanding features of these four, he got no satisfaction: no general grants for all school systems; no national prepayment plan for medical care; no FEPC, or anti-poll tax or antilynching laws; no wholesale renovation of price supports to insure good returns from general farm production. Here, if anywhere, does Elmer Davis's refrain approach reality: "Truman kept asking for all of it and getting none of it."

Why did he keep asking? From 1945 to 1950, one may concede that year by year there always seemed to be good reason to press on: reason to hope and plan for action, if not in one session then the next, reason to believe the very chance for future action might depend on present advocacy. But after 1950, after Korea, faced with a dozen hard new issues, on the defensive all the way from "communism to corruption," what then explains the Truman course? He

---

[5] The "Gearhardt Resolution" (removing certain news vendors and others from social security coverage) was pocket-vetoed August 6, 1947; regularly vetoed April 5, 1948, the latter promptly overridden. Coverage was restored in the social security amendments of 1950.

[6] An earlier McCarran Act, the Internal Security Act of 1950, vetoed August 22, 1950, is also in this category.

must have known, his actions show awareness, that there had come a real sea change in his affairs and in the country's. Why move so slowly towards a bare minimum of reappraisal, readjustment?

Perhaps the answers lie, in part, in Truman's temperament; partly in his concept of the presidency. Unquestionably he thought these measures right for the country; hence proper for the president to advocate, regardless of their chances in the Congress. He had assumed responsibility as keeper of the country's conscience on these issues; as its awakener, as well, by virtue of stands taken far ahead of the procession. For civil rights, especially, Truman could claim—like Roosevelt after the court fight of 1937—that while he may have lost a legislative battle, the forcing of the issue helped to win a larger war. "There has been a great awakening of the American conscience on the issue of civil rights," he was to say in his farewell report to Congress, "all across the nation . . . the barriers are coming down." This was happening; by his demands for legislation he conceived that he helped make it happen. On that premise, he was bound not to abandon his position, no matter what the legislative outcome, present or prospective.

Even in strictly legislative terms there was, perhaps, much to be gained by standing firm. Were not some of the fights that failed a vital stimulus to others that succeeded? Were not some votes against a measure such as health insurance, repaid by other votes in favor of reciprocal trade renewal, say? Was not a total presidential program basically advantaged if it overshot the limits of assured congressional response? There are no ready measurements providing certain answers to these questions. But presidents must seek them all the same. And on his record there is little doubt what answers Truman found.

For Truman then, each of his great outstanding issues had value as a legislative stalking horse, if nothing more. But that is not to say he saw no more in them. On the contrary, had he not thought many things attainable, still actionable in the not too distant future—still meaningful, therefore, in rallying political support—he scarcely would have bothered, during 1951, to cleanse his farm and health programs—much less Taft-Hartley—of the worst taints absorbed in the campaign of 1950, thus rendering them usable for 1952.

Those changes in approach were hardly aimed at Congress—not, anyway, the current Congress. Rather, the president was preparing new positions for his party, shifting to ground on which it could afford to stand with him and to uphold, if in adjusted guise, the Fair Deal label and the Truman cause.

Right to the last, then, Truman was persuaded that those Fair Deal issues touched felt needs, roused real response among Americans; no longer viable objectives for his time in office, but crucial undertakings in his party's future.

Robert A. Taft

THE FAIR DEAL IS CREEPING SOCIALISM

Senator Robert A. Taft, "Mr. Republican," was the intellectual and political leader of the conservative wing of the GOP. Taft argues, in this talk delivered to a Republican gathering, that Fair Deal welfare liberalism boils down to a species of socialism, which in turn must ultimately subvert individual liberty and lead to the creation of a totalitarian state.

In 1948 President Truman was elected on a personal platform which, if carried out, would have established a labor-socialist government in this country similar to that of Great Britain. Fortunately, the people at the same time elected a Congress most of whom had never endorsed or approved the Truman program. The Eighty-first Congress, while much more radical than the Eightieth Congress, still refused to accept the dictates of President Truman, although by a narrow majority and after a violent battle. The election was indecisive because, I believe, the people did not clearly understand the issues.

But in 1952 the people must decide whether they will elect a Congress whose policies will be guided by the principles of liberty which guided this country for 150 years, or one which will accept the socialist proposals of President Truman. The recent Republican statement of principles and objectives says that the basic domestic issue today is liberty against socialism. It goes on to define these

From the *Congressional Record*, 81st Congress, 2nd Session (Appendix), pp. A2530–32. Title supplied by the editor.

terms. Liberty, it says, means a free people in constant control of their government. Socialism means an all-powerful federal government with unlimited power to tax and spend, to direct and operate our agriculture, industry, labor, and local communities, and the daily lives of our citizens.

In the past four months I have traveled through the eighty-eight counties of Ohio and visited hundreds of cities and villages, schoolhouses, industrial plants, and farms. I am confident that the people of Ohio—and they are typical of the people of America—believe in liberty, and I think I know what the essential quality of that liberty is. It is the freedom of people in every walk of life and every form of activity to think their own thoughts and carry out their own ideas; the freedom of man to have his ideas taught to others if he can convince his teachers; freedom of the press; freedom of religion. It is the freedom of each community to determine how its own children shall be educated and its health, welfare, and other local activities conducted. In a country this size it is impossible to exaggerate the importance of local self-government if we are to maintain freedom at all, for the bureaus of a central government are never responsive to the will of any considerable number of the people of different sections of this great country.

It is the liberty of men and women to choose their own occupation, and to establish and operate their own business, if they so desire, as they feel it should be operated without interference from the government, or from labor-union bosses so long as they themselves do not interfere with the rights of others. It is the liberty which encourages every boy and girl to feel that the world is open to their abilities and their efforts, in occupation, in local politics, and in public and private life throughout the nation.

The results of that freedom have made this country the greatest and the happiest country in the world. An essential feature of liberty is freedom from the direction of government, and particularly a central government. We have a great system of education, probably the best in the world, and it is partly socialized in our public elementary and secondary schools, but it is free because there is no central power directing it. Power is diffused among thousands of school districts and between forty-eight states and between thousands of private schools and colleges. Many of these schools may have entirely erroneous ideas. Some may do harm rather than good, but the net result is a great system of education with more freedom than is given by any other country. It has resulted in millions of people developing their own ideas and a general opportunity to try them out to see whether they are worthwhile.

This kind of freedom made the American soldiers the greatest army in the world. Certainly it was not because they were better trained, because they were not, or better disciplined. Their discipline was poor according to military standards. But they out-fought the leading military nations of the world because every man was able to think for himself to meet the situation as it occurred.

So, in the field of economic progress. In every industrial plant I have visited the managers think their plant has a peculiar excellence, a new product, better morale, better machines or better methods and production lines. We are ahead of other countries because of the tremendous advance in tools and machinery and the productivity of every workman resulting therefrom. The American farmer is just as far ahead in his methods and productivity.

We are ahead because of freedom, because there are millions of people stimulated to develop ideas and free to put those ideas into effect without some bureaucratic interference. We would be far behind today if government had owned every little industrial plant in this country as Mr. Attlee desires to have the government own them in England. Our system has led to a production so great that it gave the basis of victory in two world wars. It has led to a standard of living in this country two and a half to three times that of Great Britain, or in Europe.

We happen to have today a very vivid comparison with the industrial system of England. The freedom of industry in England was abused, and the importance of freedom was never realized. Monopolies were encouraged rather than competition. Government control and assistance was sought and encouraged until today it is a matter of course. Neither workmen nor management had the interest in new machinery which complete liberty of ideas gave in this country. As a result today, the British workman is getting $20 a week and the American workman $55 a week. The very measures advertised as benefiting the workman have reduced him to a life of austerity. Government control and government taxation have removed any incentive to individuals to invest their money in new plants or new machinery or new methods. And England is unable to make goods cheaply enough, even with cheap labor, to compete with American goods and earn the dollars they need.

What is the greatest enemy of liberty and its accomplishments? Obviously in America today it is the concentration of power in Washington. It is the course of these mistaken individuals who cannot abide the scattered planlessness of liberty however excellent its results, and must establish a regulated order organized to carry out the particular ends they have in mind. Already we have created in our federal government the greatest monopoly in the world, an institution spending $46 billion in twelve months, one-sixth of all the activity in this great country. While the people have resisted many increases of power sought since 1939, spending has gone on until by its mere size and the weight of taxation the freedom of men is limited. If the government takes from me 20 to 50 percent of my earnings, it is depriving me of liberty to spend that money for myself. It is saying to me that the government will select the services that I shall receive, whether I want them or not. It removes the income by which men may experiment and carry out their own ideas, and also the incentive to spend their time and their money and their ability and their genius in further improvement.

Socialism is the taking over of human activity by government. Of course socialism is a relative term. Some activities have always been socialized like public schools and the post office in this country. A few socialists will carry their program to the complete control of all individual activity. But it is not necessary to go so far to bring an effective end to liberty. There is a point at which the growth of government so weakens the effective operation of liberty that government is forced into still greater expansion. In England they have effectively ended economic liberty. They think they can do that and still maintain individual liberty, but I doubt if a real socialistic regime can be continued in force in the economic field for many years except under a dictatorship.

It is said that Harry Truman is no socialist. That makes little difference if all his policies lead to socialism. We are in danger of complete government control not only because of his policies, but because the totalitarian philosophy has affected the thinking of a lot of other people in this country who ought to know better. There was a time when men expected to solve their own problems, when they were solved by cooperative effort and local effort. Today the

FIGURE 2. A conservative cartoonist's view of Fair Deal liberalism. (*Leo, Washington Times-Herald, copyright © The Washington Post*)

first thought is to turn to Washington for money and action. The organization of pressure groups has been a dangerous factor in that movement. Every pressure group, whether from business or labor or professions, concentrate their interest on Washington activity.

Their paid lobbyists find it much easier to seek a federal statute than to go out and educate the people or even their own members, to achieve by their own efforts a solution of their problems.

We have been faced in the Eightieth and Eighty-first Congresses with a detailed Truman program which would leave little freedom in the people and concentrate power in the federal government, greater even than that it exercised during the war. Every policy which Mr. Truman advocates means more power in Washington. Perhaps he does little realize the total effect of his own program, forced on him item by item by the political necessity of appeasing the CIO Political Action Committee.

In the first place he has been demanding the power of price-fixing, wage-fixing—in a very moderate way, of course—and allocation which means rationing. There was a time in the summer of 1947 when he referred to these powers as "police state controls." Since December 1947, he has continuously demanded these powers now spelled out in the Spence Bill.

He demands the power for the government to go into business. He supports the great expansion of government in the power business and incidental activities through Valley Authorities in every region of the United States.

He insists on the Brannan Plan with subsidies to farmers and consumers and the power of government to direct in detail the operation of every farm, the number of acres to be planted to wheat, to corn, to cotton and other crops; the number of animals to be raised—hogs, beef cattle, dairy cattle, chickens.

These measures have been developed by those men who believe in economic planning, and government control to order those plans to be carried out. They would mean a complete power in government to direct the detailed operation of industry, commerce, and agriculture. They would involve the control of labor and the allotment of jobs. If Harry Truman is not a socialist, then he simply does not understand the effect of the measures which he supports.

Then he advocates the socialization as well as the nationalization of medicine. Under his plan the government would levy $6 or $7 billion of new taxes and put it all in the hands of a federal bureau to set up a vast organzation to employ all the doctors and hospitals in the United States to give free medical care to 150 million people. All doctors would become employees of the government and it would destroy the freedom of the medical profession which has contributed more than any other to the remedies against human illness.

Many other proposals before us extend the activities of so-called social insurance to other contingencies of life. Of course, it is not really insurance at all, but merely a plan of additional taxation to provide the cash for free handouts of all kinds of welfare service. This year's report of the Federal Security Agency says, "The administration believes that comprehensive welfare services should in time be available to persons requesting them—whether needy or not —in all communities of the Nation."

Naturally enough, Mr. Truman has also advocated universal military training and is not at all fearful concerning a system which would take boys out of their education and occupations in time of peace and subject them for twelve months to the indoctrination of some bureau in the War Department.

As part of all this program, we have the necessary extension of spending and taxation. Already we are spending about 28 percent of our national income on government. Every man works more than one day in four for government and less than three days for himself. Taxes increase the price of every product the housewife buys by about 20 percent on the average so that this burden falls on millions who do not realize that they are paying taxes. It destroys the incentive of men to expand their business and their business activities and may soon leave voids which the government will be urged to fill up with government investment requiring more taxes. In Great Britain a tax burden of 40 percent of the national income has practically brought a stagnation of progress in industry. Even here there is doubt whether we can get the money necessary to keep up the growth of industry required to give a million new jobs every year to the young people entering the labor market and those displaced by technological improvement. Certainly, some rearrangement of taxes is required.

It is quite true that Mr. Truman does not present his program in its true light. In England the socialists are proud of their program. They admit freely its cost in taxes and the limitation of freedom, but insist that it is worth the price. Mr. Truman's advisers despair of convincing the American people along that line. They try to play down the radical nature of the proposals they make. Powers are only to be stand-by powers to be occasionally used. The medical program is to retain the liberty of choosing your own doctor. Also, the people are not asked to pay the price. We have a deficit of $5 billion a year, and no new taxes are asked for. The people are urged to accept all the programs because they are not going to have to pay for them. They are to get something for nothing.

Each step in the past has been taken without warning of those to come. Now, at last, we have the whole program before us. We know that if Mr. Truman can elect a Congress subordinate to his will and that of the labor unions, it is not just a question of socialized medicine or economic control, it is the whole program of the hand-out state and the police state which a radical Eighty-second Congress can put into effect before the end of Mr. Truman's term.

It is important that the people be not fooled by Mr. Truman's occasional hesitations and his olive branches extended to the businessmen. There has been no repudiation of any of these policies. The only way to avoid a creeping socialism is to elect a Republican Congress in 1950 and a Republican president in 1952. The only way to get rid of the Communists in the State Department is to change the head of the government. It can't be done with men in control who think they are only red herrings. The only way to get a judicial treatment of labor problems is to elect an impartial president. As long as Mr. Truman is there, he will sabotage whatever policy Congress may adopt as he has sabotaged the Taft-Hartley law.

The issue is clear. It is inconceivable to me that the American people would throw away a system at the very time that it has proved its ability to improve the condition of the great mass of the people to a standard of living far beyond anything the world has ever seen, and adopt a system which in Great Britain has failed to benefit the very workmen to which it promised utopia. The issue is, in fact, the issue between continued progress under liberty and a socialized state.

And liberty is the only key to real progress. The Republican party believes that if we follow the same principles, we can secure the same improvement as in the past. There is no limit or frontier to the productive ability or the standards of living of our people. There is no reason why they should not constantly improve, providing we follow the same principles of freedom which have succeeded in the past. We are opposed to a planned economy through federal regulation and control, but we support the policies which the federal government has pursued for one hundred years. We insist on a sound fiscal policy to maintain the value of the American dollar and the savings and insurance policies of the people, a stability which is the base of full employment and prosperity. We favor federal concern with every important problem—research, advice, and assistance to individuals and business and states and communities, and financial aid in those cases where the need is clearly shown and where the objective is clearly beyond the power of the state or community to achieve.

In the whole field of education, welfare, health, and housing the federal government must take that interest. These matters are primarily in the jurisdiction of the states and local communities, but that does not exclude an active interest on the part of the federal government. The federal government is specially concerned that there be equality of opportunity throughout this great country, particularly for every child who is born into an American family, no matter how poor the family or the community into which he may be born. I believe the American people are convinced that we are sufficiently wealthy so that we can provide a minimum decent standard of living for every family in the United States. This is the obligation recognized by most states and local communities, but all of them are not able to carry out that program, and financial help from the federal government can assist them in doing it.

Conclusive figures on illiteracy show that the poorer states in this nation are not able to provide a minimum decent education for all their children after raising taxes for education in excess of the average throughout the nation. Consequently, I favor a bill for federal aid to education in the nature of an equalization fund to see that every child shall have a primary and secondary school education.

We have as good health as any nation in the world, and we have always undertaken to see that free medical care is furnished to those who cannot afford to pay for it, but federal aid can make that service more complete in providing a sufficient number of hospitals and of doctors, and see that real insurance is available to those who desire to take advantage of it to spread the risk of every illness in one year.

I have regarded decent shelter as essential for providing minimum standards of living and supported the bill which will subsidize housing for those in the lowest income brackets.

In this whole field, it is most essential that we do not impose federal control as a condition of federal assistance. Administration must remain in the states and local communities. In general, the federal government should not be called in unless the need is clearly shown. I do not think the federal government should undertake any program to provide free services for those who are able to pay for them and that means the great bulk of the population. Above all, we cannot impose on federal government any more than on local government an excessive burden of taxation. The only way we can give free service or support to those who are not working is out of the earnings of those Americans who are working. The burden on them must not be so great as to threaten their liberty or reduce the incentive and reward for hard work, ability, and daring.

Nor do we adopt any laissez-faire principle. Federal action is often essential to maintain liberty itself in industry by preventing monopoly and unfair competition. Federal action can prevent economic oppression by setting a standard for a minimum wage. It can prevent economic inequality by some reasonable price-support program to prevent the destruction of agricultural purchasing power through forces far beyond the control of the individual or the united farmers.

Every proposal for federal action, however, must be judged by its effect on the liberty of the individual, the family, the community, industry, and labor. Such liberty cannot be sacrificed to any theoretical improvement from government control or government spending.

I am convinced that the people of this country are strong believers in liberty and I have a complete faith in their decision in 1950 and 1952. That decision involves not only the future of America. Only if the American people convince themselves and convince the world that they believe in liberty can we hope to meet the aggressive ideology of communism. Communism has spread through the world because there has been no ideal to oppose it. Our leaders have been apologizing for America for twenty years. The time has come when we must spread the banners of liberty throughout the world as did our forefathers after 1776.

Barton J. Bernstein

AMERICA IN WAR AND PEACE: THE TEST OF LIBERALISM

During Truman's years in office, most of the criticism of his administration came from conservatives such as Taft. By the later sixties, however, young revisionist historians were formulating a comprehensive critique from a left-liberal/radical perspective. In this "New Left" survey of the Truman era, Barton J. Bernstein decries both Truman's political leadership and the intellectual assumptions of American liberalism.

When the nation joined the Allies, Roosevelt had explained that "Dr. Win-the-War" was taking over from "Dr. New Deal," and there were few liberal legislative achievements during the war years. Those benefits that disadvantaged groups did receive were usually a direct result of the labor shortage and the flourishing economy, not of liberal politics. By 1944, however, Roosevelt was prepared to revive the reform spirit, and he revealed his liberal vision for the postwar years. Announcing an "Economic Bill of Rights," he outlined "a new basis for security and prosperity": the right to a job, adequate food, clothing, and recreation, a decent home, a good education, adequate medical care, and protection against sickness and unemployment.[1]

Noble as was his vision of the future society, Roosevelt was still unprepared to move far beyond rhetoric, and the Congress was unsympathetic to his program.[2] While approving the GI Bill of Rights,[3] including educational benefits and extended unemployment pay, Congress resisted most liberal programs during the war. Asserting its independence of the executive, the war Congress also thwarted

From *Towards a New Past,* edited by Barton J. Bernstein. Copyright © 1967, 1968 by Random House, Inc. Reprinted by permission of Pantheon Books, a Division of Random House, Inc.

[1] Message on the State of the Union, January 11, 1944, in Rosenman, ed., *Public Papers of Roosevelt,* 13: 41. For some evidence that Roosevelt was at least talking about a new alignment of politics, see Samuel Rosenman, *Working with Roosevelt* (London, 1952), pp. 423–29. Probably this was a tactical maneuver.

[2] Mary Hinchey, "The Frustration of the New Deal Revival, 1944–1946" (Unpublished Ph.D. dissertation, University of Missouri, 1965), chs. 1–2.

[3] President's statement on signing the GI Bill of Rights, June 22, 1944, in Rosenman, ed., *Public Papers of Roosevelt,* 13: 180–82, and Rosenman's notes, pp. 183–84. The GI Bill has generally been neglected as an antidepression measure.

Roosevelt in other ways—by rejecting a large tax bill designed to spread the cost of war and to reduce inflationary pressures,[4] and by liquidating the National Resources Planning Board, which had originated the "second bill of rights" and also studied postwar economic planning.[5]

By its opposition to planning and social reform, Congress increased the anxieties of labor and liberals about the postwar years and left the new Truman administration poorly prepared for the difficult transition to a peacetime economy when the war suddenly ended.[6] Fearing the depression that most economists forecast, the administration did, however, propose a tax cut of $5 billion. While removing many low-income recipients from the tax rolls, the law was also of great benefit to large corporations. Charging inequity, organized labor found little support in Congress or the executive, for the government was relying upon business activity, rather than on consumer purchasing power, to soften the economic decline. Significantly, despite the anticipated $30 billion deficit (plus the $5 billion tax [cut]), no congressman expressed any fear of an unbalanced budget. Clearly fiscal orthodoxy did not occupy a very high place in the scale of values of congressional conservatives, and they accepted in practice the necessity of an unbalanced budget.[7]

Before the tax bill passed, the wartime harmony of the major interest groups had crumbled: each struggled to consolidate its gains and advance its welfare before the anticipated economic collapse. Chafing under the no-strike pledge and restrictions on wage raises, organized labor compelled the administration to relax its policy and free unions to bargain collectively.[8] Farmers, fearful of depression, demanded the withdrawal of subsidies which artificially depressed prices.[9] Big business, despite anticipated shortages,

4 President's veto of the tax bill, February 22, 1944, in Rosenman, ed., *Public Papers of Roosevelt,* 13: 80–84.
5 Charles Merriam, "The National Resources Planning Board: A Chapter in American Planning Experience," *American Political Science Review* 38 (December 1944): 1075–88.
6 Bernstein, "The Truman Administration and the Politics of Inflation," chs. 3–4.
7 Bernstein, "Charting a Course Between Inflation and Deflation: Secretary Fred Vinson and the Truman Administration's Tax Bill," scheduled for *Register of the Kentucky Historical Society.*
8 Bernstein, "The Truman Administration and Its Reconversion Wage Policy," *Labor History* 6 (Fall 1965): 214–31.
9 Bernstein, "Clash of Interests: The Postwar Battle Between the Office of Price Administration and the Department of Agriculture," *Agricultural History* 40 (January

secured the removal of most controls on the allocation of resources.[10]

As the economic forecasts shifted in late autumn, the administration discovered belatedly that inflation, not depression, was the immediate economic danger. The president acted sporadically to restrain inflationary pressures, but his efforts were too occasional, often misguided, and too weak to resist the demands of interest groups and the actions of his own subordinates.[11]

Beset by factionalism and staffed often by men of limited ability, Truman's early government floundered. By adopting the practice of cabinet responsibility and delegating excessive authority to department chiefs, Truman created a structure that left him uninformed: problems frequently developed unnoticed until they had swelled to crises, and the choice then was often between undesirable alternatives. Operating in a new politics, in the politics of inflation, he confronted problems requiring greater tactical skill than those Roosevelt had confronted. Seeking to maintain economic controls, and compelled to deny the rising expectations of major interest groups, his administration found it difficult to avoid antagonizing the rival groups. In the politics of depression, the Roosevelt administration could frequently maintain political support by bestowing specific advantages on groups, but in the politics of inflation the major interest groups came to seek freedom from restrictive federal controls.[12]

So difficult were the problems facing Truman that even a more experienced and skilled president would have encountered great difficulty. Inheriting the hostile Congress that had resisted occasional wartime attempts at social reform, Truman lacked the skill or leverage to guide a legislature seeking to assert its independence of the executive. Unable to halt fragmentation of the Democratic coalition, and incapable of ending dissension in his government, he

1967): 45–57; Allen J. Matusow, "Food and Farm Policies During the First Truman Administration, 1945–1948" (unpublished Ph.D. dissertation, Harvard University, 1963), chs. 1–3.

[10] Bernstein, "The Removal of War Production Board Controls on Business, 1944–1946," *Business History Review* 39 (Summer 1965): 243–60.

[11] Bernstein, "The Truman Administration and the Steel Strike of 1946," *Journal of American History* 52 (March 1966): 791–803; "Walter Reuther and the General Motors Strike of 1945–1946," *Michigan History* 49 (September 1965): 260–77; "The Postwar Famine and Price Control, 1946," *Agricultural History* 39 (October 1964): 235–40; and Matusow, "Food and Farm Policies," chs. 1–3.

[12] Bernstein, "The Presidency Under Truman," [*Yale Political Review*] 4 (Fall 1964), 8ff.

also found that conservative subordinates undercut his occasional liberalism. Though he had gone on record early in endorsing a reform program[13] ("a declaration of independence" from congressional conservatives, he called it),[14] he had been unsuccessful in securing most of the legislation—a higher minimum wage, public housing, expanded unemployment benefits, and FEPC. Even the employment act was little more, as one congressman said, than a license to look for a job.[15] The president, through ineptitude or lack of commitment, often chose not to struggle for his program. Unable to dramatize the issues or to command enthusiasm, he was an ineffectual leader.[16]

So unsuccessful was his government that voters began jibing, "To err is Truman." Despairing of a resurgence of liberalism under Truman, New Dealers left the government in droves. By the fall of 1946, none of Roosevelt's associates was left in a prominent position. So disgruntled were many liberals about Truman and his advisers, about his unwillingness to fight for price controls, housing, benefits for labor, and civil rights, that some turned briefly to serious consideration of a new party.[17]

Achieving few reforms during his White House years, Truman, with the notable exception of civil rights, never moved significantly beyond Roosevelt. The Fair Deal was largely an extension of earlier Democratic liberalism,[18] but Truman's new vigor and fierce partisan-

[13] Truman's message to Congress, September 6, 1945, in *Public Papers of the Presidents of the United States* (8 vols.; Washington, 1961–66), pp. 263–309 (1948).

[14] Quoted in Jonathan Daniels, *The Man of Independence* (Philadelphia, 1950), p. 288. For evidence that Truman was trying to head off a bolt by liberals, see *New York Times,* August 12, 1945; Harold Smith Daily Record, August 13, 1945, Bureau of the Budget Library, Washington, D.C.

[15] Harold Stein, "Twenty Years of the Employment Act" (unpublished ms., 1965, copy in my possession), p. 2. Also see Stephen K. Bailey, *Congress Makes a Law: The Story Behind the Employment Act of 1946* (New York, 1950).

[16] Lubell, *The Future of American Politics*, pp. 8–27, while emphasizing the continuation of the prewar executive-legislative stalemate and the strength of conservative forces in the postwar years, has also been critical of Truman. "All his skills and energies . . . were directed to standing still. . . . When he took vigorous action in one direction it was axiomatic that he would contrive soon afterward to move in the conflicting direction" (p. 10). Cf. Richard Neustadt, "Congress and the Fair Deal: A Legislative Balance Sheet," in Carl Friedrich and John Galbraith, eds., *Public Policy* 5: 351–81.

[17] Curtis MacDougall, *Gideon's Army,* 3 vols. (New York, 1965–66), 1: 102–27. The National Educational Committee for a New Party, which would be explicitly anticommunist, included John Dewey, A. Philip Randolph, Daniel Bell, and Lewis Corey.

[18] On the continuity, see Mario Einaudi, *The Roosevelt Revolution* (New York, 1959), pp. 125, 334; Neustadt, "Congress and the Fair Deal"; Eric Goldman, *Rendezvous*

ship ultimately made him more attractive to liberals who despairingly watched the GOP-dominated Eightieth Congress and feared a repeal of the New Deal.

Their fears were unwarranted, as was their enthusiasm for the Fair Deal program. In practice it proved very limited—the housing program only provided for 810,000 units in six years of which only 60,000 were constructed;[19] social security benefits were extended to 10 million[20] and increased by about 75 percent, and the minimum wage was increased to 75 cents, but coverage was reduced by nearly a million.[21] But even had all of the Fair Deal been enacted, liberal reform would have left many millions beyond the benefits of government. The very poor, the marginal men, those neglected but acknowledged by the New Deal, went ultimately unnoticed by the Fair Deal.[22]

While liberals frequently chafed under Truman's leadership and questioned his commitment, they failed generally to recognize how shallow were his reforms. As the nation escaped a postwar de-

---

with Destiny (New York, 1952), pp. 314–15; and Goldman, *The Crucial Decade and After, America 1945–1960* (New York, 1960).

[19] Richard O. Davies, *Housing Reform during the Truman Administration* (Columbia, Mo.) p. 136. The original measure aimed for 1,050,000 units in seven years, at a time when the nation needed more than 12 million units to replace inadequate housing. During the Truman years, the government constructed 60,000 units of public housing (pp. 105–38). Rather than creating programs to keep pace with urban needs, the government in these years fell further behind. In contrast, private industry was more active, and it was assisted by noncontroversial federal aid. Under Truman's government, then, the greatest achievement in housing was that private capital, protected by the government, built houses for the higher-income market.

[20] Under the old law, the maximum benefit for families was $85 a month and the minimum was $15, depending on prior earnings. The new minimum was $25 and the maximum $150. (*Social Security Bulletin,* September 1950, p. 3). Unless couples also had other sources of income, even maximum benefits ($1,800 a year) placed them $616 under the BLS "maintenance" standard of living and $109 above the WPA-based "emergency" standard of living—the poverty level. (Calculations based on Kolko, *Wealth and Power,* pp. 96–98.) Since the payments were based on earnings, lower-income groups would receive even fewer benefits. They were the people generally without substantial savings or significant supplementary sources of income, and therefore they needed even more, not less, assistance.

[21] *Congressional Quarterly Almanac* 5 (1949): 434–35.

[22] Bernstein, "Economic Policies of the Truman Administration." Truman had achieved very little: improved unemployment benefits, some public power and conservation projects, agricultural assistance, and a National Science Foundation. He failed to secure the ill-conceived Brannan Plan and two programs suggested by Roosevelt: federal aid to education and health insurance. For his health insurance programs, see his messages of November 19, 1945, in *Public Papers of Truman* (1945), pp. 485–90, and of May 19, 1947, in *ibid.* (1947), pp. 250–52. In 1951, when the BLS calculated that a family of four needed $4,166 to reach the "maintenance" level, 55.6 percent of the nation's families had incomes beneath that level (Bureau of the Census, *Income Distribution in the United States,* p. 16).

pression, American liberals gained new faith in the American economy. Expressing their enthusiasm, they came to extoll big business for its contributions. Believing firmly in the success of progressive taxation, they exaggerated its effects, and congratulated themselves on the redistribution of income and the virtual abolition of poverty. Praising the economic system, they accepted big agriculture and big labor as evidence of healthy pluralism that protected freedom and guaranteed an equitable distribution of resources.[23]

Despite the haggling over details and the liberals' occasional dismay at Truman's style, he expressed many of their values. Like Roosevelt, Truman never challenged big business, never endangered large-scale capitalism. Indeed, his efforts as well as theirs were directed largely to maintaining and adjusting the powers of the major economic groups.

Fearing that organized labor was threatened with destruction, Truman, along with the liberals, had been sincerely frightened by the postwar rancor toward labor.[24] What they failed to understand was that most Americans had accepted unions as part of the political economy. Certainly most major industrialists had accepted organized labor, though smaller businessmen were often hostile.[25] Despite the overwrought rhetoric of debates, Congress did not actually menace labor. It was not seeking to destroy labor, only to restrict its power.

Many Americans did believe that the Wagner Act had unduly favored labor and was creating unions indifferent to the public welfare and hostile to corporate power. Capitalizing on this exaggerated fear of excessive union power, and the resentment from the postwar strikes, businessmen secured the Taft-Hartley Act.[26] Designed to weaken organized labor, it tried but failed to protect the membership from leaders; it did not effectively challenge the power of established unions. However, labor chiefs, recalling the bitter industrial warfare of the thirties, were still uneasy in their new positions. Condemning

[23] Bernstein, "Economic Policies of the Truman Administration."

[24] Truman to William Green, September 13, 1952, PPF 85, Truman Papers, Truman Library.

[25] Wilcock, "Industrial Management's Policies Toward Unionism," pp. 305–11; "Public Opinion on the Case Bill," OF 407B, Truman Papers, Truman Library; Robert Brady, *Business as a System of Power* (New York, 1943), pp. 210–15; Harry Millis and Emily Clark Brown, *From the Wagner Act to Taft-Hartley* (Chicago, 1950), pp. 286–98.

[26] R. Alton Lee, *Truman and Taft-Hartley: A Question of Mandate* (Lexington, Ky., 1966), pp. 22–71.

the legislation as a "slave-labor" act, they responded with fear, assailed the Congress, and declared that Taft-Hartley was the major political issue.[27]

Within a few years, when unions discovered that they were safe, Taft-Hartley faded as an issue. But in 1948 it served Truman well by establishing the GOP's hostility to labor and casting it back into the Democratic ranks. Both the president and union chiefs conveniently neglected his own kindling of antilabor passions (as when he had tried to draft strikers).[28] Exploiting Taft-Hartley as part of his strategy of patching the tattered Democratic coalition, Truman tied repeal of the "slave-labor" law to price controls, farm benefits, anticommunism, and civil rights in the campaign which won his election in his own right.

In courting the Negro the Truman administration in 1948 made greater promises to black citizens than had any previous federal government in American history. Yet, like many Americans, Truman as a senator had regarded the Negro's plight as peripheral to his interests, and with many of his generation he believed that equality was compatible with segregation.[29] As president, however, he found himself slowly prodded by conscience and pushed by politics. He moved cautiously at first and endorsed only measures affirming legal equality and protecting Negroes from violence.

Reluctant to fragment the crumbling Democratic coalition, Truman, in his first year, had seemed to avoid taking positions on civil rights which might upset the delicate balance between Northern and Southern Democrats. While he endorsed legislation for a statutory FEPC that the Congress would not grant, his efforts on behalf of the temporary FEPC (created by Roosevelt's executive order) were weaker. Having already weakened the power of the temporary agency, he also acquiesced in the legislative decision to kill it.[30] Despite the fears of Negro leaders that the death of FEPC would leave Negroes virtually unprotected from discrimination in the post-

[27] Lee, *Truman and Taft-Hartley*, pp. 79–130.
[28] Truman's message to Congress, May 25, 1946, in *Public Papers of Truman* (1946), pp. 277–80.
[29] Truman's address of July 14, 1940, reprinted in *Congressional Record*, 76th Cong., 3rd Sess., 5367–69.
[30] Ruchames, *Race, Jobs & Politics*, pp. 130–36. This section relies upon Bernstein, "The Ambiguous Legacy: The Truman Administration and Civil Rights" (paper given at the AHA, December 1966; copy at the Truman Library).

war job market, Truman would not even issue an order requiring nondiscrimination in the federal service and by government contractors.[31]

Though Truman was unwilling to use the prestige or power of his great office significantly on behalf of Negroes, he did assist their cause. While sidestepping political conflict, he occasionally supported FEPC and abolition of the poll tax. When Negroes were attacked, he did condemn the racial violence.[32] Though generally reluctant to move beyond rhetoric during his early years, Truman, shortly before the 1946 election, found conscience and politics demanding more. So distressed was he by racial violence that when Walter White of the NAACP and a group of white liberals urged him to assist the Negro, he promised to create a committee to study civil rights.[33]

The promise of a committee could have been a device to resist pressures, to delay the matter until after the election. And Truman could have appointed a group of politically safe men of limited reputation—men he could control. But instead, after the election, perhaps in an effort to mobilize the liberals for 1948, he appointed a committee of prominent men sympathetic to civil rights. They were men he could not control and did not seek to control.[34]

The committee's report, undoubtedly far bolder than Truman's expectations,[35] confirmed charges that America treated its Negroes as second-class citizens. It called for FEPC, an antilynching law, an anti-poll tax measure, abolition of segregation in interstate transportation, and the end of discrimination and segregation in federal agencies and the military. By attacking Jim Crow, the committee had moved to a redefinition of equality and interpreted segregation as incompatible with equality.[36]

Forced by the report to take a position, he no longer could easily remain an ally of Southern Democrats and maintain the wary allegiance of Negro leaders and urban liberals. Compelled earlier to yield to demands for advancement of the Negro, pressures which

---

[31] Truman to David Niles, July 22, 1946, and drafts (undated) of an order on nondiscrimination; and Philleo Nash to Niles (undated), Nash Files, Truman Library.
[32] Truman to Walter White, June 11, 1946, PPF 393, Truman Papers, Truman Library.
[33] Walter White, *A Man Called White* (New York, 1948), pp. 331–32.
[34] Robert Carr to Bernstein, August 11, 1966.
[35] Interview with Philleo Nash, September 19, 1966.
[36] President's Committee on Civil Rights, *To Secure These Rights* (Washington, 1947), pp. 1–95.

he did not wish fully to resist, Truman had encouraged these forces and they were moving beyond his control. On his decision, his political future might precariously rest. Threatened by Henry Wallace's candidacy on a third-party ticket, Truman had to take a bold position on civil rights or risk losing the important votes of urban Negroes. Though he might antagonize Southern voters, he foresaw no risk of losing Southern Democrats, no possibility of a bolt by dissidents, and the mild Southern response to the Civil Rights Report seemed to confirm this judgment.[37]

On February 2, 1948, Truman asked the Congress to enact most of the recommendations of his Civil Rights Committee (except most of those attacking segregation). Rather than using his executive powers, as the committee had urged, to end segregation in federal employment or to abolish segregation and discrimination in the military, he *promised* only to issue orders ending discrimination (but not specifying segregation) in the military and in federal agencies.[38] Retreating to moderation, the administration did not submit any of the legislation, nor did Truman issue the promised executive orders. "The strategy," an assistant later explained, "was to start with a bold measure and then temporize to pick up the right-wing forces. Simply stated, backtrack after the bang."[39]

Truman sought to ease Southern doubts by inserting in the 1948 platform the party's moderate 1944 plank on civil rights. Most Negro leaders, fearing the taint of Wallace and unwilling to return to the GOP, appeared stuck with Truman and they praised him. Though they desired a stronger plank, they would not abandon him at the convention, for his advocacy of rights for Negroes was unmatched by any twentieth-century president. To turn their backs on him in this time of need, most Negroes feared, would be injuring their own cause. But others were prepared to struggle for a stronger plank. Urban bosses, persuaded that Truman would lose, hoped to save their local tickets, and prominent white liberals sought power and principle. Triumphing at the convention, they secured a stronger plank, but it did not promise social equality. By promising equality when it was still regarded as compatible with segregation, they

[37] Clark Clifford, "Memorandum for the President," November 17, 1947, Clifford Papers (his possession), Washington, D.C.
[38] Truman's message to Congress, February 2, 1948, in *Public Papers of Truman* (1948), pp. 117–26.
[39] Interview with Nash.

were offering far less than the "walk forthrightly into the bright sunshine of human rights," which Hubert Humphrey, then mayor of Minneapolis, had pledged in leading the liberal effort.[40]

When some of the Southerners bolted and formed the States' Rights party, Truman was freed of any need for tender courtship of the South. He had to capture the Northern vote. Quickly he issued the long-delayed executive orders, which established a federal anti-discrimination board, declared a policy of equal opportunity in the armed forces, and established a committee to end military discrimination and segregation. (In doing so, Truman courted Negro voters and halted the efforts of A. Philip Randolph to lead a Negro revolt against the draft unless the military was integrated.)[41] Playing politics carefully during the campaign, Truman generally stayed away from civil rights and concentrated on inflation, public housing, and Taft-Hartley.

In the new Democratic Congress Truman could not secure the civil rights program, and a coalition of Southern Democrats and Northern Republicans blocked his efforts. Though liberals were unhappy with his leadership, they did not question his proposed legislation. All agreed on the emphasis on social change through legislation and judicial decisions. The liberal way was the legal way, and it seldom acknowledged the depth of American racism or even considered the possibility of bold new tactics. Only occasionally—in the threatened March on Washington in 1941, in some ride-ins in 1947,[42] and in the campaign of civil disobedience against the draft in 1948—had there been bolder means. In each case Negroes had devised and carried out these tactics. But generally they relied upon more traditional means: they expected white America to yield to political pressure and subscribe to the dictates of American democracy. By relying upon legal change, however, and by emphasizing measures to restore a *modicum* of human dignity, Negroes and whites did not confront the deeper problems of race relations which they failed to understand.[43]

---

[40] On the struggle, see Clifton Brock, *Americans for Democratic Action: Its Role in National Politics* (Washington, 1962), pp. 94–99; quotation at p. 98.

[41] Grant Reynolds, "A Triumph for Civil Disobedience," *Nation* 166 (August 28, 1948): pp. 228–29.

[42] George Houser and Bayard Rustin, "Journey of Reconciliation" (mimeo, n.d., probably 1947), CORE Files, Schomburg Collection, New York Public Library.

[43] There was no urging of special programs to assist Negroes left unemployed

Struggling for moderate institutional changes, liberals were disappointed by Truman's frequent unwillingness to use his executive powers in behalf of the cause he claimed to espouse. Only after considerable pressure did he create a FEPC-type agency during the Korean War.[44] His loyalty-and-security program, in its operation, discriminated against Negroes, and federal investigators, despite protests to Truman, apparently continued to inquire into attitudes of interracial sympathy as evidence relevant to a determination of disloyalty.[45] He was also slow to require the Federal Housing Administration to stop issuing mortgages on property with restrictive covenants, and it continued, by its policies, to protect residential segregation.[46]

Yet his government was not without significant achievements in civil rights. His special committee had quietly acted to integrate the armed forces,[47] and even the recalcitrant army had abolished racial quotas when the president secretly promised their restoration if the racial imbalance became severe.[48] And the Department of Justice, despite Truman's apparent indifference,[49] had been an active warrior in the battle against Jim Crow. Entering cases as an *amicus curiae,* Justice had submitted briefs arguing the unconstitutionality of enforcing restrictive covenants and of requiring separate-but-equal facilities in interstate transportation and in higher education.[50] During the summer of 1952, the Solicitor General's Office even won the administration's approval for a brief directly challenging segregated primary education.[51]

(at roughly double the white rate) in the mild recession of 1949–1950, nor was there open acknowledgement of race hatred.

[44] National Council of Negro Women to Truman, November 18, 1950, Nash Files, Truman Library; Senator William Benton to Truman, October 21, 1951, OF 526B, Truman Library.

[45] Carl Murphy to Truman, April 10, 1950, OF 93 misc.; Walter White to Truman, November 26, 1948, OF 252K; both in Truman Library.

[46] NAACP press release, February 4, 1949, Schomburg Collection, New York Public Library; Hortense Gabel to Raymond Foley, February 26, 1953, Foley Papers, Truman Library; Housing and Home Finance Agency, *Fifth Annual Report* (Washington, 1952), p. 413.

[47] President's Committee on Equality of Treatment and Opportunity in the Armed Forces, *Freedom to Serve* (Washington, 1950); Dalfiume, "Desegregation of the Armed Forces."

[48] Gordon Gray to Truman, March 1, 1950, OF 1285B, Truman Library.

[49] Interview with Philip Elman, December 21, 1966.

[50] *Shelley* v. *Kraemer,* 334 US 1; *Henderson* v. *United States* 339 US 816; *McLaurin* v. *Board of Regents,* 339 US 641.

[51] Interview with Elman; *Brown* v. *Board of Education,* 347 US 483.

The accomplishments of the Truman years were moderate, and the shortcomings left the nation with a great burden of unresolved problems. Viewed from the perspective of today, Truman's own views seem unduly mild and his government excessively cautious; viewed even by his own time he was a reluctant liberal, troubled by terror and eager to establish limited equality. He was ahead of public opinion in his legislative requests, but not usually in his actions. By his occasional advocacy, he educated the nation and held high the promise of equality. By kindling hope, he also may have prevented rebellion and restrained or delayed impulses to work outside of the system. But he also unleashed expectations he could not foresee, and forces which future governments would not be able to restrain.

Never as committed to civil rights as he was opposed to communism at home and abroad, Truman ultimately became a victim of his own loyalty-and-security policies. Mildly criticized in 1945 and 1946 for being "soft on communism," the administration belatedly responded after the disastrous election of 1946.[52] Truman appointed a committee to investigate loyalty and security, promptly accepted its standard of judgment ("reasonable grounds of belief in disloyalty"), and created a system of loyalty boards.[53]

Outraging many liberals, his loyalty program provoked vigorous criticisms—for its secret investigations, for the failure to guarantee the accused the right to know the identity of and cross-examine the accuser, for its loose standards of proof, for its attempt to anticipate disloyal behavior by inquiring into attitudes.[54] In seeking to protect the nation, the government seemed to be searching for all who *might* be disloyal—"potential subversives," Truman called them.[55]

[52] "The Report of the President's Temporary Commission on Employee Loyalty," Appendix 3, Charles Murphy Papers, Truman Library; Rep. Jennings Bryan to Truman, July 25, 1946, OF 2521, and Stephen Spingarn, "Notes on Meeting of Subcommittee of February 5, 1947," Spingarn Papers, Truman Library.

[53] E.O. 9806, 11 Fed. Reg. 13863; "The Report of the President's Temporary Commission on Employee Loyalty," quotation at 3; E.O. 9835, 12 F.R. 1935. On earlier programs, see Eleanor Bontecou, *The Federal Loyalty-Security Program* (Ithaca, N.Y., 1953), pp. 1–19.

[54] Letter by Zechariah Chafee, Jr., Erwin Griswold, Milton Katz, and Austin Scott, in *New York Times,* April 13, 1947; L. A. Nikoloric, "The Government Loyalty Program," *American Scholar* 19 (Summer 1950): 285–98; Bontecou, *Federal Loyalty-Security Program,* pp. 30–34.

[55] Quoted from Bontecou, *Federal Loyalty-Security Program,* p. 32, who suggests that Truman may have really meant Communists who might be subject to future

Dangerously confusing the problems of loyalty and security, the administration, in what might seem a burst of democratic enthusiasm, decided to apply the same standards to diplomats and gardeners. Disloyalty at any level of government would endanger the nation. "The presence within the government of any disloyal or subversive persons constitutes a threat to democratic processes," asserted Truman in launching the program.[56] Anxious to remove communism in government as a possible issue, Truman had exaggerated the dangers to the nation. And by assuming that disloyalty could be determined and subversives discovered, Truman seemed also to be promising *absolute* internal security.[57]

Shocked by earlier lax security procedures and unwilling to rely exclusively upon counterintelligence to uncover spies, the administration had responded without proper concern for civil liberties. So extreme was the program that it should have removed loyalty and security as a political issue. But by failing to distinguish between radical political activity and disloyalty, the administration endangered dissent and liberal politics: it made present or past membership in organizations on the attorney general's list evidence of possible disloyalty. Thus, in justifying investigations of political activity, it also legitimized occasional right-wing attacks on the liberal past and encouraged emphasis on the radicalism of a few New Dealers as evidence of earlier subversion.[58]

In their own activities, many liberals were busy combating domestic communism. Taking up the cudgels, the liberal Americans for Democratic Action (ADA) came often to define its purpose by its anticommunism. As an enemy of those liberals who would not renounce association with Communists, and, hence, as vigorous foes of the Progressive party, the ADA was prepared to do battle. Following Truman's strategy, ADA members assailed Wallace and his

orders by the party. Also see Truman's statement of November 14, 1947, in *Public Papers of Truman* (1947), pp. 489–91.

[56] Quoted from E.O. 9835, 12 Fed. Reg. 1935.

[57] Much of the analysis of this program and its contribution to the rise of McCarthyism is indebted to Athan Theoharis, "The Rhetoric of Politics: Foreign Policy, Internal Security and Domestic Politics in the Truman Era, 1945–1950" (paper delivered at the Southern Historical Association, November 1966). Cf. Daniel Bell, ed., *The New American Right* (New York, 1955). On the need for absolute security, see Tom Clark to A. Devitt Vanech, February 14, 1947, OF 2521, Truman Library; "Report of the President's Temporary Commission on Employee Loyalty"; Theoharis, "Rhetoric of Politics," pp. 26–32.

[58] Theoharis, "Rhetoric of Politics," pp. 29–31.

supporters as Communists, dupes of the Communists, and fellow travelers. To publicize its case the ADA even relied upon the tactic of guilt by association and paid for advertisements listing the Progressive party's major donors and the organizations on the attorney general's list with which they were or had been affiliated.[59] (Truman himself also Red-baited. "I do not want and will not accept the political support of Henry Wallace and his Communists. . . . These are days of high prices for everything, but any price for Wallace and his Communists is too much for me to pay.")[60] In the labor movement liberals like the Reuther brothers led anti-Communist crusades, and the CIO ultimately expelled its Communist-led unions. ("Granting the desirability of eliminating Communist influence from the trade union movement," later wrote Irving Howe and Louis Coser, "one might still have argued that mass expulsions were not only a poor way of achieving this end but constituted a threat to democratic values and procedures.")[61]

Expressing the administration's position, Attorney General J. Howard McGrath proclaimed a "struggle against pagan communist philosophies that seek to enslave the world." "There are today many Communists in America," he warned. "They are everywhere—in factories, offices, butcher stores, on street corners, in private business. And each carries in himself the death of our society."[62] ("I don't think anybody ought to be employed as instructors [sic] for the young people of this country who believes in the destruction of our form of government," declared Truman.)[63]

Calling for a crusade against evil, viewing communism as a

[59] Karl M. Schmidt, *Henry A. Wallace: Quixotic Crusade, 1948* (Syracuse, N.Y., 1960), pp. 159–60, 252–53, 261–62. On the strategy of letting the liberal intellectuals attack Wallace, see Clifford, "Memorandum for the President," November 17, 1947. On the split in liberal ranks on cooperation with Communists, see Curtis MacDougall, *Gideon's Army* 1: 122–25.

[60] Truman's address of March 17, 1948, in *Public Papers of Truman* (1948), p. 189.

[61] Howe and Coser, *The American Communist Party*, 2d ed. (New York, 1962), p. 468; see pp. 457–68 for the activity of labor.

[62] McGrath's address of April 8, 1949, McGrath Papers, Truman Library, which was called to my attention by Theoharis. Also see Theoharis, "Rhetoric of Politics," n. 37.

[63] Quoted from transcript of President's News Conference of June 9, 1949, Truman Library. Also see Sidney Hook, "Academic Integrity and Academic Freedom," *Commentary* 8 (October 1949), cf., Alexander Meiklejohn, *New York Times Magazine,* March 27, 1949, pp. 10ff. In his veto of the McCarran Act, Truman failed to defend civil liberties effectively and instead emphasized that the act would impair the government's anticommunist efforts. Veto message of September 22, 1950, *Public Papers of Truman* (1950), pp. 645–53.

virulent poison, the administration continued to emphasize the need for *absolute* protection, for *absolute* security. By creating such high standards and considering their fulfillment easy, by making success evidence of will and resolution, the administration risked assaults if its loyalty-and-security program was proved imperfect. To discredit the administration, all that was needed was the discovery of some Red "spies," and after 1948 the evidence seemed abundant—Alger Hiss, William Remington, Judith Coplon, Julius and Ethel Rosenberg.[64]

In foreign policy, too, Truman, though emphasizing the danger of communism, had promised success. Containment could stop the spread of communism: military expansion could be restrained and revolutions prevented. Since revolutions, by liberal definition, were imposed on innocent people by a small minority, a vigilant American government could block them. By his rhetoric, he encouraged American innocence and left many citizens little choice but to believe in their own government's failure when America could not thwart revolution—when the Chinese Communists triumphed. If only resolute will was necessary, as the administration suggested, then what could citizens believe about America's failure? Was it simply bungling? Or treason and betrayal?[65]

By his rhetoric and action, Truman had contributed to the loss of public confidence and set the scene in which Joseph McCarthy could flourish. Rather than resisting the early movement of anti-communism, he had acted energetically to become a leader, and ultimately contributed to its transformation into a crusade which threatened his administration. But the president could never understand his own responsibility, and his failure handicapped him. Because he had a record of vigorous anticommunism, Truman was ill-prepared to respond to McCarthy's charges. At first the president could not foresee any danger and tried to dispense with McCarthy as "the greatest asset the Kremlin has."[66] And later, as the senator terrorized the government, Truman was so puzzled and pained that he retreated from the conflict and sought to starve McCarthy without publicity. Rather than responding directly to charges, the president

[64] Theoharis, "Rhetoric of Politics," pp. 32–38.
[65] See Truman's addresses of March 17, 1948, in *Public Papers of Truman* (1948), pp. 182–86; and of June 7, 1949, in *ibid.* (1949), pp. 277–80. See Theoharis, "Rhetoric of Politics," pp. 17–27.
[66] Quoted from transcript of President's News Conference, March 30, 1950, Truman Library.

tried instead to tighten his program. But he could not understand that such efforts (for example, revising the loyalty standard to "reasonable doubt as to the loyalty of the individual")[67] could not protect the administration from charges of being soft on communism. He only encouraged these charges by seeming to yield to criticism, admitting that the earlier program was unnecessarily lax.

The president was a victim of his own policies and tactics. But bristling anticommunism was not simply Truman's way, but often the liberal way.[68] And the use of guilt by association, the discrediting of dissent, the intemperate rhetoric—these, too, were not simply the tactics of the Truman administration. The rancor and wrath of these years were not new to American politics, nor to liberals.[69] Indeed, the style of passionate charges and impugning opponents' motives may be endemic to American democratic politics. Submerging the issues in passion, using labels as substitutes for thought, questioning motives, these tactics characterized much of the foreign policy debate of the prewar and postwar years as well—a debate in which the liberals frequently triumphed. Developing a more extreme form of this rancorous style, relying upon even wilder charges and more flagrant use of guilt by association, McCarthy and his cohorts flailed the liberals and the Democratic administration.

In looking at the war and postwar years, liberal scholars have emphasized the achievements of democratic reform, the extension of prosperity, the movement to greater economic and social equality. Confident that big business had become socially responsible and that economic security was widespread, they have celebrated the triumph of democratic liberalism. In charting the course of national progress, they frequently neglected or minimized major problems, or they interpreted them as temporary aberrations, or blamed them on conservative forces.[70]

[67] E.O. 10241, 16 Fed. Reg. 9795.

[68] On liberal confusion about this period, see Joseph Rauh, "The Way to Fight Communism," *Future*, January 1962. For the argument that liberal naiveté about Stalinism had led to McCarthyism, see Irving Kristol, "Civil Liberties, 1952—A Study in Confusion," *Commentary* 13 (March 1952): 228–36.

[69] For earlier antitotalitarianism, see Freda Kirchway, "Curb the Fascist Press," *Nation* 154 (March 28, 1942): 357–58.

[70] Although there are no thorough, scholarly histories of these years, there are many texts that embody these characteristics. In addition, much of the monographic literature by other social scientists conforms to the pattern described in this para-

Yet the developments of the sixties—the rediscovery of poverty and racism—suggest that the emphasis has been misplaced in interpreting these earlier years. In the forties and fifties white racism did not greatly yield to the dictates of American democracy, and the failure was not only the South's. The achievements of democratic liberalism were more limited than its advocates believed, and its reforms left many Americans still without adequate assistance. Though many liberal programs were blocked or diluted by conservative opposition, the liberal vision itself was dim. Liberalism in practice was defective, and its defects contributed to the temporary success of McCarthyism. Curiously, though liberalism was scrutinized by some sympathizers[71] who attacked its faith in progress and by others who sought to trace McCarthyism to the reform impulses of earlier generations,[72] most liberals failed to understand their own responsibility for the assault upon civil liberties or to respond to the needs of an "other America" which they but dimly perceived.

graph. For a discussion, see Bernstein, "Economic Policies of the Truman Administration."

[71] In particular see the works of Reinhold Niebuhr and the new realism that he has influenced: Niebuhr, *Moral Man and Immoral Society* (New York, 1932); *The Children of Light and the Children of Darkness* (New York, 1944); Arthur Schlesinger, Jr., *The Vital Center* (Cambridge, Mass., 1947). What is needed is a critical study of wartime and postwar liberalism, an explanation for many on "Where We Came Out" (to use the title of Granville Hicks's volume). See Jason Epstein, "The CIA and the Intellectuals," *New York Review of Books* 7 (April 20, 1967): 16–21.

[72] See Bell, ed., *The New American Right,* and the tendency to trace McCarthyism back to earlier reform movements and often to populism. The volume, interestingly, is dedicated to the managing editor of the *New Leader.* For a former radical's attempt to reappraise the liberal past, see Richard Hofstadter, *The Age of Reform* (New York, 1956).

III THE POLITICS OF REFORM

Harry S. Truman, January 3, 1946

THE RECONVERSION CRISIS AND
THE NEED FOR CONGRESSIONAL ACTION

In this abridged version of a nationally broadcast speech appealing for public support, Truman outlines his approach to the complex problems of postwar reconversion and discusses his problems with Congress.

Nineteen forty-six is our year of decision. This year we lay the foundation of our economic structure which will have to serve for generations. This year we must decide whether or not we shall devote our strength to reaching the goal of full production and full employment. This year we shall have to make the decisions which will determine whether or not we gain that great future at home and abroad which we fought so valiantly to achieve.

I wish I could say to you that everything is in perfect order—that we are on the way to eternal prosperity. I cannot.

The months ahead will be difficult. We are well along the road toward our goal, but at every turn we run the risk of coming upon a barrier which can stop us.

In the message to the Congress on September 6, 1945, and in other messages, I have outlined legislative proposals to meet the problems which lie ahead. Many of these proposals are pending before the Congress. A few have been adopted. Progress on most of them has been distressingly slow.

Now, at the beginning of this new year, is a good time to take stock.

First, I can say with emphasis that the legislative branch of our government has done its full share toward carrying out its responsibility in foreign affairs.

*   *   *

When we turn to our domestic problems, we do not find a similar record of achievement and progress in the Congress.

From *Public Papers of the Presidents of the United States: Harry S. Truman, 1946* (U.S. Government Printing Office, 1962), pp. 1–8.

And yet our domestic postwar problems are just as serious and, in many ways, just as difficult as our international problems. Unless we can soon meet the need of obtaining full production and full employment at home, we shall face serious consequences. They will be serious not only in what they mean to the American people as such, but also in what they can do to our position as a leader among the nations of the world.

With the surrender of Japan last August, we set certain domestic goals to be attained. The tasks before us were clear then; they are clear now.

We had to reconvert our economy from war to peace—as rapidly as possible.

We had to keep employment and wages and purchasing power on a high level during the changeover.

We had to keep the prices of commodities from going up too high. We had to get civilian goods produced and put upon the market promptly.

In other words, our primary aim was to bring about an expanded production and steady, well-paid jobs and purchasing power for all who wanted to work—we had to maintain high farm income—and good profits based on big volume.

Reaching that goal means better homes, better food, better health, better education, and security for every citizen of the United States. It means bigger and steadier markets for business. It means world confidence in our leadership.

We [have] gone a long way in getting our workers and factories back on a peacetime basis. War plants have been cleared in large numbers, and their war contracts settled. Men, machines, and raw materials are already back in peacetime production in greater numbers, and are producing more goods, than any one of us had dared to expect a few months ago.

But we are a long way from our goal.

The return of the United States to a peacetime economy in 1946 requires the same cooperation that we had during the war years. Industry, labor, agriculture, the Congress, the president—each one of these—is called upon to do certain things. None of them can do the job alone. Together they can.

There is one vast difference, however, between 1941 and 1946. While we were producing to meet the needs of war, we had the great stimulus of the war itself. That stimulus is now gone. The cooperation and teamwork in some quarters, I am sorry to say, have suffered proportionately.

The reconversion period through which we are now passing has as many elements of danger to our economy as the war period. Whether we fall into a period of great deflation because of unemployment and reduced wages and purchasing power, or whether we embark upon a period of great inflation with reduced production and spiraling prices—the result will be equally disastrous.

Immediately after the surrender of Japan, in the full flush of our victory, representatives of the Congress, of industry, of labor, and of farm organizations called upon me. From them I received promises of cooperation and teamwork during this reconversion period.

I regret to say that those promises have not all been kept. As a result, many obstacles have been thrown in our path as we have tried to avert the dangers of inflation and deflation.

First among those obstacles have been labor-management disputes.

Immediately after V-J Day, the government announced a policy of taking off the wartime controls which it had exercised over wages and over industrial relations as a whole. It was thought, particularly by labor and management, that through collective bargaining, labor and management would be able to find common ground, that they would be able to agree upon ways to avoid stoppages of work and to continue the production that is so necessary to our economic life.

Unfortunately, industrial disputes soon began, and many strikes were called. Many of these disputes and strikes were settled or conciliated. But there were some strikes of nationwide importance in which collective bargaining and conciliation both failed.

In order to enable management and labor to make a common effort to find means for preventing work stoppages, and to consider many other aspects of industrial relations, the government invited their representatives to meet in a conference of their own, in Washington.

Although it did reach agreement on some matters, and although it did pave the way for future meetings and discussions, the Labor-Management Conference could not agree upon a solution of the most immediate and pressing problem—what to do about strikes when bargaining, conciliation, and arbitration had all broken down.

As industrial strife has increased, with automobile workers out on strike, and with steel workers, electrical workers, and packinghouse workers scheduling strikes very soon, I have been deeply concerned about the future. I am sure that all of us, including these workers themselves, share that concern.

When the Labor-Management Conference ended, it became my responsibility as the president of the United States to recommend a course of action. This I did in a message to the Congress on December 3, 1945.

I recommended certain fact-finding procedures which I believe can go a long way toward meeting these problems.

I had hoped that the Congress either would follow my recommendations or would at least propose a solution of its own. It has done neither.

The purposes of my recommendations have been misrepresented by some of the spokesmen of both labor and management. The recommendations, however, are very clear.

I proposed that in the few nationwide industries where a stoppage of work would vitally affect the national public interest, after all other efforts had failed, the government should step in to obtain all the facts and report its findings to the country.

Experience has repeatedly shown that once the public knows the facts it can make its opinion felt in a practical way. In order to give a fact-finding board a reasonable chance to function before a strike is actually called, I suggested that there be a thirty-day "cooling-off period." I further recommended that the power of subpoena be given to the fact-finding board so that it could get all the pertinent facts. . . .

I have indicated my opposition, and I repeat it now, to the antilabor bills pending in the Congress which seek to deprive labor of the right to bargain collectively, or which seek to deprive a union of its ultimate right to strike. That is why I am so anxious to have on our books an effective statute which will have none of the evil effects of some of the legislation now pending.

Of equal importance with the settlement of management-labor disputes during this reconversion period is the question of keeping prices on an even keel. Here too there are pressure groups at work in the Congress and outside the Congress, constantly pushing, lobbying, arguing to take off price controls and let prices go up without interference.

We cannot keep purchasing power high or business prosperous if prices get out of hand. There is no use talking about the expanded production upon which steady jobs depend, unless we keep prices at levels which the vast majority of the people can afford to pay. . . .

People have a right to protection for their savings. They should be assured that their earnings will give them a decent standard of living. Businessmen who want to plan ahead have the right to know now that the prices of the things they will have to buy in the future will remain predictable. They must have confidence now that the purchasing power upon which their markets depend will be protected.

We are all anxious to eliminate controls just as rapidly as we can do so. The steps that we have already taken show that. But price and rent controls will have to be maintained for many months to come, if we hope to maintain a steady and stable economy. The line must be held. I shall urge the Congress after it reconvenes to renew the act as soon as possible and well in advance of its expiration date, June 30, 1946.

*   *   *

One essential part of our program, designed not only to tide us over the reconversion period but also to carry us to our goal of full production and a higher standard of living, is the adoption of full employment legislation. A satisfactory full employment bill was passed by the Senate. Another bill was passed by the House of Representatives which is not at all acceptable, and which does not accomplish any of the purposes sought. These two bills are now in conference between the Senate and the House of Representatives.

It was my fervent hope, and I am sure that it was the hope of all progressive Americans, that before the recess of the Congress for the Christmas holidays the conferees would have reported a satisfactory full employment bill for adoption by both houses. No such bill has been reported. It is most important that the conferees report a satisfactory bill immediately upon the reconvening of the Congress.

One of the measures which I have been urging upon the Congress ever since May of last year is that the federal government make provision to supplement the unemployment insurance benefits now provided by the different states.

While unemployment has not reached anything like the level which was feared, there is still need to provide at least some measure of subsistence to those men and women who do lose their jobs by the end of war production.

The Senate has passed an acceptable measure along these lines. But in the House of Representatives the bill is now locked up in the Ways and Means Committee. It will remain locked up in that committee unless *you* the people of the United States insist that it be reported out and passed.

On several occasions I have also asked that the Congress outlaw by permanent statute un-American discrimination in employment. A small handful of Congressmen in the Rules Committee of the House have prevented this legislation from reaching a vote by the Congress. Legislation making permanent the Fair Employment Practices Committee would carry out a fundamental American ideal. I am sure that the overwhelming mass of our citizens favor this legislation and want their Congressmen to vote for it.

I have also asked that the Congress raise substantially the amount of minimum wages now provided by law. There are still millions of workers whose incomes do not provide a decent standard of living. We cannot have a healthy national economy so long as any large section of our working people receive wages which are below decent standards. Although hearings have been held on this question in the Congress, no action has been taken. . . .

In any discussion of action at this time, housing must be considered. In this field the Congress *is* cooperating, and there is much to be done.

Of the three major components which make up our standard of living—food, clothing, and housing—housing presents our most difficult problem. As for food, there is every prospect that 1946 will be a peak year of production. As for clothing, it is expected that production will reach a satisfactory level sometime this year. But in housing the situation is different.

We urgently need about 5 million additional homes. This does not include the replacement of millions of existing substandard dwellings in the cities and on the farms. The greatest number of homes constructed in any one year before the war was less than a million. It is clear, therefore, that this is an emergency problem which calls for an emergency method of solution.

We must utilize the same imagination, the same determination that back in 1941 enabled us to raise our sights to overcome the Nazi and Japanese military might. With that imagination and determination we can mobilize our resources here at home to produce the housing we require.

Because of the critical need, I have appointed an emergency housing expediter. He will be empowered to use every agency of the government and every resource of the government to break the bottlenecks and to produce the materials for housing. The government is determined to give private enterprise every encouragement and assistance to see that the houses are produced—and produced fast. Where private enterprise is unable to provide the necessary housing, it becomes the responsibility of the government to do so. But it is primarily a job for private enterprise to do—a job which is a challenge as stimulating as any goal we set during the war.

*   *   *

I seek no conflict with the Congress. I earnestly desire cooperation with the Congress. Orderly procedure in the Congress is indispensable to the democratic process. But orderly procedure does not mean needless delay.

Stable world relationships require full production and full employment in the United States.

There are voices of defeat, dismay, timidity among us who say it cannot be done. These I challenge. They will not guide us to success, these men of little faith.

We cannot shirk our leadership in the postwar world. The problems of our economy will not be solved by timid men, mistrustful of each other. We cannot face 1946 in a spirit of drift or irresolution.

The men and women who made this country great and kept it free were plain people with courage and faith.

Let us justify this heritage.

Mary H. Blewett

ROOSEVELT, TRUMAN, AND THE ATTEMPT TO REVIVE THE NEW DEAL

An important theme of the early years of the Truman presidency was the effort to carry out Roosevelt's design of reviving New Deal liberalism. Contrasting the approaches which both presidents employed in dealing with Capitol Hill, Mary H. Blewett concludes that neither FDR's aggressiveness nor Truman's conciliation were sufficient to overcome the resistance of an ideologically hostile Congress.

World War II halted the New Deal of Franklin D. Roosevelt and the Democratic party. Roosevelt had already faced stiff opposition from Congress and the public against extending New Deal programs in the late 1930s, but the war replaced domestic reform as the central political issue of the early 1940s. Despite Roosevelt's public avoidance of reform issues during wartime, the possibility of a postwar revival of the New Deal obsessed liberals and conservatives. When in the 1944 campaign the president championed a policy of postwar full employment and new programs to raise standards of health, education, and social security, liberals cheered and conservatives organized to fight. Roosevelt died as the battle over reviving the New Deal began, but his successor Harry S. Truman pledged his new administration to the effort. Truman's cautious attempts to persuade Democratic conservatives to support his legislative program failed; by the end of 1945 he had lost control of Congress and had won the enmity of liberals and labor. In spite of demonstrated conservative strength and serious postwar inflation, the president tried to force Congress to vote for the legislative program vitally needed to secure urban votes in the upcoming elections. Lacking public support and in trouble with the Democratic left, Truman had no influence on Congress. The Democrats, weakened by disunity and the president's inability to solve the problems of reconversion, lost the 1946 elections.

The Roosevelt administration's planning for reconversion to a full

Adapted by the author from "The Frustration of the New Deal Revival" by Mary H. Hinchey Blewett (Ph.D. Dissertation, University of Missouri, 1965). Copyright © 1965 by Mary H. Hinchey Blewett.

employment economy after the end of World War II centered in the National Resources Planning Board (NRPB). An executive agency assigned this function in 1940, the NRPB quickly became the vehicle for the ideas of Keynesian economists, such as Alvin Hansen of Harvard, who used the board's close relationship to the president to promote a revival of the New Deal. Because of the strong anti-administration tide in the 1942 elections and the reformist nature of the board's recommendations, especially what conservatives called a "cradle to grave" social security program, Congress abolished the NRPB in 1943. The leadership in this fight fell to Southern Democrats and to an important Republican conservative, Senator Robert A. Taft of Ohio. The abrupt demise of the NRPB was a defeat for the administration and a clear victory for the conservatives in Congress. Roosevelt was forced to assign Congress a large role in postwar planning and to hold the NRPB's recommendations discreetly in abeyance. But in his 1944 State of the Union message, written in part by Hansen, the president outlined a new Economic Bill of Rights and endorsed the concept of a revival of the New Deal.

As the presidential election approached, Roosevelt considered steps to strengthen the liberal-urban coalition which had become the basis of the national Democratic party. A light Democratic vote in the 1942 congressional elections had produced the strongest Republican gains since the 1920s—and what Roosevelt privately dubbed the "impossible" Seventy-eighth Congress. Organized labor resented the conservatism of Congress, grumbled about frozen wartime wages, and feared postwar unemployment and reaction. Liberals complained about the postponement of postwar domestic planning. Roosevelt needed to reassure the Democratic left while avoiding a revolt on the right.

Conservative opposition to the administration emerged most strongly over the issue of tax policy in early 1944. Roosevelt had been unable to get substantial tax increases in 1942 or 1943, and his economic advisers warned that government borrowing in lieu of higher taxes would produce dangerous postwar inflation and a subsequent depression. The 1944 tax bill failed to produce the increase urgently demanded by the administration, and the president inadvertently precipitated a serious political conflict with the Democratic leadership by vetoing the bill. Believing that the tough veto message impugned their motives, the congressional leaders struck back. The veto was overridden. Alben Barkley of Kentucky resigned as Senate majority leader and was immediately reelected by a unanimous vote of the Senate Democrats. The revolt in the Senate prompted Roosevelt to improve his relations with Capitol Hill.

One of the irritants in this relationship was Vice-President Henry Wallace, who was actively seeking renomination. The Democratic leadership disliked both Wallace's behavior as presiding officer of the Senate and his strenuous commitment to postwar reform, which he tried to make the issue of his renomination fight. Wallace was no more popular with the Democratic bosses in cities vital to the Roosevelt coalition. Instead of naming his vice-president, as he had done in 1940, the president allowed contending factions to promote possible candidates. Roosevelt needed a man who possessed a liberal record but was acceptable to Congress. He chose Senator Harry S. Truman of Missouri and promised Wallace a position in the cabinet.

Wallace's defeat made it even more imperative for Roosevelt to reassure the Democratic left on postwar full employment. In the last weeks of the campaign the president acted on the advice of former NRPB economists, many of them now in the Bureau of the Budget, and delivered a speech on this issue in Chicago on October 28. The administration, he said, expected serious economic difficulties in the reconversion period. Large-scale unemployment would occur as government spending on war production stopped. To maintain full employment for the postwar period, Roosevelt argued that the administration must revive the New Deal with new programs to provide work for all and to raise standards of health, education, and social security. Maintenance of full employment—60 million jobs—required a rekindling of reform. He dramatically told his enthusiastic audience at Soldiers' Field: "We are not going to turn the clock back!" The Chicago speech relieved the anxieties of organized labor and urban liberals. It inspired the newly organized Political Action Committee of the CIO to get out a heavy labor vote. Roosevelt won easily over Republican Thomas E. Dewey of New York, and the Democrats gained twenty-five seats in the House while holding their own in the Senate.

The president intended to feature a proposal to expand the social security program in his 1945 State of the Union message, but this section of the draft message was deleted in December 1944 after the Allied military reverses in the Battle of the Bulge. Preoccupied with problems of diplomacy abroad and the politics of foreign policy at home, Roosevelt temporarily postponed a showdown with Congress on a postwar New Deal. Instead he waited for the Republican foreign-policy leader, Senator Arthur Vandenberg of Michigan, to pledge bipartisan support for the administration's outline for a peace settlement. Then on January 20, a few days after Vandenberg's announcement, Roosevelt removed conservative Texan Jesse Jones as secretary of commerce and head of the powerful Reconstruction Finance Corporation and designated Henry Wallace to replace him.

The appointment of Wallace to this influential position aroused bitter opposition among conservatives in Congress. The Senate Commerce Committee hearings on the appointment made clear that Wallace intended to use the RFC's lending powers to promote full employment. Dominated by Wallace's opponents, the committee reported out the George Bill to sever the RFC from Commerce and it also advised the Senate to reject Wallace. A motion to vote first on the nomination before consideration of the George Bill, a move designed to maximize anti-Wallace votes, was defeated in an extremely close vote. In this fight the administration got crucial support from eight Southern Democrats. Vice-president Truman had managed to get those votes by agreeing to refer a bill for a public power project in the Missouri River Valley to the hostile Commerce Committee which would kill it. Truman spent some of his hard-won influence in this maneuver and received sharp criticism from the liberal press. The George Bill passed, separating the RFC from Commerce, and later Wallace won confirmation. The confirmation of the Wallace appointment was one of Roosevelt's few victories on domestic policy during the war. The fact that the administration had operated skillfully to regain the upper hand from Congress on a key postwar domestic issue far overshadowed the limited nature of the victory, and the left wing of the Democratic party felt secure in the knowledge that Roosevelt and Wallace were working on behalf of postwar full employment. The death of Roosevelt on April 12, 1945, shattered this security.

Truman's relationship with FDR had been distant during the campaign and after. He thought at the convention that Roosevelt had wanted him on the ticket to aid the passage of foreign-policy legis-

lation through the Senate. However, his absence from the meetings of
the Democratic leadership on legislative strategy was noted with
some surprise by Dean Acheson, assistant secretary of state for
congressional relations. Truman had few important assignments as
vice-president other than the Wallace confirmation. He possessed
no illusions about the vice-presidency and had been a reluctant
candidate. Once elected he had been acutely aware of the power-
lessness of his new position and of the way it upset his old patterns
of association in the Senate.

As successor to the dead president, Truman realized he had no
personal political base from which to operate, no public following.
He knew far less about the administration's programs and plans
than those who now looked to him for leadership. As an administrator he would have to control and direct a collection of strangers in
the Executive Office who owed him nothing and who generally felt
that he was tragically inadequate to take on Roosevelt's responsibilities. At the suggestion of congressional leaders, the new president dropped a public attitude of self-effacing humility after a few
days. In public statements and in his first address to Congress, he
pledged to continue Roosevelt's policies. His forceful behavior and
willingness to learn in the first week of his presidency impressed
the White House staff.

Truman's political vulnerability and his background as a senator
convinced him of the necessity of working with Congress on domestic policy. He sought to continue Roosevelt's postwar program and
believed he could obtain cooperation from the legislative branch by
increasing the role of Congress in policymaking. He appreciated
the dangers of this course—Congress would support him only as
long as it remained politically advantageous, he told Budget Director
Harold D. Smith in May. But he also felt deeply that only congressional approval of legislation would give him the power he needed
to be a successful president and party leader.

As a senator and as vice-president, Truman had observed un-
necessary conflict between the Congress and Roosevelt. Disorderly
administrative organization in the Executive Office caused trouble;
cabinet officers fought publicly; the Democratic leadership was
often ignored; Roosevelt appealed across party lines for support.
Truman himself had been treated in a cavalier fashion by the Roosevelt White House before attaining national prominence during World

War II. The result was clear to the new president: annoyed Democrats rebelled, and much important legislation was either compromised or lost. The antagonism between the Congress and the presidency, as Truman saw it, lay not in ideological conflicts over the welfare state and Keynesian economics but in the distribution of political power between the White House and Capitol Hill. The key to FDR's difficulties thus had been his insensitivity to the political requirements of congressmen.

During the first four months of his administration, Truman attempted to establish a closer relationship between the executive branch and the Congress. He proposed legislation to reorganize the executive and to eliminate FDR's tangled strands of authority and jurisdiction. He replaced Roosevelt appointees in the cabinet with former members of Congress, such as James F. Byrnes at the State Department and Fred Vinson at the Treasury. He appointed Tom C. Clark as attorney general after Clark had been recommended by the powerful Texas delegation in Congress. Representative Clinton Anderson, who had investigated wartime food problems, became secretary of agriculture. He hoped that the legislative skills, experience, and connections of these men would help him persuade Congress to act favorably on legislation. By midsummer only Wallace in Commerce and Secretary of the Interior Harold Ickes remained of the old Roosevelt cabinet, primarily because of their strong followings among liberal Democrats and independents.

Truman resolved to make important use of his meetings with the Democratic leadership. He smoothed the last vestiges of irritation over the Wallace confirmation by appointing a St. Louis banker, John Snyder, as head of the RFC, an appointment warmly received by Jesse Jones and his congressional friends. Truman dealt deferentially with powerful committees in Congress, lunching informally with them on Capitol Hill. He took a seat in the Senate, listened to major speeches in favor of the United Nations Charter, then rose and made his own supporting speech. He participated actively in legislative strategy to get votes on important foreign policy bills and agreed to a two-month summer recess beginning August 1 after the passage of the legislation on foreign policy.

Although foreign policy issues and the Potsdam Conference absorbed most of Truman's time in the summer of 1945, he also sought the cooperation of Congress on domestic policy. Most of Roosevelt's staff stayed on as speechwriters and planners, serving as his source of information on FDR's postwar domestic plans. The staff seemed satisfied with its continuing role in domestic planning and with Truman's commitment to a postwar New Deal. The president, however, shaped his own strategy with Congress. In late May he sent his first message on domestic policy, a request for unemployment compensation during reconversion. The document picked up the prediction of full employment advocates that large scale unemployment would require action by the federal government; it especially reflected the fears of West Coast Democrats who worried about the political consequences of joblessness resulting from the heavy concentration of war industries there. The message fit the economic forecasts and political anxieties of liberals, but it was carefully planned to avoid exciting congressional opposition.

Truman's recommendation on unemployment compensation was limited to the period of reconversion, no farther. The message did not endorse the comprehensive legislation to expand social security introduced by Democratic liberals, and against the advice of Budget Director Smith, the president refused to attach a draft of the administration's bill to the message. Instead he dealt directly with the chairmen of the committees involved, Senator Walter George of Finance and Congressman Robert Doughton of the House Ways and Means Committee. Truman asked them if they wished to see the administration's draft bill; they did not. He then cultivated the two chairmen for weeks and finally got their grudging cooperation. Doughton introduced the administration's bill in the House on July 9, and, more importantly, both committees scheduled hearings on unemployment compensation before considering tax reduction. In persuading them to put aside the politically irresistible subject of lower taxes, the president scored an important victory.

However, liberal Democrats in Congress became restless under Truman's cautious strategy. As the August 1 recess approached, they began to press the administration to reveal its plans for domestic policy. The victory of the British Labour party over the Churchill government in July seemed instructive to them. On July 30 twelve progressive senators led by Harley Kilgore of West Virginia and Claude Pepper of Florida met to draft a full employment program which they intended to present to their constituents during the recess. Prompted by Majority Leader Barkley's refusal to hold a party caucus on reconversion problems, the protest meeting reflected deep dissatisfaction with the administration's view of the congressional recess as a reward for cooperation and as a needed period of calm.

On August 1 a fight took place on the Senate floor over control of domestic policy. Barkley, speaking for Truman, made it clear that full employment legislation would be introduced when Congress reconvened in October. This was not enough. To satisfy the angry liberals Barkley had to list a specific fifteen-point program. He then spent the rest of the afternoon listening to speeches by liberal Democrats warning the administration of the political and economic dangers of mass unemployment during reconversion. The Senate then recessed as planned until October 8, but political pressure from the left wing of the party had forced the administration to reveal the outlines of domestic policy before the president was ready. Truman needed to assert his leadership in this area if he meant to control political strategy.

The decision to use atomic weapons and the sudden Japanese surrender on August 14 created a public sense of crisis over reconversion. Orderly conversion to civilian production seemed impossible; government war orders were automatically canceled. The national press predicted industrial turmoil and high unemployment; liberal journalists feared another major depression. Labor leaders forecast 10 million unemployed in six to eight weeks.

Truman's response to the crisis was to submit a lengthy domestic program for reconversion to Congress on September 6. He did not, however, abandon the political strategy which had seemed so successful during his first months in office. The purpose of this twenty-one point message was to unite the party under his leadership by a commitment to reform coupled with an approach to Congress that would assure the passage of legislation. The end of wartime politics and the beginning of reconversion did not alter the president's views on the correct strategy to use with Congress. He believed that Democratic members of Congress would support the administration's program in return for cooperation on local projects. Congress would regain power in the legislative process, and he would gain stature as president and party leader.

Truman specifically rejected the advice of liberals in the Congress and in the executive who urged him to seize the moment of economic crisis, use it to arouse the public, and force Congress to act. The liberals predicted a boom-and-bust pattern which would disrupt the economy as it had after World War I. They expected Truman, whose Kansas City haberdashery had failed in the post–World War I depression, to understand this and act vigorously. Instead the president gambled that his approach would produce satisfactory legislation which would keep the confidence of organized labor and liberals. His whole political experience in the Senate told him it would work.

The twenty-one point message read like a catalog of liberal-labor demands for postwar full employment and economic stability. But it was curiously vague and formless. The list lacked stated priorities, and the administration drafted no bills to go up with it. While the document was still in the drafting process, Budget Director Smith sent the speechwriters a blistering critique of its organization. The message, he argued, violated all canons of presidential leadership. It had no specifics, only generalities; it stated no well-thought-out program for which the president could fight. The suggestions were noted and discarded. At this time Truman rejected Smith's view of presidential activity. He wanted Congress to set the priorities, commit itself to policy, and use the legislative process to draft bills. This would assure passage of legislation and success for his administration. The message openly invited congressional initiative, and Truman was not overly worried that the initiative lay in conservative hands. He strongly believed in a mutuality of interest between Congress and the president.

On unemployment compensation, on tax policy, and on full employment legislation, Truman worked personally with the committee chairmen, paid them deference, and offered to visit their home districts. Still they did not give him what he wanted. On September 19 the Senate Finance Committee reported an unsatisfactory unemployment compensation bill. But it was a bill; it could be amended. With joblessness rising rapidly in early September, this issue was labor's most urgent demand. On September 22 and 23 Truman held a weekend stag party at a resort on Chesapeake Bay to charm the House Democrats. There, in shirt sleeves, the president played poker, pitched horseshoes, and entertained on the piano; but bourbon and good fellowship failed to produce results. On September 24 the Ways and Means Committee voted to report no bill on unemployment compensation at all, thereby killing any chance of legislation. Truman summoned the committee to the White House and bluntly told them to report some kind of a bill. They refused, and, responding in their own way to the politics of reconversion, angrily voted to take up tax reduction.

Secretary of the Treasury Vinson, a former member of Ways and Means, did little better on taxes. After a conference with Vinson and Ways and Means Chairman Doughton, Finance Committee Chairman George quickly announced that he opposed the administration's tax program. In the Ways and Means Committee, Republican members dealt shrewdly with Doughton and produced a bill which featured their demands for substantial tax cuts, respected Doughton's opposition to a repeal of the excess profits tax, but rejected Vinson's proposals. The bill passed the House by a large majority, provoking a storm of criticism from organized labor, which wanted the repeal of special excise taxes which fell heavily on low-income groups. Instead the House bill simply cut income taxes 10 percent across the board. The Senate did not substantially alter the tax bill, and another key demand of labor was lost. At the same time, the House Committee on Expenditures in the Executive bottled up legislation to commit the federal government to maintain full employment. Truman's appeal to senior Democrats on the committee to report a bill produced nothing.

The president's mistake was to rely on the congressional system to respond to the needs of the national party. The seniority rules produced committee chairmen who held power because they were loyal first of all to the economic interests and political philosophies of their constituents. The chairmen were likewise supported by senior committee members who, for the same reason, could be independent of the national party. When the national interests of the Democratic party conflicted with those of the constituencies of these congressmen, the party lost, but the men stayed in power. The Democratic party depended heavily on the votes of organized labor in the industrial states. However, the chairmen of committees that handled legislation on urban unemployment and taxes were interested in the problems of rural voters and felt no pressure to take a national view. Rural areas faced scarcities of labor, not unemployment, and wanted above all to end wartime restrictions on the economy, particularly price controls. That mutuality of interest between Congress and the executive which Truman hoped to exploit did not exist on the most vital policy issues.

By the end of October, the president's proposals to protect labor against widespread unemployment and loss of purchasing power had been defeated or stalled in Congress. His strategy was in shambles, and the liberal press attacked him for his failures. Labor leaders, disgusted with Congress and disillusioned with the White House, planned major strikes in the steel and automotive industries. On November 13 the Office of Economic Stabilization admitted that inflation, not unemployment, was the most serious threat to the economy. With this announcement the rationale for the domestic reform program disappeared. On November 20 the United Auto Workers struck General Motors. On November 28 the United Steel Workers voted for a national steel strike. These disruptive stoppages would greatly accelerate inflation, and Truman concluded that he had to act. On December 3 the president called for legislation to protect the economy from major strikes by employing cooling-off periods, fact-finding procedures, and federal mediation. His support for antistrike legislation deeply shocked labor, and CIO President Philip Murray publicly denounced Truman as a traitor to Roosevelt's labor policy. Added to the failures of the domestic program, the situation provoked an open breach between the Truman administration and the Democratic left.

Pressured by the specter of a crumbling party in an election year, Truman made a major attempt in early 1946 to force Congress to act on the administration's domestic program. He appealed directly to the public in a national radio broadcast on January 3. In effect the president resubmitted his twenty-one point program to Congress, but, responding to inflation, he highlighted his strike mediation bill and the extension of price controls. Over and over in the speech, Truman called on his listeners to convince their representatives in Congress, spending the Christmas holidays in their home districts, to vote for the administration's legislative agenda. This strategy was perilous. If public pressure failed to develop, it would demonstrate the political weakness of the president and his party in an election year. The response was disappointing. Congressional mail was light; even the liberals were not impressed. Press reports indicated that

Congress sensed no overwhelming public sentiment on behalf of the president's program. When the second session of the Seventy-ninth Congress opened, conservatives were in a fighting mood.

As executive influence declined in 1946 and Truman's prestige as party leader continued to fade, Congress became increasingly dominated by an organized coalition of conservatives. Led by GOP Representative Fred Hartley of New Jersey and Senator Taft, Republicans and Southern Democrats organized caucuses to draft proposals on price controls and to work out crippling amendments and floor strategy to defeat Truman's domestic legislation. They functioned effectively in the Rules Committee to reject fact-finding legislation and to substitute the antilabor Case Bill. The minimum wage increase and full employment legislation emerged from committee so changed that many liberal Democrats walked off the Senate floor in disgust. Southern Democrats openly attacked Democratic National Chairman Robert Hannegan for his activities on behalf of minorities and tried to force his resignation.

As relations between Truman and Democratic conservatives worsened, the administration found itself unable to prevent the deterioration of relations with the left. Truman had recommended a permanent Fair Employment Practices Committee in his twenty-one point program and in his January 3 radio speech, but the president refused to interfere with a Southern filibuster designed to kill the FEPC. Minority groups had resented Truman's lukewarm support for the temporary FEPC in 1945, and when the president refused to see a delegation of their leaders in early February during the filibuster, they despaired over the future of civil rights in the Democratic party.

The resignation of Interior Secretary Ickes in mid-February further alienated liberals. Ickes, who with Wallace symbolized the Roosevelt tradition in the cabinet, objected to the appointment of Edwin Pauley, former treasurer of the Democratic National Committee, as undersecretary of the Navy. Ickes objected to Pauley's links with California oil interests and intimated that Pauley was too corrupt to be trusted with the Navy's oil reserves. Surprised by Ickes's refusal to support the nomination, Truman publicly defended Pauley. Unable to negotiate an arrangement to have both men in the administration, the president reluctantly accepted the resignation of the old progressive. Pauley, now a hot political issue, withdrew his own nomination in the interests of the party. The episode damaged all of the principals, the president most of all.

The bitterest blow to the political ties between the Truman administration and organized labor came in May 1946 over a railroad strike which threatened a national transportation crisis. As the railroad union leaders defied the administration's attempts to mediate the dispute, the conservative caucus in the Senate drafted amendments to strengthen the Case Bill. To prevent the passage of these amendments and to rebuke and discipline the rebellious union heads, Truman called a joint session of Congress on May 25 to appeal personally for emergency strike-control legislation, although by then the railroad unions had settled. The tough nature of the Truman proposals, especially the provision to draft strikers into the army, stunned organized labor. Congress ignored the president's proposal and passed the amendments to the Case Bill. Although Truman successfully vetoed the new legislation, union leaders denounced him and his labor policy as fascist.

The only protection in the spring of 1946 for the purchasing power of low-income groups was price control. However, the conservative caucuses in the House and the Senate sabotaged the price control extension bill with amendments freeing agricultural and retail prices. The Democratic leadership advised the president to accept another humiliation; OPA Director Chester Bowles resigned and headed for Connecticut politics.

Truman's decision to veto the OPA bill on June 29 represented his final attempt to define an issue on which the Democrats could campaign in the 1946 elections. By vetoing the bill and allowing the OPA to expire on July 1, the president used the pressure of soaring prices to outrage the public and goad the Congress into new legislation. For once during reconversion, economic pressures helped the administration politically. Truman also cast the OPA fight in highly partisan terms, hoping to encourage party loyalty and thus to break the back of the conservative coalition. Liberals and labor spokesmen applauded his aggressive behavior; the White House mail ran heavily in favor of the veto. Republican party leaders angrily tried to blame the president for rising prices.

Although Truman had repaired some of the damage to his political standing, he could not get satisfactory price control legislation from Congress. Again, conservatives attached crippling amendments to the bill, and the president finally signed it on July 25. Truman was hopeful that his initial veto would at least help the party in the fall elections, but his acquiescence in the second bill blurred the responsibility for inflation. When Truman lifted all price controls on meat, just three weeks before election day, in order to ease widespread discontent over shortages, it seemed clear to the consumer that he was directly responsible for high prices.

Despite the president's best efforts to make the issue of the campaign a contest between Democratic progressivism and Republican reaction, apathy on the left became the major problem for the Democratic organization in the 1946 elections. The trend of the summer primaries in the Midwest and in New York was conservative. The need for labor's support was urgent to help Democrats in Pennsylvania and in West Virginia, and Truman hoped a liberal Democrat in New York would cut into Governor Dewey's political base and dampen his presidential ambitions.

As the elections approached, Truman lost the support of the last remaining New Dealer in his cabinet. Secretary of Commerce Wallace publicly criticized United States policy toward the Soviet Union in a September campaign speech in New York City. Truman had counted heavily on Wallace's appeal to labor to help the Democrats survive the elections. Faced with the threat of resignation by Secretary of State Byrnes over the speech, which the president himself had hastily approved, Truman fired Wallace. He then kept himself out of sight until the elections were over. On election day, in despair over party apathy, the St. Louis Democratic City Committee offered a raffle ticket on a 1946 Ford to any Democrat who would go to the polls and vote.

In the November elections the Republican party won control of both houses of Congress for the first time since 1928. It was a crushing defeat for Truman. The politics of reconversion had wrecked the revival of the New Deal and had crippled the Democratic party. Truman's chances for election in 1948 seemed slight, and Republican presidential candidates began to plan their strategies. The president might have reflected that neither his long experience as a Democratic politician nor his knowledge of the legislative process had enabled him to prevent this disastrous turn in the fortunes of his party. Economic events had overtaken his strategy for reform, and his attempts at reconciliation with Congress had failed to heal the Democratic divisions inherited from Roosevelt. It was a bitter time for a man who believed in his party.

Had Truman in September 1945, heeded the advice of liberals and moved earlier and more aggressively to get domestic legislation from Congress, formidable barriers to reform would have remained. The political atmosphere of the days of the New Deal was over: conservatives, having greatly increased their strength in Congress and in the Democratic party during the war, were behaving in an organized and defiant manner toward the White House. The economic assumptions of New Deal reform did not meet the problem of a postwar inflation which called for less government spending. Truman, a moderate, had neither Roosevelt's skill in dealing with the Democratic left nor the acceptance FDR had enjoyed with liberals and independents. Suddenly hurled into the presidency, Truman relied too much on his ordered view of the legislative process, a product of the lessons he had learned as a senator. With the elections of the Republican Eightieth Congress, he could now adopt a new and more promising stance toward Capitol Hill—that of political adversary.

Harry S. Truman, September–October, 1948
WHISTLE-STOP TALKS

Truman's upset victory in the 1948 election was in large measure a vindication of the president's shrewdness as a political strategist and his considerable talents as a campaigner. Crisscrossing the nation by rail, he delivered some 355 speeches, most of them at "whistle-stops" from the rear platform of his train. The following excerpts demonstrate Truman's feistiness, folksiness, and use of an extraordinarily wide range of issues.

Colorado Springs, Colorado, September 20, 1948

I am very happy to be in Colorado Springs again. I have been here on numerous occasions. It's a lovely place, beautifully situated, and you don't dare talk about the climate of Colorado Springs in California—or Florida either, for that matter.

From *Public Papers of the Presidents of the United States: Harry S. Truman, 1948* (U.S. Government Printing Office, 1964), pp. 512, 641–642, 690–692, 880–881.

One of the reasons you are prosperous and happy is because you've learned how to use your resources to the very best advantage, especially your water resources.

You know, the Reclamation Act has been on the books for more than thirty years, but nothing much was done about it or the development of this part of the world until 1932, when you elected Franklin D. Roosevelt.

Most of you in 1932 had given up hope and were thinking of going somewhere else, along with the Okies and the other people who were moving around the country; but much to your satisfaction you didn't do that.

At that time the income of the great state of Colorado was about $350 million. Do you know what it was last year? It was a billion, five hundred million dollars. And that wasn't due to any accident. That was due to the development of the resources of this great state.

It's a wonderful thing that has happened to this part of the world in the last decade, and I am wondering whether you are going to let the present propaganda machine fool you into turning the clock back to 1932 again. I am very sure you won't do that. If you'll just study the facts and the figures, you can't do anything else but keep an administration in power that has been trying to do things for this part of the world.

I made a speech in Denver at noon, in which I made the statement that due to the example of that terrible Eightieth Republican Congress elected in 1946, I could say definitely that the Republicans are trying to sabotage the West.

In 1946, you know, two-thirds of you stayed at home and didn't vote. You wanted a change. Well, you got it. You got the change. You got just exactly what you deserved.

If you stay at home on November the second and let this same gang get control of the government, I won't have any sympathy with you. But if you go out to the polls on that day and do your duty as you should I won't have to worry about moving out of the White House; and you won't have to worry about what happens to the welfare of the West. Those two things go together.

Eldorado, Illinois, September 30, 1948

Thank you very much. I never had a more cordial welcome on the whole trip. I appreciate it very much. I had the pleasure of riding with your mayor, and with your Mr. Powell, who has entertained me most highly on this trip, and he told me all about Illinois and this part of the state—a great Democratic stronghold, this is. I am certainly glad to be here in this great Democratic stronghold, and I wish I had all afternoon to discuss with you the issues that are before us in this campaign; but the issues are clearly drawn.

It is merely the people against the special interests. The Democratic party has always represented the people in these fights with the special interests, and the Republican party has been the special interest party. And this Eightieth Congress—I call it the "do-nothing" Eightieth Congress—has conclusively proven that they are still for that viewpoint of the public servant.

Now, the way you can cure that is to elect a Democratic Congress, and if you do that, of course you will return me to the White House, and I won't have any trouble with the housing shortage.

Here are just a few examples to prove it to you that this Congress is a special interest Congress. The first thing they did when they got there was to vote themselves a rich man's tax bill, which I vetoed. Then they took it back and modified it, and I vetoed it again. Then they passed it over my veto. It is a rich man's tax bill, if you analyze it.

Then the next thing they did was to take some freedom away from labor, and to pass the Taft-Hartley Act which tried to emasculate the Wagner Act. Now labor got its magna charta from President Roosevelt under the Wagner Act back in 1935, the act that gives to labor the right to free collective bargaining, and guarantees that right. Well, this Taft-Hartley law endeavored to take that right away from labor.

And if the laboringmen stay at home, as they did in 1946, I have just received information as to what the Republicans intend to do further to labor.

Then they took on the farmer, and they are going right down the line to undo everything that has been done to keep his income on an even keel, to evenly distribute the income so that everybody will have his fair share. Then, on the price support program, they almost wrecked it by a joker which they put into the recharter of the CCC, which does not allow the government to furnish storage space for the grain on which they make loans.

Corn, right now, in this vicinity is selling 45 percent below the support price just for that reason, and the speculators will get the benefit of the Republican change in that Commodity Credit law. And it isn't fair. It isn't right.

I have been going up and down this country pointing out specific examples of what happened. We wanted to build a steamplant—a standby plant for TVA, which would be of some benefit to you people right here and cost $4 million. They knocked that out. I asked them to put it in again at the special session, but they never did it. They did not intend to do anything for the welfare and benefit of the people. The power trust lobby stood out here at the rat hole and wouldn't let them do it. There are bigger lobbies in Congress this time—in that Eightieth Congress—than ever before in history.

We have been making a crusade up and down this country, trying to convince the people that their interests are with the Democratic party, and if you believe that, you will send me back to the White House, and you will elect a Democratic Congress to take the place of this "do-nothing," good-for-nothing Eightieth Congress.

Thank you.

Elizabeth, New Jersey, October 7, 1948

Mr. Mayor, Mr. Chairman, ladies and gentlemen, and Democrats of Elizabeth, New Jersey:

I appreciate very much this very cordial welcome which you have accorded me. This is my first stop in the great state of New Jersey, and it is right in line with the other first stops. In every state, through which I have been, they were all just like this. People want to see their president, they want to hear what their president has to say; and I can't tell you how very much I thank you for that interest.

You are here because you are interested in the issues of this campaign. You know, as all the citizens of this great country know, that the election is not all over but the shouting. That is what they would like to have you believe, but it isn't so—it isn't so at all. The Republicans are trying to hide the truth from you in a great many ways. They don't want you to know the truth about the issues in this campaign. The big fundamental issue in this campaign is the people against the special interests. The Democratic party stands for the people. The Republican party stands, and always has stood, for special interests. They have proved that conclusively in the record that they made in this "do-nothing" Congress.

FIGURE 3. "Down by the Station." (*Courtesy, the Washington (D.C.) Star-News*)

I have been trying to get the Republicans to do something about high prices and housing ever since they came to Washington. They are responsible for that situation, because they killed price control, and they killed the housing bill. That Republican Eightieth "do-nothing" Congress absolutely refused to give any relief whatever in either one of those categories.

What do you suppose the Republicans think you ought to do about high prices?

Senator Taft, one of the leaders in the Republican Congress, said, "If consumers think the price is too high today, they will wait until the price is lower. I feel that in time the law of supply and demand will bring prices into line."

There is the Republican answer to the high cost of living.

FIGURE 4. In this cartoon and the one facing, cartoonist Jim Berryman accurately conveys both the tone and strategy of Truman's 1948 campaign. (*Courtesy, the Washington (D.C.) Star-News*)

If it costs too much, just wait.

If you think 15 cents is too much for a loaf of bread, just do without it and wait until you can afford to pay 15 cents for it.

If you don't want to pay 60 cents a pound for hamburger, just wait.

That is what the Republican Congress thought you ought to do, and that is the same Congress that the Republican candidate for president said did a good job.

Some people say I ought not to talk so much about the Republican Eightieth "do-nothing" Congress in this campaign. I will tell you why I will talk about it. If two-thirds of the people stay at home again on election day as they did in 1946, and if we get another

Republican Congress like the Eightieth Congress, it will be controlled
by the same men who controlled that Eightieth Congress—the
Tabers, and the Tafts, the Martins and the Hallecks would be the
bosses. The same men would be the bosses the same as those who
passed the Taft-Hartley Act, and passed the rich man's tax bill, and
took social security away from a million workers.

Do you want that kind of administration? I don't believe you do—I
don't believe you do.

I don't believe you would be out here interested in listening to my
outline of what the Republicans are trying to do to you if you intended to put them back in there.

When a bunch of Republican reactionaries are in control of the
Congress, then the people get reactionary laws. The only way you
can get the kind of government you need is by going to the polls and
voting the straight Democratic ticket on November second. Then you
will get a Democratic Congress and I will get a Congress that will
work with me. Then we will get good housing at prices we can
afford to pay; and repeal of that vicious Taft-Hartley Act; and more
social security coverage; and prices that will be fair to everybody;
and we can go on and keep 61 million people at work; we can have
an income of more than $217 billion, and that income will be dis-
tributed so that the farmer, the workingman, the white-collar worker,
and the businessman get their fair share of that income.

That is what I stand for.

That is what the Democratic party stands for.

Vote for that, and you will be safe!

Framingham, Massachusetts, October 27, 1948

Thank you, thank you very much. I certainly appreciate most highly
that cordial introduction. I have had a most wonderful reception in
this great state, and I certainly wish I could visit every corner of
New England and every town in it.

Now, this city of Framingham has a reputation of being a forward-
looking community. I had heard about it long before I ever arrived
here. I know that you want to keep right on going forward along the
lines laid down by the Democratic party in the last sixteen years.
You proved that in 1946 when you sent a fine Democrat to Congress,
Harold D. Donohue. If more cities and congressional districts had

followed your example, how much better off we would all be! We would never have had that backward-looking Eightieth Congress if every city and community had done what you did the last time.

I am satisfied that the American people are very sorry that they let so many mossback Republicans slip into that Eightieth Congress. I believe the voters all over the country are going to send those reactionary Republicans back to private life in November. I believe the voters are going to turn thumbs down on the Republican candidate for president, a candidate who won't tell you where he stands or what he believes in. He goes around preaching platitudes. You know, he has given "G.O.P." another meaning. It now means "Grand Old Platitudes." I believe the American people are entitled to hear from the Republican leaders the full and honest convictions of the candidate.

You certainly know where the leaders of the Democratic party stand. I have gone all over the country, from one end to the other —north and south and east and west—and you understand exactly where I stand; and I have tried to make it perfectly clear to you where the Republicans stand too. I defy you to say what the Republicans stand for—what the Republican candidate for president stands for except for the Republican party. And if he can stand for that, he can stand for anything!

In the last sixteen years your government has been headed by men who have done everything possible to promote the welfare of the people as a whole. By "the people" I mean all the citizens of the United States. We don't restrict our sympathies to the people who make $100,000 a year. We mean everybody in the country. We want to build millions of low-priced houses for workingmen and their families. We want to get rid of the vicious Taft-Hartley law, passed by the Republican Congress under the whip of the millionaire manufacturers. We want to provide federal aid to education so that all our children will have a chance to get a decent schooling. We want to put a national health program into effect so that all Americans can get good medical care and good dental care.

We can do all these things if everybody goes to the polls and votes the Democratic ticket straight in November. You can vote for a federal housing program, a federal aid to education program, a federal health program, by marking your ballot for the Democratic candidates.

You have a stake in this election. It will affect your job, your chance to get a raise, your chance to get a better home, your chance to control the high prices that rob you of all gains you had before those prices went up. It will mean the difference between moving ahead and going backward.

The people's campaign is rolling to victory. I can assure you of that. The West is with us, the Central states are with us, and the East is swinging into line. If you would see the people I have been talking to since I came East, you would understand what I mean when I say the East is beginning to find out what side its bread is buttered on.

All I ask you to do is vote for yourself, vote for your family. When you come right down to the analysis of our government, our government is the people, and when the people exercise their right to vote on election day they control that government. When they don't exercise that right then you get—then you get an Eightieth Congress. So, two-thirds of the people of the United States entitled to vote in 1946 stayed at home. They didn't have energy enough to go and look after their political interests on election day—and they got the Eightieth Congress. Don't do that again. Don't do that again.

The Democrats are not afraid of the people. The Democrats know that when the people exercise their rights the country is safe.

I am urging you with everything I have: on November 2, everyone of you, get up early and go to the polls and vote the Democratic ticket straight.

Irwin Ross

WHAT HAPPENED IN 1948

Truman's 1948 victory was a major embarrassment to political pollsters and analysts who had almost universally predicted his defeat. Irwin Ross closely examines the election results and concludes that the outcome demonstrated the continuing strength of the political coalition established by Franklin D. Roosevelt. Particularly provocative is his speculation that the interests of the nation might have been better served by a Dewey triumph.

On the evening of the day after the election, Truman attended a victory celebration in the courthouse square at Independence, where some 40,000 people gathered on a few hours' notice. Thanking the crowd, Truman announced that "Protocol goes out the window when I am in Independence. I am a citizen of this town and a taxpayer and I want to be treated just like the rest of the taxpayers. . . ." The next day he set out on his "Victory Special" to return to Washington. When the train reached Union Station in St. Louis, the waiting crowds pushed aside police barriers and scrambled over the tracks. Truman delighted his admirers by holding aloft the previous day's early edition of the Chicago *Tribune,* with the memorable headline "DEWEY DEFEATS TRUMAN." The president also made a little speech. "The reason I am so happy," he said, "is because my home state stood by me so well. You must continue to stand by me, because I have got the biggest job in the world now." The next day, when he reached Washington, he was greeted by an estimated 750,000 people massed along the route from the railway station to the White House. Bands blared, schoolchildren cheered, confetti spiraled through the air, fire trucks made triumphal arches with their ladders, the parade passing underneath. Few wartime heroes have received a more ardent welcome.

For the journalists and the pollsters, the shock of the election lingered after the disbelief had worn off. Some adopted a bantering tone to cover their embarrassment; thus, the Alsop brothers: "There is only one question on which professional politicians, polltakers, political reporters and other wiseacres and prognosticators can any longer speak with much authority. That is how they want their crow cooked. These particular reporters prefer their crow fricasseed." The pollsters were even more dismayed. On every side, they were ridiculed and abused, an inevitable development given the omniscience to which they had laid claim. In his first postelection column, Elmo Roper sounded completely deflated: "I could not have been more wrong. The thing that bothers me most is that at this moment I don't know why I was wrong." He promised to find out. A few newspapers canceled their subscriptions to the Gallup Poll. Many people recalled how the *Literary Digest* had gone out of business after the 1936 election, when its celebrated poll had predicted Alfred M. Landon's victory, only to have Franklin D. Roosevelt carry every state in the union but Maine and Vermont. The *New York Times* asked Wilfred J. Funk, the last editor of the *Literary Digest,* for a comment on the current plight of the pollsters. "I do not want to seem to be malicious," said Funk, "but I can't help but get a good chuckle out of this."

The postmortems began the day after the election and continued for years afterward. The figures told a paradoxical story: Truman had won by a decisive majority and yet the election had been close. In popular votes, the president had polled 24,179,345 to Dewey's 21,991,291—a plurality of 2,188,054. In electoral votes, the score was Truman, 303; Dewey, 189; Thurmond, 39. The minority candidates had done poorly, with Wallace polling a mere 1,157,326 votes; Thurmond, 1,176,125; Norman Thomas, 139,572; and all the other fringe parties, including the Prohibition party, 150,167. The Wallace and Thurmond candidates, however, had attracted enough Democratic votes to deny Truman an absolute majority; the final tally showed him with 49.6 percent of the popular vote to Dewey's 45.1 percent. The total vote had been low, with only 51.2 percent of the electorate going to the polls.

A plurality of over 2 million votes was substantial, but Truman's lead in three states was so slender that the outcome might easily have been reversed in the Electoral College. Truman carried Ohio by only 7,107 votes, California by 17,865, Illinois by 33,612; his total plurality in the three states came to 58,584 votes. The arithmetic irony was clear: a swing to Dewey of less than 30,000 votes, appropriately distributed in the three states, would have given him an additional 78 electoral votes and the presidency; the electoral vote would then have been 267 for Dewey to 225 for Truman and 39 for Thurmond. A switch of any two of these three states to Dewey (Ohio and California each had 25 electoral votes and Illinois 28) would have left Truman with the lead in the Electoral College but without the majority of 266 necessary to win, thereby throwing the election into the House of Representatives. All of which explained, of course, why Dewey waited until Wednesday morning before conceding.

There were other paradoxes. Truman had won despite the loss of four of the largest industrial states—New York (47 electoral votes), Pennsylvania (35), Michigan (19), New Jersey (16), all of which (with the exception of Michigan in 1940) had been carried by Roosevelt in the two preceding presidential elections. On the other hand, Truman won three Midwest states—Iowa, Ohio, and Wisconsin—in which the farm vote was important and which Roosevelt had lost to Dewey in 1944.

Equally surprising was the impact of the Wallaceite and Dixiecrat defections. Truman was hurt, but not as badly as anticipated. His loss in the South was limited to the four states in which the Dixiecrats took over the Democratic party label—Alabama, Louisiana, Mississippi and South Carolina—whose electoral vote totaled 38. (Thurmond's thirty-ninth electoral vote came from a Democratic elector in Tennessee who could not abide Truman.) Wallace was responsible for Truman's defeat in three states—New York, Maryland and Michigan; in New York, for example, Wallace polled 509,559 votes—nearly half his national total—and Dewey won the state by 60,959. On the other hand, Wallace's vote in California—190,381—was far short of expectations and he was not on the ballot in Illinois. Had Wallace done just a trifle better in California and had he not been kept off the ballot in Illinois, Truman would have lost both states and the election of the president would have been decided by the House of Representatives. The Constitution provides that when the House elects a president, during January of the following year, each state delegation has but one vote; and the winning candidate must win a majority—which would have been 25 votes in 1948. One can assume that each state delegation would vote along party lines. On that assumption, Truman would have won, for the Democrats controlled 25 state delegations after the 1948 election; the Republicans had 20; three were evenly split.

As things turned out, Truman's winning coalition of states bore a remarkable resemblance to the design sketched by Clark Clifford in his memorandum of November 1947. The president took every state in the West but Oregon, won seven of the eleven states of the old Confederacy, the four Border states of Kentucky, Oklahoma, Missouri, and West Virginia, and five states in the Midwest—Illinois, Iowa, Minnesota, Ohio, and Wisconsin; his only victories in the Northeast were in Massachusetts and Rhode Island.

Not only had the experts failed to anticipate the specific design of Truman's victory, but neither the pollsters nor the journalists foresaw that Truman would poll over 2 million more votes than Dewey. The New York *Star* had the rare distinction of being able to boast that two of its writers, columnists Jennings Perry and Gerald Johnson, had predicted that the election would be close. In September, Robert Bendiner had also published an article in *The Nation* entitled "Don't Count Truman Out." It was largely a review of a book by Louis Bean, *How to Predict Elections,* which described the rise and fall of the Democratic and Republican electoral "tides," over long spans of years, and argued that the Republican tide had begun to ebb by 1947. Bean foresaw the possibility of Truman's victory, but did not predict it.

How had almost all the experts been so wrong? As regards the journalists, the *New York Times* provided some instructive answers after querying the forty-eight correspondents who had provided the newspaper's state-by-state survey on the Sunday preceding the election. The correspondents reported that in taking their soundings, they had talked with local political leaders, checked with their colleagues, interviewed some rank-and-file voters and, of course, studied the polls, both local and national. An inordinate amount of reliance had been placed on the polls, far more than on "grass roots" reporting. One correspondent confessed: "I was too gutless to put stock in my own personal hunch, based on nothing better than tours of the area, chats with businessmen, union men, miners, ranchers, farmers, political leaders." He felt that he could not "pin down" his hunch, so he followed the trend indicated in the polls. Local political leaders also relied heavily on the polls in assessing the situation in their areas; the consequence was that when a reporter interviewed a politician, he often only picked up an echo of a poll which he had already read.

Newsmen traveling on the campaign trains were at an inevitable disadvantage in reporting the sentiments of the voters, for they lingered so briefly in a town that they had little opportunity to talk either to the voters or the local politicians. They were meticulous, as we have seen, in reporting crowd turnout and in describing the demeanor and attitude of the crowds, but they were usually unwilling to draw conclusions which hindsight showed to be obvious. Thus the great throngs which Truman attracted in the last two weeks of the campaign led almost no one to hazard the guess that he might just conceivably win; the tendency remained to attribute the crowds to idle curiosity or to Truman's "entertainment value" rather than to partisan zeal. The journalists were unwilling to credit the reality of what they saw and heard, so firmly had they accepted the assumption of Dewey's victory. In large part, this was a result of the polls; it was also a consequence of the political diagram of the campaign, with the Dixiecrat and Progressive party breakaways apparently making it impossible for Truman to win a majority in the Electoral College. If the electoral vote were the only error in prediction, it would have been understandable (the outcome in the Electoral College, after all, was narrowly decided). The more grievous error was the complete misreading of the popular vote.

The press had clearly been led astray by the myth of Dewey's invincibility. In a letter to his own paper, the *New York Times*'s James Reston wrote: "There were certain factors in this election that were known (and discounted) by almost every political reporter. We knew about the tradition that a defeated candidate had never been nominated and elected after his defeat. We knew that the national income was running at a rate of $210 billions a year, that over 61 million persons were employed at unprecedentedly high wages, and that the people had seldom if ever turned against the administration in power at such a time. . . . In a way our failure was not unlike Mr. Dewey's: we overestimated the tangibles and under-estimated the intangibles . . . just as he was too isolated with other politicians, so we were too isolated with other reporters; and we, too, were far too impressed by the tidy statistics of the polls."

Time's judgment on its colleagues was even harsher: "The press was morally guilty on several counts. It was guilty of pride: it had assumed that it knew all the important facts—without sufficiently checking them. It was guilty of laziness and wishful thinking: it had failed to do its own doorbell-ringing and bush-beating; it had delegated its journalist's job to the pollsters."

Everybody's mistakes, in the end, could be attributed to the polls. Eight days after the election, the Social Science Research Council set up a committee of academic experts to analyze what had gone wrong. The Gallup, Roper and Crossley organizations all cooperated in the investigation, making available both their files and their personnel. On December 27, 1948, the committee issued a detailed report and subsequently published the staff studies on which it was based.

The pollsters, the committee concluded, had made many errors. All three national polls had not been alive to the possibility of a decisive swing to Truman in the last two weeks of the campaign. Gallup and Crossley stopped polling too early. Gallup's final prediction, published the day before the election, was actually based on two national samples gathered during mid-October. Crossley's final forecast was derived from a combination of state surveys taken around mid-August, mid-September and mid-October. Roper's final estimate used data he collected in August, which provided the basis for his September 9 column in which he predicted Dewey's victory and announced he was no longer going to publish periodic surveys. (Roper, however, did take a poll in the final week of the campaign, which he did not publish. It showed a slight upswing for Truman, but Dewey was still far in the lead.)

The Gallup and Crossley organizations obviously assumed that the final stages of the campaign would have no significant impact on the preference of voters. As he indicated in his September column, Roper believed that the entire campaign was likely to be irrelevant, given Dewey's enormous lead (44.2 percent to Truman's 31.4 percent). The absurdity of these assumptions was proven when Gallup and Roper conducted postelection surveys. Respondents were asked if they had voted, whom they had voted for, and when they had made their decisions. One out of every seven voters claimed to have made up his mind within the last fortnight of the campaign; *three-quarters of these delayed decisions favored Truman.* Other data corroborated these findings. A postelection poll conducted by the Survey Research Center of the University of Michigan reported that 14 percent of the Truman voters recalled making up their minds in the two weeks prior to the election; 3 percent decided on election day. The figures for Dewey voters were 3 and 2 percent, respectively. "Even if one makes allowance for errors in such reports," said the Social Science Research Council analysis, "one must conclude that failure to detect and measure changes of mind about voting during the closing days of the campaign account for a considerable part of the total error of the prediction."

Some of the voters who made up their minds toward the end of the campaign had previously been undecided; others switched candidates. The Michigan survey showed that, on balance, the last-minute vote changes favored Truman. Thus, of the voters who said they were for Dewey in October, 14 percent switched to Truman and 13 percent did not vote. Of the Truman supporters in October, more failed to vote—25 percent—but only 5 percent switched to Dewey. Thus Truman benefited; as a report on the Michigan survey pointed out, "To lose a vote because of non-voting is only half as penalizing as to lose a vote through its going to one's opponent."

Gallup, Crossley, and Roper made equally grievous errors in handling the undecided vote. Voters who would express no choice, but said they planned to vote, were nearly twice as numerous in 1948 as in 1944; in the Gallup figures, they accounted for 15 percent of the total. The pollsters either disregarded the undecided, on the grounds that they were unlikely to vote, or divided them among the candidates in the same proportions as the decided voters. In past elections going back to 1936, such simple solutions had created no embarrassing distortions, because of Roosevelt's substantial lead, but in 1948 not only did the undecided bulk large, but over half of them voted—and they voted for Truman in the ratio of about two to one, according to the postelection surveys.

The pollsters also failed accurately to gauge intent to vote. "The error in predicting the actual vote from expressed intention to vote was undoubtedly an important, although not precisely measurable, part of the over-all error of the forecast," the SSRC report stated. "The prediction of human behavior from an expression of intent is, in the present state of knowledge, and particularly with the actual methods used, a hazardous venture. This is a central problem for research, which has been largely ignored in preelection poll predictions."

The polls' difficulties were further compounded by errors in sampling and interviewing techniques, which resulted in too few interviews with people of grade school education. The Democratic vote thus tended to be underestimated. Finally, the polls added to their own problems by an exuberant desire to make flat predictions, not distracting the reader with qualifications or "technicalities." The reader was not taken behind the scenes and shown how the forecast was put together. Instead of merely trying to indicate the state of public opinion at some particular point of time and within stated margins of error, the polls insisted on picking the winner. The polls had made many of the same errors in the three previous presidential elections, but they did not result in the wrong choice of the winner, given Roosevelt's large lead over his opponents. And, in the past, luck had enabled some of the pollsters' errors to cancel each other out. For example, underestimation of the Northern Democratic vote had been compensated for by overrepresentation of the South, which had been solidly Democratic until 1948. After 1948 the polltakers became a more modest and chastened lot, and their techniques improved considerably.

Dissecting the errors of the polls did not demonstrate, however, how Truman had managed to assemble his plurality out of the diverse elements in the electorate that have to coalesce to elect any president. Where had the voters come from?

They came from the same sources that FDR had tapped. On an electoral-vote basis, as previously mentioned, Truman did not recreate the old Roosevelt coalition, for he lost New York, Pennsylvania, New Jersey, and Michigan as well as four states in the previously Solid South. When the constituents of the popular vote are analyzed, however, it is apparent that Truman retained the basic elements of the old Roosevelt coalition. That is to say, he held most of the South; he ran well in the urban North though not as well as Roosevelt; he successfully appealed to the conservation-minded West, where he won more states than Roosevelt had in 1940 and 1944; and he also had considerable success in the Midwest farm belt, where Roosevelt's support had begun to erode in 1940.

Throughout the campaign, it had been widely assumed that the Roosevelt coalition had been shattered, largely because of expected defections in the South to the Dixiecrats and in the metropolitan centers of the North and West to the Wallaceites. Such defections did of course occur, but, as we have seen, they were marginal, in terms of both the popular and electoral votes. Samuel Lubell, in his brilliant 1952 volume, *The Future of American Politics,* persuasively argued that the States' Rights and Progressive campaigns actually strengthened Truman. While they siphoned off some votes, they simultaneously solidified support for Truman among certain groups of traditionally Democratic voters, who had either defected in 1944 or were likely to defect in 1948. Thus, Henry Wallace's campaign took the Communist curse off Truman. With the Wallace movement being openly supported (as well as covertly manipulated) by the Communists, and with Truman denouncing him for the liaison, the president was much less vulnerable than he might otherwise have been to charges of being "soft" on communism. His strength went up among Catholic voters.

Lubell provided considerable data to support this contention. His research method was to collate the county returns in successive presidential elections, determine which geographic areas typified the shifting voting patterns of various economic or ethnic groups, and then go out and talk to the voters to determine why they had voted as they had; it was a new technique that combined scientific opinion-sampling with journalistic interrogation.

In Boston, for example, Lubell found that the heavily Irish Catholic wards voted more overwhelmingly for Truman than they had for any Democratic presidential candidate since Al Smith, in 1928. In Massachusetts, to be sure, a birth-control amendment was on the ballot and there were other referendum proposals which the unions opposed, all of which brought out a heavy Catholic vote, but had there been a measure of Catholic hostility to Truman on the Communist issue, Dewey might have been the beneficiary of some normally Democratic votes. (It will be recalled that Truman, in his Boston speech late in the campaign, had emphasized his anti-Communist credentials.) Moreover, Lubell described the same pattern elsewhere in the country. St. Paul, Minnesota, which had a large Catholic population, gave Truman 10 percent more votes than Roosevelt received four years before, whereas in nearby Minneapolis, which was predominantly non-Catholic, Truman's vote was 6 percent under Roosevelt's. In East Pittsburgh, the local leadership of the United Electrical Workers put on a strong drive for Wallace. The result was a record Democratic presidential vote from the predominantly Catholic union members; Truman polled nearly 25 percent more votes in East Pittsburgh than Roosevelt had in 1944.

Similarly, the Dixiecrat rebellion against Truman's civil rights program assured him of the loyalty of the great bulk of Negro voters, many more of whom might otherwise have been attracted to Wallace or even to Dewey, under whose administration New York had been the first state to enact a law against discrimination in employment. Wallace held some appeal for Negroes, but far less than his managers had expected. In the Negro ghettos of the North, Lubell found that Wallace did best in Harlem, where he polled 29,000 votes to 108,000 for Truman and 34,000 for Dewey. Throughout the country, according to the Michigan postelection poll, nearly twice as many Negroes voted for Truman as for Dewey. The figures showed that 18 percent of the Negro respondents voted for Truman, 10 percent for Dewey, less than 0.5 percent for Wallace; the great bulk of Negroes did not vote at all (many said they could not, apparently because of Southern election customs). The irony, of course, is that if the administration's civil rights plank had been adopted by the Democratic convention, the president's appeal to Negroes would have been considerably undercut.

As in the Roosevelt years, the less affluent citizens, the trade union members, the ethnic minorities remained steadfastly Democratic. Such was the common impression at the time, validated by what studies we have of the socioeconomic characteristics of the 1948 voter. The Michigan survey showed that 57 percent of the Truman voters had annual incomes of under $3,000, as compared with 33 percent of the Dewey voters; 53 percent of the Truman voters came from working-class homes, as did only 21 percent of the Dewey voters; a mere 9 percent of the Truman voters, or their head of family, held managerial or professional positions, as against 37 percent of the Dewey voters; 39 percent of the Truman voters were members of trade-union families (the figure for Dewey voters was 11 percent). Lubell's researches led to similar findings, though he generally did not deal in percentage figures; so did the exhaustive study of the voting habits in 1948 of the citizens of Elmira, New

York. "The higher the socioeconomic status, the more Republican the vote," said the Elmira study; "put crudely, richer people vote Republican more than poorer people." Lubell also detected an interesting wrinkle in ethnic preferences: a marginal decline in the predominantly Democratic sentiments of Jewish voters, with some defecting to Wallace and others to Dewey. Lubell attributed the movement to the fact that Jews had been the most pro-Roosevelt sector of the electorate and hence were proportionately more disillusioned by Truman's performance.

The rallying of the blue-collar vote and the ethnic minorities allowed Truman to maintain the normally Democratic hold on the cities, though declines occurred in most places. In the twelve biggest cities in the nation (New York, Chicago, Philadelphia, Pittsburgh, Detroit, Cleveland, Baltimore, St. Louis, Boston, Milwaukee, San Francisco, Los Angeles), Truman's plurality was one-third below that of Roosevelt in 1944, but his margin of victory was still substantial—1,443,000 votes—nearly three-quarters of his countrywide plurality.

"Labor did it," Truman was quoted as saying the day after the election, and many commentators attributed his victory, in large part, to the efforts of the unions to get their members to the polls. It was observed that in many states, such as Illinois, Minnesota, Michigan, Truman had run behind the state tickets, leading to the obvious—though unprovable—conclusion that the "coattail" effect had been reversed in this election; that is to say, that Truman had benefited from the greater popularity of lesser candidates. Whether that had in fact occurred, it was certainly reasonable to assume that the union drive had helped Truman simply by bringing out a larger Democratic vote, even if the intended beneficiaries were liberal congressmen and senators.

A major surprise of the election, however, was Truman's showing in farm areas. His victory in Iowa was the great shocker; and it was apparent that he had done well in the farm country of Wisconsin, Ohio, Illinois, Minnesota. These facts were duly commented upon immediately after the election; after a while a theory developed that the farm vote had been the crucial element in Truman's victory. Professor Arthur Holcombe, for example, argued that "the losses to Dewey in the industrial states of the northeast would have cost Truman the election but for his extraordinary gains in the grain-growing and stock-raising states. His ability to recapture Wisconsin, Iowa, Colorado and Wyoming, which Dewey had carried in 1944, and to hold Minnesota and Washington, which had voted for Roosevelt at the earlier election, secured his victory. . . . The grain-growing and stock-raising interests . . . held the balance of power." In a memorandum to Elliott V. Bell, dated March 2, 1949, Gabriel Hauge argued that "the margin for the Truman victory came, not from labor, but from the turnabout of farm votes in the midwest, a fact which appears to be closely allied with the drop in corn prices before election." He pointed out that of the "eight leading corn states"—Illinois, Iowa, Indiana, Minnesota, Nebraska, Ohio, Wisconsin, and Missouri—Truman carried all but Indiana and Nebraska; in those two states, Dewey's plurality dropped sharply from 1944.

The theory that the farmer elected Truman attained a certain vogue, probably because of its ironical overtones: the Democratic leader loses strength in his city strongholds while suddenly blossoming forth as the farmer's friend. But the theory cannot be sustained merely by showing that certain farm or stock-growing states went to Truman. The relevant question is what segment of the electorate caused the state to shift—the farm areas, the small towns, the big cities, or perhaps some combination of these areas. Conclusive proof that a shift in the farm vote caused a state to go Democratic would be a demonstration that while the Democratic vote in the cities, normally the party's largest source of strength except in the South, remained stable or declined, a swing in the farm areas put the state in the Democratic column. A majority of farmers would not have had to vote Democratic, only a large enough number to tip the balance.

A detailed analysis prepared for *The Loneliest Campaign* by Victor A. Soland of Louis Harris & Associates proves that there was a significant shift in the farm vote to Truman, but that it by no means won him the election. The county returns were analyzed in twelve Midwest and Western states where the farm vote could have been significant. In each state the counties were grouped according to percentage of persons employed in agriculture, the spectrum being divided into segments of 10 percentage points each—less than 10 percent, 10 to 19.9 percent, and so on. For purposes of analysis, any county with more than 30 percent of the working population engaged in agriculture was regarded as a farm county, inasmuch as census data indicated that in such areas the number of people engaged in manufacturing was generally 10 percent or less. The remainder of the employed—people working in commerce and the service trades—could fairly be assumed to share the economic interests of their farm customers. Those counties with between 10 and 30 percent employed in agriculture contained small and medium-sized towns and were not especially dependent on farming. The counties with less than 10 percent employed in agriculture basically represented the cities. The division of the two-party vote, in 1944 and 1948, was then compared for each group of counties in each state studied. This made it possible to determine just where the vote-swing occurred and what its magnitude was.

Only in Wisconsin and in Iowa was the farm swing the crucial element in Truman's victory. In 1944, Dewey won Wisconsin with a plurality of 24,119 votes; in 1948, Truman's plurality was 56,351 votes. In the cities, Truman had a plurality of 61,581 votes— a decline of 14,347 from Roosevelt's plurality in 1944. In the small towns, on the other hand, the Republican plurality of 25,716 in 1944 was transformed into a Democratic plurality of 3,070 in 1948—a swing to the Democrats which negated their losses in the cities and wiped out much but not all of Dewey's 1944 plurality. Thus, if the remainder of the state had voted the way it had in 1944, Dewey would have won again with a small plurality. In the farm areas, however, Truman cut Dewey's 1944 plurality of 74,331 to 8,300. This swing gave Truman the state.

Similarly in Iowa. Had there been no Republican defections in the farm belt, Dewey would have won the state with a plurality of about half the 47,000 which he had in 1944, for Truman ran better than Roosevelt did in 1944 in both Iowa's cities and small towns. In addition, however, Dewey's 1944 plurality in the farm belt was cut by 52,030, which was more than enough to give the state to Truman. (Truman's statewide plurality was 28,362.) Moreover, even if Truman had not improved on Roosevelt's showing in the cities and small towns, the swing in the farm country would have been sufficient to bring him victory by a scant 4,639 votes.

In Ohio, Truman's performance in agricultural districts occasioned considerable comment, but it was not sufficient to win the state for him, even though his plurality was a mere 7,107 votes out of more than 2,800,000 cast. Truman had a plurality of 100,332 in the cities, a decline of 89,971 from Roosevelt's 1944 plurality. The farm areas showed a decline in the Republican plurality of 22,375 —far less than needed to compensate for the decline in the Democratic urban plurality and to overcome Dewey's statewide plurality of 11,530 in 1944. However, in the small towns the Republican plurality declined 85,233 from the 1944 figure—almost but not quite canceling out the decline in the Democratic city plurality. This development, together with the Republican losses in the farm areas, moved the state into the Truman column. The farmers alone did not do it. Had there not been defections from Dewey in the normally Republican small towns, Truman would have lost Ohio.

In Illinois the farm swing was not decisive, in view of Truman's small-town vote. In 1944, Roosevelt won Illinois with a plurality of 140,165; in 1948, Truman won by 33,612. Truman had an urban plurality of 169,883, a decline of 155,979 from 1944. If the Republican vote had remained stable elsewhere in the state, Truman would have lost. In the farm areas, however, the Republican plurality declined in 1948 by 20,433 votes—enough to have put Truman over. But the same phenomenon occurred in the small towns, where the Republican 1944 plurality declined by 28,993. Thus Truman was not dependent on the farm swing for his victory; it merely increased the size of his slender plurality. But there was one other crucial factor: Henry Wallace was not on the ballot in Illinois. Had his name appeared, there is no doubt that he would have attracted enough support to have wiped out Truman's plurality of 33,612. In New York State, after all, Wallace polled over 500,000 votes, and in California, 190,000.

In Minnesota, there was a substantial swing in the farm areas; it accounted for the largest proportion of the increase in the Democratic plurality from 62,448 in 1944 to 209,349 in 1948, but even without the farm swing Truman would have improved on Roosevelt's victory. In California, where the Democratic presidential plurality dropped in every area, the farm vote had no effect on the outcome. Truman's plurality decreased less (1.2 percent) in agricultural than in other areas, but even if the decline had been as great as in the cities (7.1 percent), Truman would still have carried the state by a tiny margin.

While it was only in Wisconsin and in Iowa that the farm vote meant victory for Truman, his appeal to farmers throughout the Midwest was one of the remarkable features of the election and certainly swelled his popular vote. Lubell's interviews in Guthrie County, Iowa, showed that Truman's popularity basically derived from apprehensions that the Republicans would not continue the agricultural policies of the New Deal. The farmers had prospered under the Democrats and feared change under the Republicans; their very conservatism, Lubell pointed out, led them to discard their traditional Republican loyalties.

One voter, a lifelong Republican, explained to Lubell that he was fearful of the great "house cleaning" which Dewey promised in Washington. "What would be swept out with the house cleaning?" he asked. "Price supports and other agricultural aids? If another depression comes, what will the farmer do?" Another citizen told Lubell, "I talked about voting for Dewey all summer, but when the time came I just couldn't do it. I remembered the depression and all the good things that had come to me under the Democrats."

Truman's harangues in the farm country apparently had their effect, though it is impossible to tell which issue was most important—the shortage of grain storage bins, the doubts cast on the Republican commitment to the price-support system, the failure of Congress to ratify the International Wheat Agreement, the taxes which some Republicans sought to impose on agricultural cooperatives. The sharp decline in farm prices, as a consequence of bumper crops, doubtless added to the sense of anxiety. Corn, for example, fell from $2.25 a bushel in July to $1.26 a bushel at the end of October, well below the support level of $1.53. The price drop, combined with the inability of many farmers to store the crop and get a government loan at the support level, lent reality to Truman's charge that the Eightieth Congress had betrayed the farmer. The consequence was apparent, among other places, in the corn country of northern Iowa, where Truman won 20 counties to Dewey's 7.

There may well have been other factors, of a less tangible nature, that contributed to Truman's victory. Clearly the Republicans suffered from excessive overconfidence and let most of the arguments go to Truman by default. Somewhat less clearly, depending on one's personal preferences, Truman was a more appealing candidate than Dewey. In the retrospective wave of admiration for Truman that followed his victory, his zest, combativeness, and informality were favorably contrasted with Dewey's somewhat prim dignity and aloofness; a temporary amnesia seemed to overtake the country in regard to those other qualities of Truman (such as his lack of dignity or seeming lack of competence) which had formerly brought him disparagement. What evidence we have suggests that the voters were more critical of Dewey than of Truman; the Michigan survey reported that Dewey's personal qualities came in for twice as much unfavorable comment as Truman's. "The criticism of Dewey made most frequently was that he had too high an opinion of his own abilities. 'Patronizing,' 'superior,' 'cold' were adjectives associated only with Dewey." On the other hand, the study could not estimate what effect such personal evaluations had on the vote.

It became a commonplace to blame Dewey's defeat on overconfidence. Typically, Leverett Saltonstall, a Republican senator from Massachusetts, argued that overconfidence had "led the Republicans to put on a campaign of generalities rather than interesting the people in what a Republican administration could and would do for them if elected and, contrariwise, it led Republicans to fail to answer in sound, forceful speeches the charges of the Democrats concerning . . . the Eightieth Congress."

Might Dewey have won if he had conducted a different kind of campaign? In an election as close as this one, it is impossible to answer in the negative. A campaign less devoted to high-minded platitudes, a campaign style less suggestive of the inevitability of victory, might have made enough of a difference to have swung the three states which in the end proved decisive. The more relevant question is whether Dewey could have bested Truman in the popular vote. It hardly seems likely, given the mood and the dominant political attitudes of the country and the impact of the Wallace and Dixiecrat campaigns. From the analysis thus far presented, one can plausibly conclude that the only way Dewey might have won the popular vote would have been to campaign on Truman's platform. In no other fashion could he have cut into the big-city vote which contained the bulk of Truman's plurality. No searching analysis of voter motivation is necessary to prove that Truman's supporters reaffirmed their loyalty to the New Deal and endorsed the more ambitious program of governmental intervention in the private sector which Truman offered. But Dewey could hardly have run as a New Deal candidate. Without committing himself to specifics, he did in fact endorse much of Truman's program, as in his Pittsburgh speech. For Dewey to have sought to outflank Truman on the left would have meant the repudiation of the Eightieth Congress and the denial of support for a host of conservative Republican candidates for the House and Senate. Even with the relaxed degree of party discipline prevailing in the United States, such a course would have been unthinkable.

After the election, some prominent Republicans—among them New York's Senator Irving Ives and Representative Jacob K. Javits —did attribute Dewey's defeat to the burdens imposed on him by the record of the Congress. Javits also argued that the party had been hurt by departing "from its origins as the party of the worker and producer, and as the party of reform." The right wing of the party had a different view of why Dewey had lost and how he might have won. Immediately after the election, the Chicago *Tribune* editorialized:

> For the third time, a Republican convention fell under vicious influences and nominated a "me-too" candidate who conducted a "me-too" campaign. For the third time the strategy failed. That is why Mr. Truman was elected and with him a Democratic House and Senate.
> After this experience, we may hope the Republicans have learned their lesson. If the same forces control the next Republican convention the party is finished and the millions of patriotic men and women who have looked to it for leadership will have to look elsewhere.

This became the dominant conservative diagnosis. Dewey was defeated because he offered a pale version of the New Deal; if he had conducted a vigorous campaign providing a clear-cut conservative alternative, he would have swept the country. In his postmortem, Senator Taft stated, "It was necessary in 1948 to run on the record of the Republican Congress," a record which he insisted would have been an asset to a candidate who championed it. Senator-elect Karl E. Mundt of South Dakota criticized the Republican failure "to focus attention on the mistakes of Yalta and Potsdam. Very little was made even of the Vinson-to-Moscow travesty.[1]

---

[1] In October, Truman had made plans to send Chief Justice Fred Vinson to Moscow to meet personally with Stalin and attempt to resolve the Berlin blockade and other Cold War issues. The State Department managed to exercise a veto, but not before news of the project had leaked to the press.—Ed.

Americans apparently like both their candidates and their baseball players to be of the hard-hitting variety."

Had Dewey assaulted Truman from the right, the result would unquestionably have been a livelier campaign, but he would probably have suffered a greater defeat. To have defended the domestic record of the Eightieth Congress (its foreign policy record was not basically controversial) would have involved a defense of tax legislation which favored the more affluent sector of the population, anti-inflation measures that were inadequate, the Taft-Hartley Act (to which the whole of the labor movement was hostile), failure to pass even the housing bill which bore Taft's name, and an equal lack of action in the fields of federal aid to education and health insurance. If Dewey had mounted such a campaign, he would have provided an even easier target for Truman and the latter's urban majorities would have been much larger. The country was in no mood for the policies of governmental restraint typified by the Hoover administration; that issue had been settled in 1936, when Alfred Landon, in anything but a "me-too" campaign, carried only Maine and Vermont. Nor does it seem likely that Dewey could have picked up much support had he emphasized Democratic failings at Yalta and Potsdam; by the autumn of 1948, Truman's foreign policy was consistently anti-Communist and the existence of the Progressive party, as already noted, tended to reinforce Truman's anti-Communist *bona fides.*

The one alteration in strategy which Dewey might have adopted, also suggested by Mundt among others, would have been a fuller discussion of farm issues. In this area, the Republican record was by no means as deplorable as Truman suggested and the Democrats were not without their own vulnerabilities. On the grain storage issue, for example, the Democrats had not raised any great cry in Congress when the Commodity Credit Corporation charter had been extended in June. Dewey might well have picked up some more votes in the Midwest had he made a determined effort to assure farmers that the Republicans favored the federal-aid policies instituted by the New Deal. But it is doubtful that Dewey could have denied Truman all his gains in the farm belt.

In long-range terms, Truman's success in holding together the old Roosevelt coalition proved that the Democratic party was truly the majority party in the country. Throughout the Roosevelt era, it had been possible for Republicans to attribute their long eclipse to the accidents of depression and the Second World War and to the astonishing personal popularity of FDR. It had been possible to hope that once Roosevelt had passed from the scene and once the country had reverted to a peacetime economy, the political pattern that prevailed prior to 1932 would reassert itself. The Republican victory in the congressional election of 1946, keyed to the slogan of "Had enough?", seemed to confirm that hypothesis. It seemed further confirmed by the fissiparous tendencies at work in the Democratic party in the early months of 1948.

Then came the victory of Harry Truman, a candidate whose prospects had seemed so dim that many of his party's leaders had sought to repudiate him just a few months before. If Truman could win, there could no longer be any doubt that a basic and irreversible alteration had occurred in the political loyalties of the American electorate (irreversibility being measured in quadrennia, not eternity). The New Deal revolution had passed beyond the stage of meaningful debate and the Republicans could not readily replace the Democrats as the majority party. As Walter Lippmann put it two days after the election, "Mr. Truman's own victory, the Democratic majorities in both houses of Congress, the Democratic victories in so many states, attest the enormous vitality of the Democratic party as Roosevelt led it and developed it from 1932 to 1944 . . . the party that Roosevelt formed had survived his death, and is without question the dominant force in American politics."

The concept of majority and minority party does not imply that the minority never wins a national election. It implies, rather, that the majority party expresses the predominant political sentiment of the nation, that over a long span of years it wins more often than it loses. Only under extraordinary conditions does the minority party attain the presidency. From 1896 to 1932, the Republican party was the majority party, winning the presidency by decisive majorities at every election except in 1912 and 1916; Wilson's victory in 1912 occurred after Theodore Roosevelt split the Republicans and ran as a third-party candidate.

Lubell has argued persuasively that "two population currents" ultimately cracked the long Republican ascendancy: "Between 1910 and 1930 for the first time a majority of the American people came to live in cities. The second population shift might be described as the triumph of the birth rates of the poor and underprivileged over those of the rich and wellborn." The cities filled up with immigrants and displaced farmers whose offspring were numerous, whose conditions of life were bleak, and whose politics (and whose children's politics) were Democratic. "The human potential for a revolutionary political change had thus been brought together in our larger cities when the economic skies caved in," Lubell writes. He points out that the urban shift to the Democrats actually began, in a small way, in 1928. In the country's twelve largest cities, the Republicans had a plurality of 1,638,000 votes in 1920; nearly 400,000 votes less four years later; by 1928 there was a Democratic plurality of 38,000, which rose to 1,910,000 in 1932 and reached its peak of 3,608,000 in 1936. By 1948, the Democrats had controlled the twelve largest cities through six presidential elections. There resided the key ingredient of its majority status, in terms of both popular and electoral votes. Those twelve cities were in states controlling 231 electoral votes; in most elections in the thirties and forties, as Samuel J. Eldersveld demonstrated in a significant article in 1949, the pluralities in the twelve cities won the states for the Democrats. Without them, the Democrats would have lost the presidency in 1940, 1944 and 1948.

Truman not only perpetuated the old Roosevelt coalition but moved it several degrees to the left, both rhetorically and programmatically. As the Alsop brothers wrote soon after the election, "His campaign speeches were consistently more aggressive and more radical than any Franklin Delano Roosevelt ever uttered. At his hottest and angriest, Roosevelt never laid it into big business as Truman did. Nor did Roosevelt ever promise specific reforms, well beyond any currently popular with other politicians, as Truman did." Indeed, the Truman program—especially such items as civil rights legislation, compulsory medical insurance, federal aid to education—constituted an agenda of unfinished business most of which was not completed until the Johnson administration. Some items have not yet been enacted, such as the repeal of the Taft-Hartley Act or the provision of medical insurance for all citizens, not merely the aged or the indigent.

The pale pink glow which the election seemed to cast over the country owed much to the Democratic successes in the congressional and gubernatorial contests. Not only did the Democrats win sizable majorities in the House (263 to 171) and Senate (54 to 42), but many liberals, and most of the candidates favored by labor, were elected. The CIO's Political Action Committee supported 215 House and 21 senatorial aspirants, of whom the winners totaled 144 and 17. The AFL's Labor's League for Political Education could boast that 86 of its 105 congressional candidates had been elected and 14 of its 16 senatorial choices. In most instances, of course, the two labor groups endorsed the same men.

The Democratic class of 1948 contained an abundance of attractive liberal talent. In Illinois, both Adlai Stevenson and Paul Douglas won instant celebrity in the national press because of the astonishing margins by which they defeated the Chicago *Tribune*'s candidates. Stevenson, a former delegate to the United Nations, won the governorship by a plurality of over 570,000. Douglas, whose only previous elected office was that of alderman in Chicago, was elected U.S. senator with a plurality of more than 400,000, defeating C. Wayland ("Curly") Brooks, one of the least prepossessing relics of the old isolationist bloc in the Midwest. In Minnesota, Hubert Humphrey, whose dazzling oratorical gifts had so impressed the Democratic convention in July, trounced the incumbent senator, Joseph Ball, by 729,494 to 485,801 votes. In Tennessee, Estes Kefauver won an easy election to the Senate over B. Carroll Reece, the former chairman of the Republican National Committee. Kefauver, with his coonskin cap and shambling, folksy manner, had already received a measure of national attention when he had won a difficult primary race against the candidate of the Crump machine. In Connecticut, Chester Bowles, the former price-control administrator, surprised everyone, possibly including himself, by getting elected governor by a mere 1,400 votes. Bowles was not to win another election, but his single, unexpected triumph laid the base for an energetic career in high appointive office. Another startling upset occurred in Michigan, where thirty-seven-year-old G. Mennen Williams, a little-known lawyer who had never held elective office, defeated the incumbent Republican, the flamboyant Kim Sigler, by a decisive 163,854 votes while Harry Truman lost the state by 35,147 votes.

All the ironies of the 1948 election were not to be apparent until a few years later. Despite the great liberal victory, Truman was able to win congressional acceptance for few of the major items in his domestic program. Before long, the old coalition of conservative Republicans and conservative Southern Democrats reasserted itself, winning effective control of the Congress and becoming almost as obdurate as the "do-nothing" Eightieth Congress. By the time Truman's term was up, it was possible to speculate that more might have been accomplished had that switch of some 30,000 votes occurred in Ohio, Illinois, and California and had Dewey been elected. What would have been the likely consequences? There would certainly have been no change in the direction of American foreign policy, which continued to enjoy bipartisan support throughout the Truman years. Dewey would have been quite as inclined as Truman to respond with alacrity to the Communist invasion of South Korea in 1950, a response that was properly celebrated as one of Truman's finest hours. In domestic affairs, one can plausibly argue that Dewey might have won the enactment of more liberal measures than Truman did, assuming that Dewey confronted the same Congress (as indeed he would have, had he won in a photo finish).

The reasoning is simple: a Republican president, at least in the opening stages of his administration, could be far more persuasive with the Republican members of Congress. Dewey might well have thwarted a new Republican–Southern Democratic coalition, at least for a time, appealing for a chance to make a domestic record. Another coalition might have been created—between the congressional Republicans who were indulgent to Dewey's leadership and the bulk of the Democrats, who favored his program, which in many particulars was similar to Truman's.

This thesis is of course open to dispute, but what seems unarguable is that a Dewey victory would have spared the country the vast trauma of the McCarthy era. Senator McCarthy, it will be recalled, did not become a McCarthyite until his Wheeling, West Virginia, speech in February 1950, in which he claimed to have the names of a sizable number of Communists in the State Department. McCarthy's discovery of the Communist issue had been fortuitous. Richard Rovere, in his biography of the senator, relates how he was casting about for a usable issue early in 1950; he was up for reelection in 1952 and he felt that he needed a new sales pitch to impress the voters. One acquaintance suggested the issue of Communist subversion, which had created abundant headlines ever since the Chambers and Bentley testimony in 1948. McCarthy enthusiastically agreed and soon found within himself a fabulous talent for distortion and demagogy. By the 1952 campaign, he was filling the airwaves with denunciations of "twenty years of treason."

McCarthy's crusade could hardly have been launched had Dewey been elected president. The senator would have lacked either the target or the impulse. He could not have blamed the sins of the prior Democratic administration on the Republicans in control of the executive department. Any raking up of the past would have been of purely historical interest. Moreover, with his own party in power, McCarthy would not have obtained the (often covert) support of other Republicans who were happy seeing him belabor the Democrats. McCarthy would have had to find another issue for his reelection campaign.

Truman's success in 1948 had another ironical consequence: the Eisenhower boom in 1952. Many Republicans were not slow in appreciating the fact that the Democrats had solidified their position as the majority party. Truman's legislative initiatives could be frustrated, but clearly more voters preferred the Democrats to the Republicans when they got into the polling booth. To the moderate Republicans, at least, it became apparent that if they could not win in the favorable circumstances of 1948 with a politician of Dewey's ability, the best solution was to present a candidate who transcended party differences, a candidate who could make an effective nonpolitical appeal.

No search was required to find the man. World War II had produced two great American wartime heroes—General Dwight D. Eisenhower and General Douglas MacArthur. From the outset, MacArthur had been hopelessly compromised by involvement with right-wing Republicans; after his defeat in the Wisconsin primary of 1948, he lost what little appeal he had previously possessed to professional politicians. General Eisenhower, however, came through 1948 with his reputation intact. His popularity remained buoyant throughout the second Truman administration, during which he left his duties as president of Columbia University to organize the military machine of the newly created North Atlantic Treaty Organization. Long before the 1952 conventions, the prospect of Eisenhower's candidacy was as dazzling to liberal Republicans as it had been to the Democratic rebels who had sought to dump Truman in 1948. Eisenhower had everything—the glow of wartime military triumphs, a radiant and attractive personality, an identification with the magnanimity and military realism of America's postwar foreign policy, a total lack of identification with divisive domestic squabbles. "The chant of 'We like Ike' was more nearly a hymn of praise and entreaty to a demigod than a political war cry," Marquis Childs has written. "Eisenhower represented strength, triumph, unswerving confidence. Millions were happy to take him on faith, on his face, on his smile, on the image of American manhood, on the happy virtue of his family life."

The alternative to Eisenhower, at the Republican convention, was Taft. He had the virtue of representing the true Republican faith and of being able to inspire the party zealots. The major case against him was that his appeal would be too narrowly partisan; and, indeed, it is quite possible that Taft, had he been nominated, would have been defeated by Stevenson. Instead, Eisenhower won by a large plurality. The general put together a winning coalition by attracting two-thirds of the voters who considered themselves independents (they constituted 16 percent of the electorate) and by cutting deeply into such traditional sources of Democratic strength as the families of union members and voters of German, Irish, and Polish descent. Eisenhower also ran especially well in the new suburban areas, he reasserted the Republican hold over the farm vote, and he won four Southern states. He repeated his massive victory in 1956. But these were clearly personal triumphs, which did not dislodge the Democrats' status as majority party. The Republicans only managed to win a narrow control of the Congress in 1952; thereafter, in the elections of 1954, 1956, and 1958, the Democrats won control. They remain the majority party to this day, with roughly a five to three ratio of registered voters.

A second consequence of Truman's victory, so far as the Republicans were concerned, was further to embitter the conservative wing of the party whose hero was Senator Taft. In the view of his admirers, Taft had been unfairly denied the nomination in every convention going back to 1940. When the liberal Dewey, against all expectations, managed to lose in 1948, the Republican right felt confirmed in its judgment, previously quoted from the Chicago *Tribune,* that a "me-too" candidate could not defeat the Democrats. The conviction gradually grew—eventually becoming almost an article of religious faith—that if the voters had been offered a clear-cut choice between an aggressive conservative and a liberal Democrat, the conservative would have won.

Eisenhower's two victories by no means eradicated this conservative dogma; it reemerged in full force after Nixon's close defeat by Kennedy in 1960. Shortly after that election, Senator Barry Goldwater declared, "We who are conservatives will stoutly maintain that 1960 was a repeat performance of 1944 and 1948, when we offered the voters insufficient choice with a me-too candidate." Goldwater's admirers believed that there was truly a conservative majority in the country, which had long remained submerged because it had always been denied a presidential candidate to rally around. In *The Winning Side: The Case for Goldwater Conservatism,* published in 1963, Ralph de Toledano wrote: "Whatever the election results of the past decades may seem to indicate—or the Gallup Poll proclaim—the Republican party has represented a real or potential majority of the electorate. The battle for America must therefore first be fought to recapture the Republican party from those whose heart's desire seems to be to make it a pallid twin of the Democratic party. Once this battle has been won, the confrontation of Left and Right can take place. In 1940, 1944, 1948, 1952, 1956 and 1960, clear-cut distinctions were obscured. The voter seeking a Liberal candidate settled for the real article and not for the Republocratic imitation. The conservative voter knew that he was not being given a significant choice."

The following year, the Republican party was "recaptured" and the voter was finally offered "a choice, not an echo," as Phyllis Schlafly put it in her best-seller paperback book in 1964. In July, Barry Goldwater was the overwhelming choice of the Republican convention. In November, he led his party to its greatest presidential defeat since 1912. Had Truman not won in 1948, the Republican party would have been spared the Goldwater disaster, as well as Eisenhower's successive triumphs.

The impact of the 1948 election has been felt in other ways as well. The election undermined a theory, widely favored by many politicians, that voters made up their minds soon after the party conventions and were not greatly influenced by the campaign. Truman's mounting appeal in the latter stages of the 1948 campaign, as well as postelection analysis of what happened to the undecided voters, certainly suggested that the campaign proper was far more than an unavoidable ritual. It may well have been decisive.

The 1948 election also demonstrated that it was a mistake to take a static view of the way an intraparty coalition works. The belief that Truman was in large part doomed because of the defection of the Dixiecrats and the Wallaceites was based on a simple arithmetic calculation rather than on an understanding of the dynamics of such a coalition. As Lubell has pointed out, the defection of one or two elements in a coalition could result in a countervailing accretion of support elsewhere along the spectrum. Thus, Truman was more appealing to Negro and Catholic voters once he was deserted by the racists and the far left. Indeed, one can speculate that had the Dixiecrat and Progressive party breakaways not occurred, Truman might have lost the election through defections to Dewey on the part of other disaffected elements in the Democratic party. But once the split-offs occurred, other restive elements in the party had reason to reevaluate their loyalty, for their defection under these circumstances could be interpreted as playing into the hands of the Dixiecrats or the Progressives. This interlocking relationship is likely to persist as long as an American political party remains a broad coalition, containing mutually antagonistic groups.

In the end, the most salutary consequence of 1948 was probably a renewed awareness of the contingent quality of events, of the unpredictability of both leadership in a democracy and of the choices that voters make in the privacy of the polling booth. Not for a long time afterward were politicians likely to take the American voter for granted.

Harry S. Truman, September 5, 1949
THE PHILOSOPHY OF THE FAIR DEAL

This address at the Allegheny County Fair in Pittsburgh was the first of two nationally broadcast speeches delivered by Truman on Labor Day, 1949. The other, from Des Moines, Iowa, was a defense of the administration's agricultural program. Taken together, the two talks amounted to a plea for farmer-labor unity to serve as the political basis of a liberal Democratic party. The Pittsburgh address, slightly abridged here, sets forth the administration agenda and philosophy in the wake of the 1948 election.

I am particularly impressed by this fair, because it is both a farm show and an industrial exposition. Farmers and industrial workers together are showing their best products here today.

Farmers and industrial workers—agriculture and industry—ought to show their products together. For these two groups depend upon each other. Together, they are responsible for the tremendous production of this country's economic system. No program for prosperity in the country can ignore the interests of either group.

In recent years some people have been telling farmers, out of one corner of their mouths, that the labor unions are bad for farmers. Out of the other corner of their mouths, these same people have been telling industrial workers that programs to benefit farmers are bad for labor. If you ever meet anybody like that, you can be sure he is not interested in the welfare of either the farmer or the industrial worker. Those who are trying to set these two great groups against each other just have axes of their own to grind.

Now, about this time last year, if you remember, the country was engaged in a great political campaign. I covered a good deal of the United States in the course of that campaign, and I put the plain facts, as I saw them, before the people. I also offered a program to meet the needs of all groups in this country for growth and prosperity. The votes of the people showed that they wanted that kind of program. They were not misled by the newspapers and the magazines and the so-called experts who tried to convince them that they did not want that kind of program.

From *Public Papers of the Presidents of the United States: Harry S. Truman, 1949* (U.S. Government Printing Office, 1964), pp. 460–464.

The people knew what they wanted.

Their votes showed that the farmers and the workers stand together in demanding a government that works for the benefit of
all our citizens.

It is now almost a year since that campaign, and I think it is time
to take stock of the situation and see what progress we have made
in carrying out the program the people voted for.

I am happy to be able to report to you that we have made
progress; and we are continuing to make progress.

As a result of last fall's election, we have a new Congress in
Washington. And this new Eighty-first Congress has an entirely
different approach to the needs and desires of the people from that
of the Eightieth Congress.

The Eightieth Congress was a threat to almost every bit of forward-looking legislation passed during recent years. For example, it
repealed the Wagner Labor Relations Act and replaced it with an unfair and restrictive Taft-Hartley Act. It took social security benefits
from hundreds of thousands of people. It weakened our farm programs. It attacked our national policy for making the benefits of
electric power available to the public—to all the people—instead of
just the privileged few.

If the Eightieth Congress had not been repudiated, this tearing
down process would have gone on and on. But now the new Eighty-
first Congress has reversed this backward trend.

The Eighty-first Congress has put a stop to the piecemeal destruction of the hard-won protections and benefits that the people have
built up for themselves. It has done more than that. The Eighty-first
Congress has moved forward.

Some people are trying to make you believe that the Eighty-first
Congress has been a "do-nothing" Congress. That simply is not
true. The fact is the Eighty-first Congress has already passed many
important measures for the good of the people—and it will pass
many more progressive laws.

The Eighty-first Congress has taken wise and important steps in
foreign policy by extending the European Recovery Program and
ratifying the North Atlantic Treaty. It has enacted a far-reaching
housing program that will benefit millions of our citizens. It has
extended rent control. It has taken action to make low-cost electricity
available to more of our people. It has strengthened the soil con-

servation and reclamation programs. This Congress has restored the government's power to acquire grain storage facilities necessary to carry out the farm-price support program. This Congress has approved an International Wheat Agreement which will give our farmers a fair share of the world wheat markets at fair prices. This Congress has strengthened and improved our organization for national defense.

My friends, this is real progress. And this session is not over yet. Other important measures, such as those raising the minimum wage and extending the Reciprocal Trade Agreements Act, are well on their way to final passage.

The Eighty-first Congress has taken these actions over the fierce opposition of the selfish interests. The organized conspiracy of the selfish interests has gone right on working against the common good, in spite of the election returns.

One of the things that the special interests have managed to do up until this time is to prevent the repeal of the Taft-Hartley law. But that issue is far from settled. We are going to continue to fight for the repeal of that repressive law until it is wiped off the statute books.

The selfish interests have always been working against the common good, since the beginning of our history. Our fathers and our grandfathers had to fight against them every step of the way to make progress. They had to fight for a free public school system. They had to fight for the right of homesteaders to settle on the public lands. They had to fight for laws to protect the health and safety of industrial workers. They had to fight for labor's right to organize.

We face the same situation today. We still have a fight on our hands.

The special interests always fail to see that the way of progress, the way of greater prosperity for themselves, as well as others, lies in the direction of a fuller and happier life for all.

Too many people who can afford big insurance policies for themselves are not concerned over the need of expanding social security. Too many who are making money out of the rents from slums are not in favor of expanding public housing to provide decent shelter for low-income families. Too many with big incomes are not interested in raising minimum wages. Too many who can freely organize themselves in business associations or employers' groups are not anxious to protect the same right to organize among industrial workers.

It is hard, perhaps, for the people in comfortable circumstances to see the need for improving the well-being of the less fortunate. Furthermore, they are always being stirred up and misled by the spokesmen and lobbyists for organized selfish interests. There are a lot of paid agitators, promoters, and so-called publicity experts who make a fat living by frightening the people in the higher income groups about forward-looking legislation, and by organizing campaigns against that forward-looking legislation.

Ever since the election those spokesmen have been very busy stirring up opposition to our legislative program.

The hue and cry that has resulted, in the press, and on the air, and through the mail, has been deafening.

These propagandists do not argue the merits of our program. They know that the American people will always decide against the selfish interests if all the facts are before them. So they have adopted the age-old device to hide the weakness of their case.

This is the device of the "scare-word" campaign.

It is a device that has been used in every country and every age by the propagandists for selfish interests. They invent slogans in an effort to scare the people. They apply frightening labels to anything they happen to oppose. These scare words are intended to confuse the people and turn them against their own best interests.

Scare words change with the times.

When Franklin D. Roosevelt and the New Deal saved our country from the Great Depression, the selfish interests raised the scare words of "socialism" and "regimentation."

But the American people didn't scare.

Year after year the selfish interests kept up their refrain. They tried new words—"bureaucracy" and "bankruptcy."

But the American people still didn't scare.

Last November the people gave the selfish interests the surprise of their lives. The people just didn't believe that programs designed to assure them decent housing, adequate wages, improved medical care, and better education were "socialism" or "regimentation."

So the selfish interests retired to a backroom with their high-priced advertising experts and thought things over. They decided that the old set of scare words had become a little mildewed. Maybe it was time for a change.

So they came up with a new set of scare words. Now they're talking about "collectivism," and "statism," and "the welfare state."

The selfish interests don't know—in fact, they don't care—what those words mean. They are using those words only because they want to turn the American people against the programs which the people want, and need, and for which the people voted last fall.

Let's see how the selfish interests are using these scare words.

The people want public housing for low-income families. The selfish interests are opposed to this because they think it will cut down their own incomes; so they call it "collectivism."

Well, we don't care what they call it.

We are for public housing. It is the democratic way to provide decent homes in place of slums.

The people want fair laws for labor. The selfish interests are against these laws because they mistakenly fear that their profits will be reduced; so they call that "statism."

Well, we don't care what they call it.

We believe that the workers in this country have a fundamental right to square treatment from employers.

The people want a fair program for the farmers, including an effective price support system. The selfish interests fight against this because it keeps them from profiteering at the farmers' expense; so they call this "socialism."

Well, we don't care what they call it.

We know that the well-being of the country depends upon the well-being of the farmers, and that farm prosperity must be protected in the interest of all of us.

The people want a better social security system, improved education, and a national health program. The selfish interests are trying to sabotage these programs because they have no concern about helping the little fellow; and so they call this the "welfare state."

Well, we don't care what they call it.

We know that the little fellow is the backbone of this country, and we are dedicated to the principle that the government should promote the welfare of all the people.

The spokesmen for these special interests say that these programs make the government too powerful and cause the people to lose their freedom. Well now, that just is not so. Programs like these make the people more independent—independent of the government, independent of big business and corporate power.

People who have opportunity to work and earn, and who have an assured income in their old age, are free. They are free of the fear of poverty. They are free of public or private charity. They can live happier, more useful lives. That's real freedom. And that is something we should be proud of—that's not something to be slandered by trumped-up slogans.

Along with this campaign of scare words, we hear another argument against adopting any forward-looking legislation. It is to the effect that even if these programs are good things, we can't adopt them now, because they cost too much and we can't afford them.

The selfish interests say we can't afford these programs during a boom because that would be inflationary. They say we can't afford them during a recession because that would be deflationary. They say we can't afford them during a war because we are too busy with defense, we can't afford them in time of peace because that would discourage business. So, according to the selfish interests, we never can afford them.

But the truth is—we can't afford not to put these programs into effect. We can afford them, we ought to have them, and we will have them.

The sooner we have them the better it will be for the country, and the more we will save.

Take our programs for resource development, for example. If we fail to conserve our soil, we lose our most valuable resource. If we fail to build electric power facilities, we hamper the development of industry.

Take our social security system. Shall we force our old people to turn to charity? Or shall we let them have an independent and self-respecting existence through an up-to-date old-age insurance system, paid for during their working years?

Take housing. If we don't go forward with our housing and slum-clearance programs, we shall have to pay the rising costs of disease, immorality, and crime bred in slums.

Consider our schools. The hidden costs of poor education, lost opportunity, and poverty resulting from inadequate schools are costs the nation can no longer afford. Federal aid to education will be a lot less expensive than ignorance and illiteracy.

If we are to have a healthy and prosperous United States, we must have better schools, better housing, better medical care, better use of our resources, stronger social security, and the other improvements in our democracy that the people need.

Those who oppose these improvements refuse to face the facts of today's world. They don't understand the overriding urgency of proving the value of the democratic way of life, not just with words, but with deeds. They don't see that the very survival of free enterprise depends upon a rising standard of living and an expanding economy. They don't recognize that to work for the increasing security and liberty of the people of the United States is the key not only to our own prosperity, but to the prosperity and peace of the whole world.

But the people of the United States do understand these things. When they have the facts before them, they always choose progress —not reaction.

They made this clear again last fall. They chose the very same programs that are now being attacked by the selfish interests with their campaign scare words. The people were not misled about those programs then. They will not be misled about them now.

The people know that the second half of the twentieth century is going to be a time of challenge to the way of freedom and progress that our democracy represents. As we meet that challenge, we shall have to fight, as we have always fought, the selfish forces of reaction and special privilege.

The people of the United States have been winning that fight for 160 years. I am convinced that we will continue to win that fight through the years to come.

Alonzo L. Hamby

THE VITAL CENTER, THE FAIR DEAL, AND THE QUEST FOR A LIBERAL POLITICAL ECONOMY

This essay attempts to connect the Fair Deal to broader currents in American liberal thought during the 1940s, discusses three of the major thinkers and political strategists of the Truman administration, and provides a brief interpretation of the political history of Truman's second term. It argues that while the Fair Deal was a direct descendant of the New Deal there were important differences of emphasis between them, the result primarily of new perspectives created by wartime and postwar prosperity.

"Every segment of our population and every individual has a right to expect from our government a fair deal," declared Harry S. Truman in early 1949. In 1945 and 1946 the Truman administration had almost crumbled under the stresses of postwar reconversion; in 1947 and 1948 it had fought a frustrating, if politically rewarding, battle with the Republican Eightieth Congress. Buoyed by his remarkable victory of 1948 and given Democratic majorities in both houses of Congress, Truman hoped to achieve an impressive record of domestic reform. The president systematized his past proposals, added some new ones, and gave his program a name that would both connect his administration with the legacy of the New Deal and give it a distinct identity. The Fair Deal, while based solidly upon the New Deal tradition, differed from its predecessor in significant aspects of mood and detail. It reflected not only Truman's own aspirations but also a style of liberalism that had begun to move beyond the New Deal during World War II and had come to maturity during the early years of the Cold War—"the vital center."

Throughout the history of the United States the main stream of reform has been within the broad Lockean-capitalist consensus to which most Americans subscribe. The Great Depression, however, had caused liberal reformers to question capitalism as never before;

From *The American Historical Review* 77 (June, 1972): 653–678. Copyright © 1972 by the American Historical Association. Reprinted by permission of the editors of *The American Historical Review*. (Footnotes edited.)

mass unemployment at home and the rise of an aggressive fascism out of the ruins of capitalism abroad seemed to provide proof that the old system had failed beyond repair. One logical response with appeal to many reform thinkers and leaders was the movement for a popular front of all reform and radical forces, most strongly united by a determination to stop the spread of fascism but also seeking newer and better socioeconomic arrangements, even "revolutionary" ones. The New Deal itself, faced with the actual responsibility of governing, took a far more moderate course, searching for a viable middle way that would preserve capitalism; yet even the New Dealers, unable to overcome the depression, were increasingly driven to the conclusion that capitalism had become incapable of the growth needed to provide reasonably full employment.

The thirties did not exactly constitute the fabled "Red Decade" of right-wing mythologists. Most liberals who worked within the government sought American solutions to American problems and appear to have been only marginally influenced by foreign examples. Those outside the government were more likely to look toward European patterns. The most enduring appeal they found was in Scandinavian welfarism, but many were at least provisionally drawn to Soviet communism. A liberal of the thirties, quite in line with the popular-front mood, was more likely to think of himself as part of an undifferentiated Left and more prone to consider substitutes for capitalism than were earlier progressives. The failure of capitalism at home and abroad did not throw the liberals en masse into the Communist party, but it shook old assumptions to an extent that left few unaffected.

Temporarily shattered by the Nazi-Soviet Pact of 1939, popular-front foreign policy staged a resurgence during World War II and received an aura of legitimacy from President Roosevelt's effort to forge a lasting alliance with the Soviet Union. During the war and the years immediately following, advocates of Soviet-American friendship could use the Roosevelt name and symbolism as a potent appeal. Yet at the same time World War II eroded the domestic side of popular frontism. The war eliminated the depression—as the New Deal had not—and demonstrated the potential of American industry. To a large extent, moreover, businessmen managed the economic war effort, and, while the liberals frequently criticized them on matters of detail, it was hard to refute the statistics of success. One result was a widespread repudiation of the psychology of scarcity, which had grown out of the long years of the depression. Leading progressives popularized the vision of an ever-expanding capitalist economy balanced by Keynesian fiscal methods and buffered by extensive social welfare programs. Their intellectual leader was the eminent economist Alvin H. Hansen and their political leader was vice-president Henry A. Wallace, who demonstrated that it had become possible, even natural, to be a popular fronter in foreign policy and an advocate of "progressive capitalism" at home. The liberal mission was no longer to achieve a new socioeconomic system or even to prop up a "mature," worn-out economy; it was to realize capitalism's capacity for endless growth.

The Cold War completed the demise of the popular-front mood. Groups and individuals that thought of themselves as liberal came increasingly to perceive the Soviet Union as an expansionist, totalitarian force and the American Communist party as the slavish, antiliberal representative of Soviet despotism. In 1947 an influential group of liberals established Americans for Democratic Action (ADA) with the express purpose of isolating Communists and pro-Communists from the main stream of liberal politics. Key foreign-policy events that followed—the Russian rejection of the Marshall Plan, the Czech coup, and the Berlin Blockade—inclined most progressives toward the ADA position. In 1948 the *New Republic,* probably the most sensitive barometer of progressive opinion, rejected the popular-front style of Henry Wallace's presidential candidacy and endorsed Truman. Wallace's weak showing on election day demonstrated a massive liberal repudiation of the Soviet Union and the Communist party.

By 1949 the ADA was the dominant progressive organization, and signs of a transformation were appearing throughout the liberal community. The editor of the New York *Post,* T. O. Thackrey, had endorsed Wallace for president. In April 1949 the paper's owner and publisher—his wife, Dorothy Schiff Thackrey—fired him. It is significant that Mrs. Thackrey defined the break in terms of attitudes toward communism, arguing that the Communists posed "new threats to democracy" and asserting that henceforth the paper would fight with equal vigor "all totalitarianism, whether Fascist or Communist." Her new editor, James A. Wechsler, was an ADA leader and a militant anti-Communist, who quickly dismissed popular-front columnists.

The *New Republic* continued the shift it had begun in 1948. Its publisher, Michael Straight, who had once regarded Henry Wallace as a personal hero, undertook a speaking tour on behalf of the ADA and delighted its leaders by bringing his magazine into nearly total agreement with the organization's viewpoint. The Italian-American intellectual, Max Ascoli, established the *Reporter* as a new outlet for moderate, tough-minded, anti-Communist liberalism. The Congress of Industrial Organizations expelled popular-front unions. "We in American labor will fight totalitarianism from the right or the left," declared Philip Murray, the president of the CIO, "We regard the human welfare state as America's middle way."

Murray's remark epitomized a new mood that conceived of liberalism as a center doctrine midway between the totalitarian poles of fascism and communism. Implicit in the new self-image was a slight moderation, a decline of utopian hopes and aspirations, a somewhat stronger suspicion of big government, and increasing doubts about the goodness of human nature. It was no coincidence that four significant books expressing this viewpoint in one manner or another appeared in 1949.

In *Target: You,* Leland Stowe, a widely read foreign correspondent, addressed himself to "Mr. American Middle Man"—the target of fascist and Communist totalitarianism, of monopolistic "Big Capitalism" and Communist Marxism—and argued that the future of American democracy depended upon the maintenance of a "strong political Center" that would counter both domestic communism and right-wing extremism by providing economic security and securing civil liberty under a rule of law.

Max Ascoli in *The Power of Freedom* depicted the earth as caught up in a worldwide civil war with one side struggling to maintain freedom by finding the middle way between unrestrained capitalism and total socialization, the other attempting to achieve "the total subjection of men on a world-wide scale." Stressing the limitations of human nature and the unattainability of utopias, Ascoli unabashedly admitted that he was a disciple of such thinkers as Edmund Burke, Alexander Hamilton, and Alexis de Tocqueville. Yet he found no inconsistency in declaring: "I am a liberal, and I don't want to add any qualifying adjectives."

In *Strategy for Liberals* the political journalist Irwin Ross used militant rhetoric and projected an ambitious reform program. Yet he carefully typed his ideal polity as the "Mixed Economy" and distinguished it not simply from fascism and communism but also from socialism, which, with its complete control of industry, detailed planning, massive bureaucracy, and control of communications, contained within itself "if not the seeds of decay, certainly the seeds of totalitarianism."

Arthur M. Schlesinger, Jr. gave the new liberalism a name with the publication of *The Vital Center.* An exercise in political philosophy and an exhortation to American progressives, the volume won an impressive reception. "It seemed to me one of those books which may suddenly and clearly announce the spirit of an age to itself," wrote Jonathan Daniels. Deeply influenced personally and intellectually by Reinhold Niebuhr, Schlesinger castigated the popular-front liberals as sentimental believers in progress and human perfectionism who, yearning for utopias, had been seduced by the surface idealism of communism and the Soviet experiment. Awake only to the evils of fascism, they had sympathized with at least some aspects of the Soviet experience and had accepted the Communists as allies in a common struggle, not understanding that such a tactic could lead only to self-destruction. The "restoration of radical nerve" had come with the rise of a non-Communist left in Europe and the United States, largely through the efforts of younger liberals whose impressions of the Soviet Union stemmed from the Stalinist purges of the 1930s rather than the idealism of the Russian Revolution. The new liberalism—or "radicalism" as Schlesinger preferred to call it—unconditionally rejected all varieties of totalitarianism. Applied to foreign affairs it stood for a dual policy of vigilantly containing communism and encouraging the democratic left abroad. Believing "in the integrity of the individual, in the limited state, in due process of law, in empiricism and gradualism," it was acutely aware of the weaknesses of human nature and of the dangers of excessive concentration of power. Devoted to the furtherance of individual liberty, it stood for a mixed economy, featuring partial government planning and ownership, antitrust action to discipline private big business, and welfare programs to provide a minimum of security and subsistence to all. The conception of liberalism as a sort of centrism had its liabilities. Schlesinger found it natural to identify with "responsible conservatives" such as Charles Evans Hughes and Henry L. Stimson; liberals, he suggested, might find common cause with this group, especially on matters of civil rights and civil liberties. Doubtless he was correct, and it was tempting, after militantly rejecting the revolutionary totalitarian ideology of communism, to conceive of the liberal effort to preserve humane, democratic values as akin to an intelligent conservatism; yet even the creed of a Hughes or a Stimson provided few answers for the problems that preoccupied the liberals. Unfortunately it was but a short step from the vital center to the superficialities of the "New Conservatism" of the 1950s.

Whatever its inner weaknesses, the vital-center approach gave the liberal movement a moral integrity and consistency that had been absent during the popular-front era. Its implications, moreover, went beyond the affairs of diplomacy or the tactical wisdom of a liberal-Communist alliance: its approach to political economy rejected what remained of domestic popular frontism and idealized the New Deal as an effort to establish a mixed economy that would preserve the essentials of capitalism while mitigating its abuses. Even the business community was recognized as a potentially constructive, if frequently wrongheaded, force in American life. The vital-center liberals looked to Niebuhr for a sociopolitical theory and to Keynes for an approach to economics, convinced that this combination provided the best possible foundation for human freedom. In 1948 a group of Keynesians published the major liberal economic manifesto of the Truman era, *Saving American Capitalism.* The title accurately represented the way in which vital-center liberalism was a return to the traditional American progressive impulse.

The legislative goals Truman announced for his administration, while not devised to meet the needs of an abstract theory, were well in tune with the vital-center approach: anti-inflation measures, a more progressive tax structure, repeal of the Taft-Hartley Act, a higher minimum wage, a farm program based on the concepts of abundant production and parity income, resource development and public power programs, expansion of social security, national medical insurance, federal aid to education, extensive housing legislation, and civil rights bills. The president's most controversial request was for authority to increase plant facilities in such basic industries as steel, preferably through federal financing of private enterprise but through outright government construction if necessary. Roundly condemned by right-wing opponents as "socialistic" and soon dropped by the administration, the proposal was actually intended to meet the demands of a prosperous, growing capitalist economy and emerged from the Fair Deal's search for the proper degree of government intervention to preserve the established American economic structure. "Between the reactionaries of the extreme left with their talk about revolution and class warfare, and the reactionaries of the extreme right with their hysterical cries of bankruptcy and despair, lies the way of progress," Truman declared in November 1949.

The Fair Deal was a conscious effort to continue the purpose of the New Deal but not necessarily its methods. Not forced to meet the emergencies of economic depression, given a solid point of departure by their predecessors, and led by a president more prone than FDR to demand programmatic coherence, the Fair Dealers made a systematic effort to discover techniques that would be at once more equitable and more practical in alleviating the problems of unequal wealth and opportunity. Thinking in terms of abundance rather than scarcity, they attempted to adapt the New Deal tradition to postwar prosperity. Seeking to go beyond the New Deal while preserving its objectives, the Truman administration advocated a more sweeping and better-ordered reform agenda. Yet in the quest for political means, Truman and the vital-center liberals could only fall back upon one of the oldest dreams of American reform—the Jacksonian-Populist vision of a union of producing classes, an invincible farmer-labor coalition. While superficially plausible, the Fair Deal's political strategy proved too weak to handle the burden thrust upon it.

The Fair Deal seemed to oscillate between militancy and moderation. New Dealers had frequently gloried in accusations of "liberalism" or "radicalism"; Fair Dealers tended to shrink from such labels. The New Dealers had often lusted for political combat; the Fair Dealers were generally more low keyed. Election campaigns demanded an aggressiveness that would arouse the Democratic presidential party, but the continued strength of the conservative coalition in Congress dictated accommodation in the postelection efforts to secure passage of legislative proposals. Such tactics reflected Truman's personal political experience and instincts, but they also developed naturally out of the climate of postwar America. The crisis of economic depression had produced one style of political rhetoric; the problems of prosperity and inflation brought forth another.

The Fair Deal mirrored Truman's policy preferences and approach to politics; it was no more the president's personal creation, however, than the New Deal had been Roosevelt's. Just as FDR's advisers had formulated much of the New Deal, a group of liberals developed much of the content and tactics of the Fair Deal. For the most part these were the men who had formed a liberal caucus within the administration in early 1947 shortly after the Republican triumph in the congressional elections of 1946, had worked to sway the president toward the left in his policy recommendations and campaign tactics, and had played a significant, if not an all-embracing, role in Truman's victory in 1948. Truman's special counsel, Clark M. Clifford, was perhaps the most prominent member of the group, but Clifford, although a shrewd political analyst, a persuasive advocate, and an extremely valuable administrative chief of staff, was neither the caucus's organizer nor a creative liberal thinker. Others gave the Fair Deal its substance as a program descending from the New Deal yet distinct from it.

The founder of the liberal caucus, Oscar R. Ewing, exemplified better than any other prominent member of the Truman administration the linkage between the New Deal and the Fair Deal. Even as a young man in turn-of-the-century Indiana he had possessed a consuming interest in Democratic politics and social welfare problems. At the age of sixteen he was secretary to the state Democratic committee, and for a time he planned to become a social worker. Instead, after graduating from the Harvard Law School, he settled in New York and pursued a highly successful practice as a partner of first the elder, then the younger, Charles Evans Hughes. By the 1940s he had also become one of the most prominent Democrats in the state and was frequently mentioned as a possible candidate for high office. During Robert E. Hannegan's tenure as chairman of the Democratic National Committee (1944–1947), Ewing was vice-chairman and, after Hannegan's health collapsed, acting chairman. Appointed administrator of the Federal Security Agency[1] in 1947, he began a drive to revitalize the agency and secure cabinet status for

---

[1] Established during the New Deal, the Federal Security Agency became one of the major components of the present-day Department of Health, Education, and Welfare.

it. It was he who took the initiative in mobilizing the liberals within the Truman administration for the crucial struggles of 1947 and 1948.

Ewing's advocacy of comprehensive social welfare legislation—a popular magazine described him as "Mr. Welfare State himself"—was the end result of a tradition that had begun with the social workers of the Progressive era, had found partial realization during the New Deal, and was now struggling for complete fulfillment. Ewing also represented a type of Democrat who had developed during the New Deal—the staunch, partisan regular who was nevertheless committed to social welfare liberalism and identified his party with it. The strongest fighter within the administration for expanded welfare programs, he did not shrink from debate with the opposition. "It is the fate of the American liberal to be a scrapper," he remarked. Accepting the Sidney Hillman Award from the Amalgamated Clothing Workers Union in March 1950, he defined the key to America's future as "the protection and extension of equal opportunity for all our people—opportunity to live, to advance, to think, to achieve." Especially in 1949 and 1950 he engaged in lusty verbal combat with his conservative opponents—"the League of Frightened Men," he called them. Ewing demonstrated the way in which the New Deal, and indeed the whole progressive social welfare tradition, provided a solid basis for the Fair Deal, but his ideas, although they went beyond New Deal welfare programs, did not give the administration its claim to a separate identity. His style, as it turned out, was not especially productive; someone doubtless had to speak out against the bitter-end opponents of social welfare reforms, but Ewing only exposed himself to defeat by doing so. His militant advocacy of national health insurance not only failed to put the proposal over; it led to a backlash and caused Congress to reject an administration reorganization plan that would have created a cabinet-level Department of Welfare with Ewing as its first secretary. His personal defeat on this issue exemplified many of the difficulties the Fair Deal encountered when it adopted the militant tones of years past.

While Ewing represented continuity, Leon H. Keyserling and Charles F. Brannan gave the Fair Deal much of its distinctive approach. Both men served their political apprenticeships during the New Deal, but both formulated important criticisms of it and sought new techniques to achieve the objectives of liberal reform.

Keyserling, educated at Columbia University—where he was influenced by Rexford G. Tugwell—and the Harvard Law School, had gone to Washington in the early days of the Roosevelt administration to work for Jerome Frank in the Agricultural Adjustment Administration. He attracted the attention of Senator Robert F. Wagner, who made him an administrative assistant; during the next several years he was a central figure in the drafting of some of the most important legislation of the 1930s, including the National Labor Relations Act. Subsequently he was general counsel of the U.S. Housing Authority, later the National Housing Agency. In 1944 he took second prize in a widely publicized contest on the achievement of postwar prosperity with an essay urging an expansion of the economy to provide jobs for all. In 1945 he was active in the struggle for full-employment legislation. With Senator Wagner's backing he was a natural choice for the new Council of Economic Advisers, established by the Employment Act of 1946.

During 1947 and 1948 Keyserling was a valuable member of the administration liberal caucus. At the same time he was gaining a public reputation as the most imaginative and articulate economist in the government. When the bland and moderate Edwin Nourse resigned as chairman of the Council of Economic Advisers in October 1949, Keyserling was automatically the liberals' candidate for the post, and the ADA spearheaded an intensive lobbying campaign in his behalf. After a long delay, in the spring of 1950 the president gave Keyserling the appointment.

Although he had won formal appointment as the chief economic spokesman of the administration and had long been valued by the most able members of the president's staff, Keyserling appeared rather insecure. Academic economists were cool toward him because he lacked the appropriate pedigree of university degrees, though in mobilizing support for his promotion, the ADA found most liberal economists willing to support him, not as the best man for the job, but simply as the best possible alternative. Within the administration he had to live down his reputation as an Ivy League liberal ideologue; he seized opportunities to remind listeners that he had been born in South Carolina and could produce a letter of commendation from Robert A. Taft. Perhaps such difficulties were responsible for his enormous vanity and stuffy manner. Yet his brilliant mind transformed Truman's style and aspirations into an economic program.

FIGURE 5. Secretary of the Treasury John W. Snyder, the administration's leading conservative, is alarmed by Leon Keyserling in the driver's seat. (*Courtesy Dan Dowling, New York Herald Tribune*)

In line with the mood of the Fair Deal, Keyserling assiduously avoided labels more specific than "forward-looking" or "the middle way" for his ideas. He noted on the first page of his essay in *Saving American Capitalism* that he rejected "classification within any 'school of thought' or endorsement of any 'general theme' or 'purpose' which this collection may be deemed by some to represent." Adamantly refusing to be typed as a Keynesian, he frequently criticized New Deal economics: "Neither those 'liberals' who betray nostalgia for the New Deal of the thirties which accomplished much but not nearly enough, nor those 'conservatives' who would reincarnate the brutal and reckless economic philosophy of the twenties should be allowed to say the last word."

On the surface his ideas and advice seemed an odd mixture of liberalism and conservatism. Writing to Clark Clifford in December 1948 with suggestions for the State of the Union message, he sounded like a conservative: "I am particularly concerned about the discussion of the economic program, which seems to imply that the Government is going to do the whole job. . . . The first responsibility for employment and production rests with business." Yet a few days later he was advocating more ambitious public-housing schedules than those proposed by the National Housing Authority. He sounded like a conservative when he emphatically disclaimed responsibility for the controversial proposal to expand basic industrial plants. He sounded like a New Dealer when he urged delegates to the convention of the Meat Cutters Union to push for higher wages and when he declared that "accruals of fat earnings" justified such demands. Shortly thereafter, however, he was reassuring business that "nobody in Washington has ever taken the position that the American economy could expand without profits."

Keyserling's critique of New Deal economics had several themes. First of all, the New Deal had failed to grasp the virtual impossibility of the task it had undertaken: the lifting of the nation out of the depression. Those who argued that the New Deal would have been successful with a more massive spending effort were probably wrong. Government alone simply could not solve great economic crises, and if the New Deal could not be blamed for its failure, the New Dealers could be blamed for not learning the lessons of that failure.

The New Dealers also had become too dogmatic in their adoption of the antitrust persuasion. "Today some industries which are organized on a large, integrated basis are charging prices under the limit of what the traffic will bear," Keyserling wrote in 1948. By contrast, home building, the most fragmented industry in the country, "has been notoriously inefficient, highly resistant to technological change, and periodically prices its product out of the market." The antitrust laws should be used to prosecute monopolistic wrongdoing, but "we cannot re-create the pre–Civil War pattern." The liberals needed instead to ask if there were not instances in which monopolistic concentration might be "used to stabilize rather than to exploit the economy." Conversely, they needed to undertake a more searching analysis of the problems that competition presented to economic stability. Some degree of economic coordination, as voluntary as possible, would always be desirable and, during times of economic difficulty, essential.

The adoption of Keynesianism by the New Dealers had not provided American liberalism with an economic panacea, Keyserling argued. Keynesianism might be useful during a depression, but it raised more problems than it solved by its remedies for inflation. Higher taxes and interest rates bore most heavily upon the lower and lower-middle classes. Cutbacks in government spending meant the sacrifice of "national objectives which we should not forgo merely because we are prosperous."

Finally, he charged, the New Dealers had lost faith in the potential of capitalism. Considering the system pathologically unstable, even if for some reason worth saving, they awaited the inevitable onset of a major depression armed with vast government programs, which probably would be no more successful than the New Deal itself. They had failed to address themselves to the potential of the American economy; they had not formulated theories for the maintenance of prosperity. "The people of America need to be electrified by our limitless possibilities, not frightened into action by prophets of disaster."

American capitalism, as Keyserling envisioned it, had virtually unlimited opportunities for growth; an ever-expanding economy could produce undreamed-of abundance and material gain for all classes. The liberals should concentrate not on reslicing the economic pie but rather on enlarging it. Business could expect higher profits, labor better wages, farmers larger incomes, and, above all, those at the bottom of the economic scale could experience a truly decent life. The federal government should publicize these possibilities; it should provide education and guidance to the private forces whose responsible cooperation would be imperative. Keyserling recommended the initiation of a "National Prosperity Budget" in which the government would lay down targets for employment and production, indicate priority needs, and sketch out price and wage recommendations. It would be purely advisory, depending upon the cooperation of the private sectors for implementation.

The government would not be passive. It would continue to police the economy against monopolistic abuses, dictate minimum wages, use Keynesian fiscal and monetary techniques, and even impose selective controls if conditions demanded. It would provide important programs and services—such as low-cost housing, social insurance, education, and resource development—that fell outside the realm of private enterprise. Washington, however, could not keep the economy growing by itself. Expansion demanded voluntary co-operation: "The widening of this area of voluntary cooperation, through common study of common problems, is the only way that our highly industrialized and integrated economy can steer between the danger of periodic collapse and the danger of excessive governmental centralization of power."

To those who feared that expansion meant boom-and-bust inflation, Keyserling replied that the growth years 1927–1929 had constituted an era of remarkable price stability. Economic policy should concentrate less on prices as such and more on the relationship between wages, prices, and profits; it should work for the optimum balance between consumer purchasing power and corporate income in order to maintain full employment and expansion. The New Dealers, he believed, had turned too frequently toward controls to fight inflation after World War II. Selective controls might be necessary at times, but the way to deal with inflation was to enlarge productive capacity to meet demand. Keyserling did not shrink from stimulative government spending in times of prosperity, and although he would not admit it, he was willing to trade a mild inflation for growth. Such an alternative was greatly preferable to the achievement of price stability via a "downward 'correction' " or recession. Higher unemployment and lower production might keep prices stable but hardly contributed to the overall health of the economy. "The idea that we can protect production and employment by reducing them 'a little bit,' " he warned, "is about as safe as the ancient remedy of blood-letting."

During the first half of 1949 Keyserling transformed his vision of abundance to solid figures. Assuming an annual growth rate of 3 percent and constant dollar values, the gross national product could rise from $262 billion in 1948 to $350 billion in 1958, national income from $226 billion to $300 billion. In 1948 almost two-thirds of all American families had lived on incomes of less than $4,000 a year; by 1958, $4,000 could be the minimum for all families. It would require only about half of the GNP increase to attain this goal, leaving a substantial sum for government programs and the enhancement of private incomes at other levels. Poverty thus could be eliminated without a redistribution of wealth. Progressive reform did not necessarily mean social conflict; rather it required intelligent cooperation.

Truman adopted Keyserling's figures and rhetoric. Speaking to a Kansas City audience in the fall of 1949, he acclaimed the nation's history of economic growth and increasingly higher standards of living and declared his determination to continue the process. He talked of the $300 billion national income and the $4,000 family minimum. "That is not a pipe dream," he asserted. "It can be done."

Keyserling had not discovered the idea of economic growth, although his ego seemed at times to tempt him to imply that he had. The growth levels of World War II had awakened many economic thinkers—Alvin Hansen and Henry Wallace, for example. Nor was Keyserling fair in his assertions that the New Deal Keynesians really accepted the business cycle and that their remedies could not be put into effect until a depression had already hit the economy. The Keynesians sought at the least to smooth out the business cycle so that depressions would be eliminated altogether, at best to maintain a constant growth without even periodic recessions.

If some of Keyserling's polemics rested on artificial assertions, his broad conception of economic expansion was nevertheless inspiring and enormously constructive. The major difficulty in the program he advocated was his reliance on voluntarism, his faith in education, his belief that group conflict could be mitigated by alluring vistas that promised gains for all. In accord with the general approach of the Fair Deal, Keyserling sought to base his economics on a politics of consensus, which neither he nor other Fair Dealers were ever able to achieve. His dream of an ever-prosperous society based on voluntary cooperation was almost as utopian as the scheme of a nineteenth-century anarchist. Fortunately there were surer, if less perfect, ways of promoting economic growth. Keyserling defined important goals for the administration and captured the ear of a president who respected his intellectual ability and liked him as an individual.

Charles F. Brannan, who was as much a product of the New Deal as Keyserling, had begun his career in Colorado politics as a disciple of the old progressive, Edward Costigan, and an associate of Oscar L. Chapman, a dedicated liberal whom Truman appointed secretary of the interior in 1949. During the Roosevelt era Brannan had worked as an attorney for the Resettlement Administration and had been a regional director of the Farm Security Administration. Long close to the neo-Populist National Farmers Union, he was a personal friend of its president, James G. Patton. Moving to Washington as assistant secretary of agriculture in 1944, Brannan quickly established himself as a loyal and capable lieutenant. In 1948 he took command of the department with the blessings of the outgoing secretary, the moderate Clinton Anderson, and the enthusiastic endorsement of the Farmers Union, which had bitterly fought Anderson. No man, not even the elder or the younger Henry Wallace, had entered the office of secretary of agriculture with clearer credentials as an aggressive liberal. Like Keyserling, Brannan used the concept of abundance as an intellectual foundation. The politicoeconomic strategy that he formulated constituted the Fair Deal's clearest break with the New Deal.

In the fall of 1948 Brannan's astute advice on political strategy and his vigorous campaigning won the attention of Truman and brought him into the White House inner circle. Almost alone Brannan grasped that Midwestern farmers were apprehensive about the future of price supports and that the Republican Eightieth Congress, by failing to enlarge government storage facilities, had practically guaranteed that grain prices would decline during the presidential campaign. Truman and his liberal advisers quickly adopted Brannan's counsel of attacking the GOP as the party of opposition to price supports, and the secretary himself carried the message into farm areas with a tirelessness that shamed other cabinet members. Truman's unexpected success in the rural Midwest made Brannan one of the major figures of the administration. It also suggested new political strategies to liberals both inside and outside the government.

Many progressives believed that the farm results represented a new trend in liberal politics. To the influential columnist Samuel Grafton, 1948 had been "a year of deep and quiet decision" for farmers; the election indicated that they had overcome their conservative biases in favor of their practical need for government support and would turn increasingly to the Democratic party. If such were the case, then the task of the liberals was to encourage and consolidate this trend. The ultimate result would be a new Democratic party with a more solidly liberal base than ever before, a liberalism that would fuse the outlook and voting power of labor with an apparently reborn Midwestern agrarian insurgency. The liberal cause would be greatly strengthened and the conservative forces proportionately weakened. Within the Republican party the number of Midwestern reactionaries would decline; within the Democratic party the Southern conservatives would have less leverage.

The first imperative was to establish lines of communication between the farmers and the liberal-labor forces. The ADA began the process by calling a conference of about thirty farm and labor leaders, which met in Chicago at the end of February 1949. The farm leaders included James Patton from the Farmers Union, Murray Lincoln and some other progressive dissenters from the Farm Bureau, Jerry Voorhis and others from the cooperative movement, and several local Grange officials. Among the labor delegates were representatives of the Railway Trainmen, the Textile Workers, the International Ladies Garment Workers Union, and the United Auto Workers. The meetings amounted simply to an exchange of views; the conference made no effort to hammer out a legislative program or draft a call to action. Yet James Loeb, the ADA's executive secretary, found the sessions "an exciting experience." The discussions were friendly despite some disagreements, and many of the participants favored more conferences at the state and local levels. "The farm and labor groups are moving, slowly but definitely, in the direction of mutual understanding," declared Loeb. "The encouragement of this process can have a lasting effect on the future history of America."

The administration took the next step in April with the introduction in Congress of a new farm program, which had been drawn up under Brannan's direction. The Brannan Plan was difficult and complex in detail, but essentially it was an effort to maintain farm income at the record high level of the war and immediate postwar periods while letting market prices fall to a natural supply-demand level. Brannan thus proposed to continue the New Deal policy of subsidizing the farmers, but he broke dramatically with the New Deal technique of restricting production and marketing in order to achieve artificially high prices.

Many agrarian progressives, including Henry A. Wallace himself, had long been troubled by the price-support mechanisms and had sought methods of unleashing the productive capacity of the farms. Brannan seemed to show the way. He proposed the maintenance of farm income through direct payments to farmers rather than through crop restriction. In order to encourage and protect the family farm, moreover, he recommended supporting a maximum of about $26,100 worth of production per farm. To the consumer he promised milk at fifteen cents a quart, to the dairy farmer a sustained high income. To the Democratic party he offered an apparently ingenious device that would unite the interests of farmers and workers.

Liberals generally were enthusiastic over both the principles and the politics of the Brannan proposals. "The new plan lets growers grow and eaters eat, and that is good," commented Samuel Grafton. "If Brannan is right, the political miracle of 1948 will become a habit as farmers, labor and consumers find common political goals," wrote agricultural columnist Angus MacDonald. James Patton called the Brannan Plan "a milestone in the history of American agriculture," and the *Nation* asserted that the average consumer should devote all his spare time to support of the program.

The plan immediately ran into the opposition of the conservatives who dominated Congress. Republicans feared that the political coalition Brannan was trying to build would entrench the Democrats in power. Large producers, most effectively represented by the powerful Farm Bureau Federation, regarded the plan as discriminatory, and many Democrats with ties to the Farm Bureau refused to support it, among them Senate majority leader Scott Lucas and Clinton Anderson, now the freshman senator from New Mexico. By June it was obvious to most political analysts that the Brannan Plan had no chance of passage in 1949. The administration and most liberals nevertheless remained optimistic. The issue seemed good, the alignment of interests logical and compelling: enough political education and campaigning could revive the scheme and revolutionize American politics.

Both the CIO and the Farmers Union undertook campaigns to spread the message of farmer-labor unity. An article in the *National Union Farmer* typified the effort:

> *Workers today are in a tough spot, just like farmers. Production has been steadily declining, and that means fewer jobs and lower wages. And that means smaller markets for farm products. This worries everybody but Big Business, but these advocates of scarcity still rule the roost. Monopoly wants less production, less employment, lower wages, fewer family farmers, less collective bargaining, lower farm prices and less competition except for jobs. . . . There is little basic difference between the labor fight against the Taft-Hartley law and our fight against attempts to tax cooperatives out of existence. . . . Labor's strong objections to 40¢ an hour as a minimum is no different than our equally strong objections to 60% of parity.*

Brannan campaigned extensively for his program. "Farm income equals jobs for millions of American workers," he told a labor gathering in a typical effort. "Together, let workers and farmers unite in achieving a full employment, full production economy." The administration sponsored regional farmer-labor conferences around the country. The one attracting the most attention was held in June at Des Moines, Iowa, and featured prominent labor leaders, important Democratic congressmen, and Vice-President Alben Barkley. Other such grass-roots meetings were organized as far east as upstate New York, and the Democratic National Committee prepared a pamphlet on the Brannan Plan for mass distribution. On Labor Day the president devoted two major appearances, one in Pittsburgh and the other in Des Moines, to the Brannan Plan and to farmer-labor unity. "Those who are trying to set these two great groups against each other just have axes of their own to grind," he warned his Pittsburgh audience. "Price supports must . . . give consumers the benefit of our abundant farm production," he told his Des Moines listeners.

Many liberals and Democratic politicians remained convinced that they had an overwhelming political strategy. "In 1950 and '52, the Brannan Plan will be the great issue in the doubtful states," wrote journalist A. G. Mezerik. "After that, Congress will enact a new farm bill—one which is based on low prices for consumers and a high standard of living for family farmers." In early 1950 the Brannan Plan seemed to be gaining popular support. Liberals inside and outside the administration continued to hope for vindication at the polls in November. They could not, of course, foresee the Korean War and the ways in which it would change the shape of American politics.

Even without the Korean War, however, even without the disruptive impact of McCarthyism, it is doubtful that the Brannan Plan would have worked the miracles expected of it. The liberals inside and outside the administration who had created or worked for it assumed that urban and rural groups could be united simply on grounds of mutual self-interest. They failed to understand that these groups were not deeply concerned with *mutual* self-interest; both sides had practiced with some success methods that had taken care of their own self-interest. The rhetoric about urban-rural interdependence was extremely superficial, talked but not deeply felt. Most farm and labor leaders, even those progressive in their outlook, hardly had a basis for communication. The ADA conference of February 1949 included some of the best-informed figures from the unions and the farms. Yet one of the labor leaders had to ask for an explanation "in simple language" of the concept of parity. One of the farm leaders then admitted that he had no idea what the dues check-off was or how it worked. The farm leaders also frankly commented that their constituents were strongly against such things as a minimum wage applied to farm workers, the extension of social security to cover farm labor and farmers in general, and especially the reestablishment of any sort of price controls. The situation at Des Moines seems to have been much the same. Even some of the Farmers Union officials at the conference were annoyed by the presence of the labor people. "Some farmers wondered if they weren't being sucked in to help the forces of labor fight the Taft-Hartley Act," reported journalist Lauren Soth. Such ideas, of course, were not entirely fanciful. Most of the observers at Des Moines sensed the artificiality of the whole affair, but they continued to hope that further contacts would consummate the union of city and country.

The farm leaders harbored a provincial suspicion of labor, while the reverse was true in the cities. "While labor has given general support to the Brannan plan, I have had the suggestion made, almost ironically, that labor might be given a guaranteed income if such were to be granted to farmers," remarked Jim Loeb in November 1949. Many liberals felt that, as proposed by the administration, the Brannan Plan was too generous. The Chicago *Sun-Times* and the *Nation* agreed that the principles and machinery of the Brannan system were excellent, but both dissented from Brannan's proposal to support farm income at record heights. "The country as a whole should not undertake to support farm income at a higher level than is fair and just," warned the *Sun-Times,* adding that it would always be easier to raise supports than to lower them. Chester Bowles went a step further when he proposed that the whole matter of agricultural subsidies should be tied to urban employment with no supports at all during periods of full employment. Such ideas were hardly the cement of a new urban-rural coalition.

Many urban liberals found the plan itself difficult to grasp and could not work up much enthusiasm about it. "Most of us do not understand it completely," admitted Jim Loeb a month and a half after its introduction. A group of ADA leaders had a cordial meeting with Brannan in June 1949 and pledged their support. Actually, however, the ADA did little to promote the program. In the spring of 1950 a Philadelphia liberal wrote to the organization asking for information on the issue, but Violet Gunther, the legislative director, replied that the ADA had published nothing other than an endorsement in the platform, nor could she think of any group other than the Farmers Union that might have something available. The *Nation* and the *New Republic* gave only occasional mention to the plan. Most liberals could heartily endorse and even get excited about Brannan's political objectives, but understanding and identifying with the scheme itself was quite a different matter.

For a time in early 1950 declining farm prices seemed to generate a surge of support for the Brannan Plan. At the beginning of June, Albert Loveland, the undersecretary of agriculture, won the Iowa Democratic senatorial primary on a pro-Brannan platform and thereby encouraged the administration to believe that the Midwest was moving in its direction. Just a few weeks later, however, the Korean War began, creating situations and pressures that doomed most of the Fair Deal.

Even if the Brannan Plan had become law, it is far from certain that it would have created the dream farmer-labor-liberal coalition. Most leading agricultural economists, including those of a progressive outlook, were convinced that the proposal would be unworkable and prohibitively expensive. Some liberal economists condemned its failure to give the rural poor at least as much aid as the middle-class family farm. Even assuming that the economists were wrong, there is no guarantee that a smoothly functioning Brannan program could have performed the neat trick of uniting the very different cultures of urban liberalism and rural insurgency; such a feat probably would have required more than mutual economic benefits. The down-to-earth, church-social ethos of the Farmers Union would not automatically homogenize with the sophisticated, intellectual progressivism of the city liberals or the wage-and-hour, union-shop, reformism of labor.

During 1949 and early 1950 the Truman administration managed a record of substantial legislative accomplishment, but it consisted almost entirely of additions to such New Deal programs as the minimum wage, social security, and public power. The Housing Act of 1949, with its provisions for large-scale public housing, appeared to be a breakthrough, but weak administration, local opposition, and inadequate financing subsequently vitiated hopes that it would help the poor. Acting on his executive authority, Truman took an important step by forcing the army to agree to a policy of desegregation. The heart of the Fair Deal, however—repeal of the Taft-Hartley Act, civil rights legislation, aid to education, national medical insurance, and the Brannan Plan—failed in Congress. Given the power of the well-entrenched conservative coalition and a widespread mood of public apathy about big new reforms, Truman could only enlarge upon the record of his predecessor.

Democratic strategists hoped for a mandate in the congressional elections of 1950. In the spring Truman made a successful whistle-stop tour of the West and Midwest, rousing party enthusiasm and apparently demonstrating a solid personal popularity. Loveland's victory provided further encouragement, and in California the aggressive Fair Dealer Helen Gahagan Douglas won the Democratic nomination for the Senate by a thumping margin. Two incumbent Fair Deal supporters—Frank Graham of North Carolina and Claude Pepper of Florida—lost their senatorial primaries, but, as Southerners who had run afoul of the race issue, they did not seem to be indicators of national trends. Nevertheless, the hope of cutting into the strength of the conservative opposition ran counter to the historical pattern of midterm elections. The beginning of the Korean War at the end of June destroyed any chances of success.

The most immediate impact of Korea was to refuel an anti-Communist extremism that might otherwise have sputtered out. Senator Joseph R. McCarthy had begun his rise to prominence in February 1950, but he had failed to prove any of his multiple allegations and seemed definitively discredited by the investigations of a special Senate committee headed by Millard Tydings. McCarthy, it is true, was a talented demagogue who should have been taken more seriously by the liberals and the Truman administration in early 1950, but it seems probable that his appeal would have waned more quickly if the cold war with communism had not suddenly become hot. As it was, many of his Senate colleagues rushed to emulate him. In September 1950 Congress passed the McCarran Internal Security Act; only a handful of congressional liberals dared dissent from the overwhelming vote in favor. Truman's subsequent veto was intelligent and courageous, but was issued more for the history books than with any real hope of success. In the subsequent campaign, liberal Democrats, whether they had voted for the McCarran Act or not, found themselves facing charges of softness toward communism.

The war hurt the administration in other ways. It touched off a brief but serious inflation, which caused widespread consumer irritation. By stimulating demand for agricultural products it brought most farm prices up to parity levels and thereby undercut whatever attractiveness the Brannan Plan had developed in rural areas. Finally it removed the Democratic party's most effective spokesman —the president—from active participation in the campaign. Forced to play the role of war leader, Truman allowed himself only one major partisan speech, delivered in St. Louis on the eve of the balloting.

The Fair Deal might have been a winning issue in a nation oriented toward domestic concerns and recovering from an economic recession; it had much less appeal in a country obsessed with Communist aggression and experiencing an inflationary war boom. The reaction against the administration was especially strong in the

Midwest. Indiana's Democratic aspirant for the Senate asked Oscar Ewing to stay out of the state. In Iowa, Loveland desperately attempted to reverse his identification with the Brannan Plan. In Missouri the managers of senatorial candidate Thomas C. Hennings, Jr. privately asked White House aides to make Truman's St. Louis speech a foreign policy address that would skip lightly over Fair Deal issues. A few days before the election the columnist Stewart Alsop returned from a Midwestern trip convinced that the region had never been more conservative. Nevertheless, Truman's political advisers, and probably Truman himself, felt that the Fair Deal still had appeal. Given the basic strength of the economy and the victories in Korea that followed the Inchon landing, the White House believed that the Democrats could easily rebut generalized charges of fumbling or softness toward communism. In mid-October the Democratic National Committee and many local leaders were so confident of success that their main concern was simply to get out the vote.

The November results, however, showed a Democratic loss of twenty-eight seats in the House of Representatives and five seats in the Senate. Truman seized every opportunity to remind all who would listen that the numbers were small by traditional mid-term standards. Liberal political analysts, including Kenneth Hechler, a White House staffer, and Gus Tyler of the International Ladies Garment Workers Union, subjected the returns to close scrutiny and all but pronounced a Democratic victory. All the same, most of the Democrats who went under had been staunch Fair Dealers. Republican candidates, including John Marshall Butler in Maryland, Richard M. Nixon in California, Everett McKinley Dirksen in Illinois, and Robert A. Taft in Ohio, scored some of the most spectacular GOP victories by blending right-wing conservatism with McCarthyism. The Midwestern losses were especially disappointing. Hechler argued that the corn-belt vote primarily reflected urban defections and that the Democrats had done comparatively well among farmers. Perhaps so, but for all practical purposes the results put an end to the Brannan strategy of constructing a farmer-labor coalition. Truman was probably more accurate than Hechler when, with characteristic overstatement, he privately expressed his disappointment: "The main trouble with the farmers is that they hate labor so badly that they will not vote for their own interests."

Thereafter, with the Chinese intervention transforming the Korean War into a more serious conflict and with the dismissal of General Douglas MacArthur in April 1951, Truman faced a tough attack from a Republican opposition determined to capitalize upon the frustrations of Korea. Finding it necessary to place party unity above all else, he quietly shelved most of his domestic legislative program and sought to bring the conservative wing of his party behind his military and defense policies. He secretly asked Richard B. Russell of Georgia, the kingpin of the Southern conservatives, to assume the Democratic leadership in the Senate. Russell, content with the substance of power, declined and gave his nod to Ernest W. Mc-Farland of Arizona, an amiable tool of the Southern bloc; Truman made no effort to prevent McFarland's selection as Senate majority leader. The president's State of the Union message was devoted almost entirely to foreign policy and defense mobilization and mentioned social welfare programs only as an afterthought. Subsequently Truman told a press conference that while he supported the Fair Deal as much as ever, "first things come first, and our defense programs must have top priority."

Truman's success in achieving a minimum degree of party unity became apparent in the weeks of investigation and accusation that followed General MacArthur's return to America. Russell, playing the role of parliamentarian-statesman to the hilt and cashing in on his great prestige with senators of both parties, chaired the Senate committee that looked into the MacArthur incident, and he saw to it that the administration was able to deliver a thorough rebuttal to the general. The Northern liberal, Brien McMahon of Connecticut, relentlessly grilled hostile witnesses. The Western representative of oil and gas interests, Robert S. Kerr of Oklahoma, lashed out at MacArthur himself with a vehemence and effectiveness that no other Democrat could match. The tandem efforts of Russell, Mc-Mahon, and Kerr demonstrated the new party solidarity, but in terms of the Fair Deal the price was high.

In July 1951 the Federal Power Commission renounced the authority to regulate "independent" (non-pipeline-owning) natural gas producers. The ruling amounted to an administrative enactment of a bill, sponsored by Kerr, which Truman had vetoed a year earlier; Truman's close friend and most recent appointee to the

Federal Power Commission, Mon Wallgren, cast the deciding vote. Although he talked like a militant liberal in a private conversation with ADA leaders, the president stalled throughout 1951 on repeated demands for the establishment of a Korean War Fair Employment Practices Committee. In December the administration established an ineffective Committee on Government Contract Compliance. Other domestic programs were soft-pedaled to near-invisibility.

Yet even the Korean War was not entirely inimical to reform. Its exigencies forced the army to transform its policy of integration into practice. Korea also provided a test for one of the basic underpinnings of the Fair Deal—Leon Keyserling's philosophy of economic expansion. Truman did not in the end fully embrace Keyserling's policies, but in the main he followed the guidance of his chief economic adviser. The Korean War years demonstrated the extent to which Keyserling's economics diverged from conventional New Deal–World War II Keynesianism and revealed both the strengths and weaknesses of his approach.

From the outbreak of the fighting, most liberals favored either immediate strong economic controls akin to those that had held down inflation in World War II or at least the establishment of stand-by machinery that could impose them rapidly. Truman disliked such measures on the basis of both principle and politics. He and his diplomatic advisers also wanted to signal the Soviet Union that the United States regarded the North Korean attack as a limited challenge meriting a limited response. Keyserling's expansionary economics provided an attractive alternative to the liberal clamor for controls. Convinced that extensive controls would put the economy in a straitjacket and retard the expansion necessary to meet both consumer and defense needs and assuming a North Korean defeat in a few months, the administration decided to accept a short-term, war-scare inflation (probably unavoidable in any case) and concentrate on economic growth, which would be underwritten in large measure by tax incentives for business. An expanding economy would be the best long-term answer to inflation: growth policies could fit a small war into the economy, avoid the social and political strains accompanying wartime controls, and reduce inflationary pressures to a level at which fiscal and monetary policies could contain them. Liberals outside the administration watched with alarm as prices went up, but Truman and Keyserling continued to gamble on a quick end to the war and the development of an economy capable of producing both guns and butter.

Their plan might have worked fairly well had the United States not overreached itself militarily in Korea. The Chinese intervention of November 1950 wrecked hopes of a quick victory, set off another round of scare buying, and intensified war demands upon the economy. The administration quickly threw up a price-wage control structure, but by the end of February 1951, eight months after the beginning of the Korean conflict, the consumer price index had risen 8 percent (an annual rate of 12 percent). Keyserling agreed that the new situation necessitated controls, but he accepted them with reluctance and sought to keep them as simple as possible, even at the risk of benefiting profiteers. "We'll never be able to out-control the Russians," he told a Senate committee, "but we can out-produce them." Speaking to an ADA economic conference, he asserted that many liberals, in their opposition to tax breaks for large business and in their demands for stronger controls, were confusing the Korean War with World War II and "engaging merely in hackneyed slogans out of the past."

Most liberals disagreed with Keyserling's emphases. As production was his first imperative, an end to the wage-price spiral was theirs. "Unless we are willing seriously to endanger the basis of existence of the American middle class, we must stop prices from rising," wrote Hans Landsberg in the *Reporter*. The liberals assumed that economic expansion was possible within a framework of rigid, tightly administered controls. Chester Bowles observed that the controlled economy of World War II had turned out a twofold increase in industrial production. John Kenneth Galbraith rejected the idea that Keyserling's expansionary policies could outrun the inflationary pressures they themselves created. The bulk of liberals regarded the administration approach as dangerous, the product of political expediency rather than sound economic analysis.

Neither Keyserling nor the more conventional liberals won a complete victory. Truman, who understood all too well the political dangers of a prolonged inflation, made substantial concessions to the controllers, led by Michael V. DiSalle, head of the Office of Price Stabilization. In the interest of fairness Truman approved a more complex system of price controls than Keyserling thought desirable, giving DiSalle considerable leeway to roll back some prices while approving advances in other areas. By March 1951 inflation was under control; during the final ten months of the year the cost-of-living index increased by less than 2.5 percent. The waves of scare buying that followed the North Korean attack and the Chinese intervention had subsided. Higher taxes and restraints on credit were beginning to affect consumer buying. The Federal Reserve System, despite opposition from the administration, initiated a stringent monetary policy. Tax breaks for businesses expanding plant facilities presaged increased productive capacity. All these factors, along with the government stabilization program, discouraged an inflationary psychology.

At the time, however, it appeared to most economic observers that the lull was only temporary. Many of the administration's liberal critics refused even to admit the existence of a lull and called for tougher controls as if prices were still skyrocketing. More moderate analysts feared that the impact of large government defense orders would set off another inflationary spiral in the fall. Influenced by such expectations, Truman ostentatiously mounted an anti-inflation crusade, demanding that Congress not only extend his control authority, due to expire on June 30, but actually strengthen it. In fact the Defense Production Act of 1951 weakened the president's powers considerably. Truman signed it reluctantly, comparing it to "a bulldozer, crashing aimlessly through existing pricing formulas, leaving havoc in its wake." A subsequent tax bill failed to meet administration revenue requests and increased the danger of serious inflation.

Yet price stability persisted through 1952, in large measure because defense production, hampered by multiple shortages and bottlenecks, lagged far behind its timetable. In late 1951 these problems and the fear of renewed inflation led Truman to decide in favor of a "stretch-out" of defense production schedules; in doing so he overrode Keyserling's urgings for an all-out effort to break the bottlenecks and concentrate relentlessly upon expansion. Given the serious problems in defense industry, the stretch-out decision may have seemed necessary to Truman, but it also carried the dividend of economic stability.

The president had steered a course between the orthodox liberal obsession with inflation and Keyserling's easy disregard of its perils; perhaps as a result the economy failed to expand at the rate Keyserling had hoped. On balance, however, Truman's approach to the political economy of the Korean War was closer to Keyserling's, and the conflict produced a dramatic economic growth. Before the war the peak gross national product had been $285 billion in 1948; by the end of 1952 the GNP (measured in constant dollar values) had reached a rate of $350 billion. The production index of durable manufactured goods had averaged 237 in 1950; by the last quarter of 1952 it had reached 313. The expansion, even if less than Keyserling had wanted, was breathtaking. Moreover, aside from the probably unavoidable inflation that accompanied the early months of the war, this remarkable growth had occurred in a climate of economic stability. Using a somewhat more orthodox approach than Keyserling preferred, the administration had achieved one of the central goals of the Fair Deal.

In its effort to carry on with the reforming impulse of the New Deal the Truman administration faced nearly insuperable obstacles. A loosely knit but nonetheless effective conservative coalition had controlled Congress since 1939, successfully defying Franklin Roosevelt long before it had to deal with Truman. Postwar prosperity muted economic liberalism and encouraged a mood of apathy toward new reform breakthroughs, although Truman's victory in 1948 indicated that most of the elements of the old Roosevelt coalition were determined to preserve the gains of the New Deal. The Cold War probably made it more difficult to focus public attention upon reform and dealt severe blows to civil liberties. It did, however, give impetus to the movement for Negro equality.

The Fair Deal attempted to adapt liberalism to the new conditions. Under the intellectual leadership of Leon Keyserling it formulated policies that sought to transcend the conflicts of the New Deal era by encouraging an economic growth that could provide abundance for all Americans. With Charles Brannan pointing the way, the Truman administration tried to translate abundance into a political coalition that could provide the votes for its social welfare policies. The political strategy, ambitious but unrealistic, collapsed under the weight of the Korean War. Keyserling's economics, on the other hand, received a lift from Korea; in a period of adversity the Fair Deal was able to achieve at least one of its objectives.

Richard O. Davies

HOUSING REFORM: A FAIR DEAL CASE STUDY

The Housing Act of 1949 appeared to be the one great breakthrough of the Fair Deal. However, it proved to be a disappointment, underfunded by Congress, weakly managed by a housing administrator friendly to the real estate lobby, stymied in many cities by local opposition. Richard Davies argues that the ultimate failure of housing reform stemmed partly from Truman's own moderation but more fundamentally from the failure of liberals to understand that slum housing was a symptom rather than a cause of poverty.

Since leaving the White House, Harry S. Truman has frequently remarked that his place in history cannot be accurately assessed until fifty years have elapsed. In regard to foreign policy this is true, since several of the policies he inaugurated have not reached their final development and because most documents related to this critical area are not yet available to researchers. But in the field of domestic policy the historian can now, justifiably, advance interpretations based upon rich manuscript collections and the seemingly endless stream of published materials.

As indicated [in *Housing Reform during the Truman Administration*], the Truman housing program, because it was too deeply involved in the complexities of national affairs, cannot be isolated from other developments. Truman had no clear-cut policy on housing when he assumed the presidency, but early in his administration he enthusiastically assumed leadership for a comprehensive reform program that had been formulated during the war years. Truman's belief that the government should be the instrument of social improvement meshed neatly with the assumptions of social regeneration that the housing reform movement advocated, which could be traced back through the New Deal to the progressive era.

Unlike his predecessors, Truman believed in government's social role to the degree that he threw the full weight of the presidency behind housing reform. He strongly believed that slums and poor housing were inexcusable in a nation as powerful and affluent as the United States and fully realized the embarrassing incongruity in the fact that, although his nation possessed an abundance of wealth and was one of the greatest powers of the world, millions of Americans lived in squalid tenements. America could harness atomic energy, conquer Germany and Japan, and almost overnight rebuild Western Europe, but it could not arrest the growth of slums or eradicate poor housing in its own cities.

Housing reform stands as a lonely monument to the basic legislative objectives of the Fair Deal. As did other urban-oriented reforms, housing ran afoul the tenacious antireform coalition in Congress that had roots reaching deeply into rural America. Only by the narrowest of margins did the Housing Act of 1949 pass Congress; on a test vote in the House of Representatives it escaped the clutches of the conservative coalition by just five votes. Housing legislation succeeded where other Fair Deal measures failed only because it had the overwhelming support of the public. The public pressure, however, resulted from the tremendous postwar housing shortage and was only indirectly related to the problems of low-income housing and slum clearance. Had the opposition succeeded in blocking passage in 1949, the "comprehensive" legislation probably would never have become law, because public enthusiasm for reform dwindled as the housing shortage rapidly disappeared.

Housing also played a significant role in the tumultuous political arena of the Truman era. Both the annual struggle over rent controls and the far-reaching political implications of the abortive Veterans Emergency Housing Program document the explosive nature of this issue. A veteran unable to locate a house or apartment for his family posed far more than just a humanitarian problem; he confronted Truman with a political crisis. The congressional campaigns of 1946, in which Republicans asked, "Had Enough?" and the 1948 campaign in which Truman emphasized housing legislation to his urban audiences illustrate the political significance of housing.

The frequent inner contradictions of Truman's housing policies reflect the complexity of the problems that confronted the Missourian. Torn between such advisers as Wilson Wyatt, who continually urged more governmental action, and John W. Snyder, who pressed equally hard for less, or between the demands of urban liberals and those of the politically potent real estate lobby, Truman gave every appearance of staunch liberalism in his housing policies, but in the day-to-day conduct of his housing agency he closely adhered to the real estate lobby's position. While Truman echoed the demands of militant housing reformers for expansive programs of slum clearance and public housing, his administrator Raymond M. Foley continually assured the housing industry that all would be well. Significantly, the Truman administration met all of the demands of the housing industry by enacting such programs as yield insurance and expansion of the activities of the Federal Housing Administration; it differed with the industry only on the matter of public housing.

Thus, Truman's housing policies, in retrospect, seem to support Samuel Lubell's interpretation that Truman was a man who "bought time." Caught in the political vice formed by the forces of conservatism and reform, Truman frequently talked to satisfy one group and acted to please the other. The failure to convert the lofty goals of the Housing Act of 1949 into the actuality of houses and cleared slums illustrates that Truman operated in a period of political stalemate. In a national election his liberalism carried the day, but in Congress, where these objectives had to be enacted and the necessary funds appropriated, the rural coalition exerted its full power.

Hailed as a major achievement by housing reformers, the Housing Act of 1949 has proven to be a hollow victory. For an accurate analysis, the act must be judged primarily on the basis of the performance of the central part of the legislation—public housing. The widespread disaffection with public housing is perhaps best demonstrated by the lack of opposition now offered by the formerly active real estate lobby. By 1960 many of the most vocal supporters of public housing during the Truman administration had become openly critical of the program. The real estate lobby felt that organized opposition was no longer necessary. Even to its most enthusiastic supporters, public housing has been a great disappointment; to its critics, its failures have only confirmed their earlier predictions; to the social scientists, the inadequacies of public housing have further documented the growing belief that social regeneration cannot be achieved within a span of a few years or even within a generation. Indeed, in this day when neoorthodoxy is gaining wide acceptance and political conservatism is seemingly on the upswing, the failures of public housing add weighty evidence to the argument that, although the reconstruction of slums is possible, the expected simultaneous reconstruction of human nature is nearly impossible.

The Housing Act of 1949 called for the erection of 810,000 units of public housing over a six-year period. By July 1, 1964, more than fifteen years after the passage of the now oft-amended law, only 356,203 units had been built. More families lived in substandard housing in 1965 than in 1949. The inexorable spread of slums in the "inner core" of the nation's cities now threatens to spread to the suburbs constructed during the postwar period, including many jerry-built housing tracts erected under the Veterans Emergency Housing Program. While the legislation has been inadequate to provide standard housing to meet even the needs of 1949, the continued growth of the urban population has intensified the seemingly perpetual problem of slum housing.

The limited scope of the original legislation helps explain the shortcomings of the program. The authorized 810,000 units were only a fraction of the need in 1949, and Congress continually refused even to appropriate sufficient funds to construct the authorized number of dwellings. During the Korean conflict the Truman administration drastically reduced the annual maximum number of units to 50,000, and in 1954 the Eisenhower administration set as the maximum construction figure 35,000 units a year.

The major source of disillusionment, however, has been the failure of public housing to fulfill the high aspirations of the housing reformers—to reduce the social disorders of crime, vice, broken families, and juvenile delinquency. This failure is succinctly summarized in the lament of a former public housing official:

> *Once upon a time we thought that if we could only get our problem families out of those dreadful slums, then papa would stop taking dope, mama would stop chasing around, and Junior would stop carrying a knife. Well, we've got them in a nice new apartment with modern kitchens and a recreation center. And they're still the same bunch of bastards they always were.*

Even uncleanliness and dilapidation have not been appreciably reduced. As Jane Jacobs, Harrison Salisbury, various housing experts, and several social scientists have clearly demonstrated, public housing has only perpetuated the exact problems it sought to eradicate. In her perceptive criticism of slum clearance and public housing, Jane Jacobs concludes that public housing projects "have become worse centers of delinquency, vandalism and general social hopelessness than the slums they were supposed to replace." "In too many instances," Salisbury says, "we have merely institutionalized our slums." In his vivid, firsthand description of the Fort Greene project in New York City, he describes conditions that are common to many projects throughout the nation:

> *The same shoddy shiftlessness, the broken windows, the missing light bulbs, the plaster cracking from the walls, the pilfered hardware, the cold, drafty corridors, the doors on sagging hinges, the acid smell of sweat and cabbage, the ragged children, the playgrounds that are seas of muddy clay, the bruised and battered trees, the ragged clumps of grass, the planned absence of art, beauty or taste, the gigantic masses of brick, of concrete, of asphalt, the inhuman genius with which our know-how has been perverted to create human cesspools worse than those of yesterday.*

Although many exceptions to this description do exist, the general widespread criticism of public housing throughout the nation suggests that public housing, as now established, too often conforms to the Fort Greene pattern.

The failure of public housing to remake the character of the inhabitants into constructive citizens, as originally argued, has led to the inevitable conclusion that poor housing does not lie at the root of the other problems of social disorder, but is another manifestation of the same problems. Poor housing now seems to be merely another condition caused by the entire environment generally associated with poverty, low cultural aspirations, poor education, and unhealthy basic attitudes toward personal and family conduct. Thus, the specters of public housing elevators serving as convenient toilets, of staircases becoming places for muggings, of the project area becoming a breeding ground for teenage gang activities, and of the general, all-too-familiar unkempt appearance of public housing projects rise from the same psychological and cultural factors that produce tenement areas. In short, because poor housing results from and is not the basic cause of other social and cultural malconditions, public housing has proved incapable of achieving the high goals set for it by its promoters during the Truman period. The real failure, therefore, does not lie in its inability to elevate the conduct of its inhabitants, but rather in the original assumption that poor housing lies at the root of most other urban social disorders.

Many explanations are advanced for what housing reform leader Catharine Bauer has called "the dreary deadlock of public housing." Obviously, one major cause of difficulty is the administrative structure. Confined in a bureaucratic straitjacket, local housing authority officials are forced to conform to minutely described procedures. Indirectly, the opponents of public housing have increased the problems by continuously keeping public housing officials on the defensive with charges of building "luxury" apartments for low-income families and of conducting a "socialistic" program. Maximum cost ceilings have prevented imaginative construction and have produced, all too often, barrackslike architecture. The resulting institutionalized atmosphere has discouraged the inhabitants from considering the "project" as "home." Also, to prevent the rapid degeneration of the housing project into a public-built slum, the local housing authorities have been forced to impose seemingly endless lists of regulations, which quite naturally create hostility between residents and the authority.

These rigid regulations have had another effect on the dwellers in public housing. While public housing may, in theory, free the low-income family from the tyranny of the slums, ironically it has, in practice, created a tyranny of its own. The requirement that only persons earning less than a prescribed annual income be accepted as tenants has meant that the more ambitious residents have to leave when their incomes rise above the limit. Such a policy has deprived the projects of potential leadership. The weekly unannounced inspections to ascertain cleanliness, the snooping into bank accounts, the strict, often petty, restrictions forbidding even minor remodeling, the arbitrary evictions, and the general institutionalized atmosphere have prevented the development of a normal, stable social order and have frequently chased away the most desirable residents. "Life in the usual public housing projects," Catharine Bauer points out, "just is not the way most American families want to live. Nor does it reflect our accepted values as to the way people should live."

Because public housing can accept only low-income families, other problems are created. As devised and conducted, the public housing program lies outside of the mainstream of the American experience. Whereas social security and unemployment insurance, for example, have been readily assimilated into American life, public housing has been generally rejected. The ideal of private home ownership has remained a major facet of the American way of life. Since most residents view public housing as only a stop-gap measure, pride of ownership, or even pride in renting an apartment of one's choosing, is absent. The stigma of inferiority is placed upon the project dweller; his self-respect is often undermined merely by the fact that he has to accept public assistance. The myriad of regulations often complete the destruction of his own sense of individualism. Because of the low-income requirement public housing has also produced "segregation by income"—a form of social segregation based upon poverty; the physical arrangement of the typical project tends to erect a barrier between the residents and the rest of the city. The new ghettos, Salisbury suggests, are equally as bad as any other form of segregation in a free society.

The relativism of modern American liberalism, which Eric Goldman has so perceptively criticized, enabled the reformers to justify the illiberalism of public housing with the argument that it was better than slums. By using this pragmatic, "ends justifies the means" argument, however, the public housing advocate neatly trapped himself. He failed to realize that quite often the methods employed preclude any success in reaching the desired goal. In this instance, as long as the ideals of individualism and freedom of choice evoke an enthusiastic response in America, public housing, as now constituted, will conflict with these ideals and therefore prevent any widespread success.

As discontent with public housing grew during the years after Truman's departure from office, the entire emphasis toward urban problems was slowly altered. Slum clearance became divorced from public housing and thereby gained new friends, although many cities rejected federal aid as an unwanted invasion of local affairs. But, nonetheless, slum clearance and urban renewal (the Eisenhower program of revitalizing deteriorated areas before complete clearance is needed) have played an important role in the reconstruction of over 600 cities. Public housing, however, has limped along in "a kind of limbo, continuously controversial, not dead but never more than half alive." To be sure, the Housing Act of 1961 contained provisions for 100,000 units of public housing, and the Housing Act of 1965 also contained ample public housing authorizations. But in the face of the magnitude of the housing problem, these were little more than token measures. The 1965 legislation contained provisions for rent subsidies for about 375,000 low-income families, and this new approach to low-rent housing demonstrates the desire of housing officials to find a workable alternative to public housing.

The Fair Deal failed to end the long-enduring problems of slum housing; perhaps the real significance of its efforts is that the basic problems were brought into sharp focus. Poor housing results from lack of education, low income, and a general inability of impoverished groups to keep step with cultural advancement. As American life in the twentieth century became increasingly more technical, the gulf between the poor and the rest of society widened. Public housing merely helps to alleviate the product of these complex factors and does not attack the source. Only sufficient education and opportunities for employment at adequate wages will enable today's slum dwellers to enjoy the benefits of decent housing.

Nonetheless, Harry S. Truman made a concerted effort to solve the housing dilemma and was the first president to recognize clearly the importance of socially sound and economically healthy cities. Although the elimination of slums and substandard housing was not even approached, the adoption of the goal, "a decent house in a good environment for every American family," was in itself a signal accomplishment.

IV THE POLITICS OF CIVIL RIGHTS

Harry S. Truman, October 11, 1952

STRUGGLE AND ACCOMPLISHMENT IN CIVIL RIGHTS

Despite his Southern background, Truman became a stronger advocate of legal equality for the Negro than any chief executive who had preceded him. In 1948, he became the first president to deliver a speech in black Harlem. Returning in the 1952 campaign, he reviewed his civil rights record with partisan, but perhaps pardonable, pride.

Now, many people have wondered how I came to have such a deep interest in civil rights. I want to tell you about that. Right after World War II, religious and racial intolerance began to show up just as it did in 1919. There were a good many incidents of violence and friction, but two of them in particular made a very deep impression on me. One was when a Negro veteran, still wearing this country's uniform, was arrested, and beaten and blinded. Not long after that, two Negro veterans with their wives lost their lives at the hands of a mob.

It is the duty of the state and local government to prevent such tragedies. But, as president of the United States, I felt I ought to do everything in my power to find what caused such crimes and to root out the causes. It was for that reason that I created the President's Committee on Civil Rights. I asked its members to study the situation and recommend to the whole country what we should do.

Their report is one of our great American documents. When it was handed to me, I said that it was a new charter of human freedom. Five years have passed, but I have never seen anything to make me change my mind. These five years have seen some hard fighting by those who believe in civil rights for all our people—women like that great lady, Mrs. Eleanor Roosevelt, men like your own good senators, Herbert Lehman and Bob Wagner—and the fine Democrats you have sent from New York to the House of Representatives. These five years have seen a lot of progress—progress in spite of obstacles that have been placed in our way.

I want to review that progress for you today.

From *Public Papers of the Presidents of the United States: Harry S. Truman, 1952–1953* (U.S. Government Printing Office, 1966), pp. 797–800.

Right after the Committee on Civil Rights made its report to me, I sent to the Congress a special message making ten recommendations for new legislation. Only two of those ten recommendations have been approved by the Congress. The opponents of civil rights in the Congress have blocked every effort to enact such important legislation as a fair employment practices law, an anti-poll tax law, and an antilynch law. Not only that, they have succeeded in changing the rules under which Congress operates, so as to make it impossible to stop a filibuster.

Who are the opponents of civil rights? All you have to do is to look at the record. Read the *Congressional Record,* and you'll find them. I sent a good FEPC bill to Congress; but the Republicans introduced the McConnell Amendment—a toothless substitute for FEPC. And the Republicans in the House voted 2 to 1 for that amendment—beating the Democratic majority that wanted FEPC. The Republicans also introduced and got passed in the Senate the Wherry rule making it next to impossible to stop these filibusters. That is rule 22 that Governor Lehman was talking to you about.

It is no accident that these anti-civil rights measures bear the names of Republican legislators. Republicans introduced them, and Republicans approved them. The Republicans deserve this recognition, for they are always on tap to provide just enough votes to insure the defeat of civil rights measures.

When the Congress refused to act, I went ahead to do what I could within the executive branch itself. This fight of ours cannot stop just because we have been blocked in the United States Congress.

First, I acted to stop racial discrimination in the armed services. The Navy and the Air Force have now eliminated all racial distinctions. And for over two years, every soldier coming into an Army training unit in this country has been assigned on the basis of his individual merit—regardless of race or color. All the troops in Korea are now integrated, and integration is going forward elsewhere overseas.

I also had a Fair Employment Board set up in the Civil Service Commission. Today, every federal agency has a fair employment practices program that is working. Any federal employee, or applicant for federal employment, who feels he has been discriminated against because of race can now ask for and receive justice.

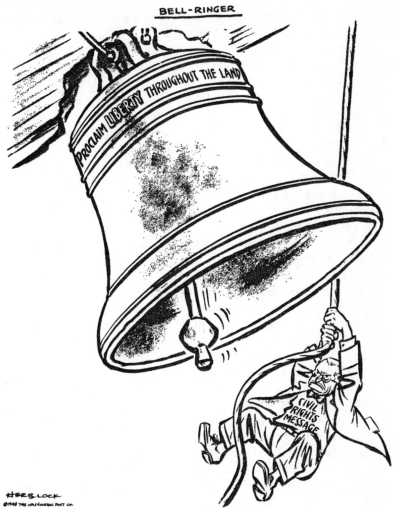

FIGURE 6. (*Copyright 1948 by Herblock in The Washington Post*)

At my request, the solicitor general of the United States went before the Supreme Court to argue that Negro citizens have the right to enter state colleges and universities on exactly the same basis as any other citizens. And we won that fight. And more than a thousand Negro graduate and professional students have been accepted by ten state universities that had barred their doors to

Negroes before. This means that this country will have more men like Louis T. Wright and Ralph Bunche.

At my request, the solicitor general again went before the Supreme Court and argued against the vicious, restrictive covenants that had prevented houses in many places from being sold to Negroes and to Jews. It was a great day in the history of civil rights when we won that case, also, before the Supreme Court.

As one result of that decision, more Negroes are homeowners today than ever before in American history.

Our locally operated public housing projects are increasingly open to families of all races and creeds. The number of integrated projects has increased eightfold in eight years. In the last few years, nine states and eight cities have forbidden discrimination or segregation in public housing.

In the last few years, eleven states and twenty cities have enacted fair employment practice laws. This is where the greatest gap exists in our federal laws on civil rights, and I have repeatedly urged the Congress to pass the kind of law we need. Such a statute must have enforcement powers if it is to mean anything. To talk about voluntary compliance with fair employment practice is just plain nonsense. Federal fair employment legislation with enforcement power is greatly needed and it ought to be on the books. And I am going to keep fighting for it, come hell or high water!

Progress has been made in assuring Negroes the opportunity to exercise their right to vote as citizens. The courts have made the infamous "white primary" a thing of the past. Thank God for that. And there are only five poll tax states left in this Union. Nevertheless, we still need laws to abolish the poll tax and otherwise protect the right to vote where intimidation or restrictions still exist.

In the last five years, two states have enacted antilynch laws. Five states and forty-five cities have passed laws against wearing masks in public—which will strip the hoods off the Ku Klux Klan. One of the finest things that has happened recently was the conviction and prosecution of those Ku Kluxers down in North Carolina and Southern states. This is splendid progress in the fight to guarantee our citizens protection against mob violence, but it is not enough. It is the clear duty of the federal government to stand behind local law enforcement agencies, and to step in if they fail to control mob action. That is exactly what we have been doing through the FBI and through the civil rights section of the Department of Justice.

Last year, a mob formed in Cicero, Illinois, and prevented a Negro veteran and his family from moving into an apartment house. Fortunately, Illinois was blessed with a great governor, who is now your Democratic candidate for president.

Governor Stevenson, who believes in action in these matters, restored law and order with the National Guard. But a local grand jury did the incredible thing of indicting—not the ringleaders of the mob—but the Negro veteran's lawyer and the property owner. At this point the federal government stepped in to prevent a gross miscarriage of justice. It obtained an indictment of the city officials who had failed in their duty to assure equal justice under the law. And the officials who had abetted the mob were tried and convicted in a federal court.

It was also last year that the nation was shocked by the bomb murder in Florida of Harry T. Moore and his wife. These tragic deaths came shortly after the bombings of synagogues and Catholic churches and of the housing project at Carver Village. For several months the FBI has been gathering evidence on the mobs responsible for these outrages. And this week the United States government began to present that evidence to a federal grand jury at Miami.

These are examples of how your federal government—under a Democratic president—stands behind the constitutional guarantees of human rights. The federal government could do a better job if we had stronger civil rights laws—and we must never let down in fighting for those laws.

Roy Wilkins

"NO CHIEF EXECUTIVE . . . HAS SPOKEN SO PLAINLY"

In the forties and early fifties, most black Americans felt that Truman had contributed mightily to the cause of civil rights. Shortly before the president left the White House, Roy Wilkins of the National Association for the Advancement of Colored People wrote to express gratitude for what at the time seemed to be substantial accomplishments.

January 12, 1953

Dear Mr. President:

You must be receiving many letters and your hours in these last days of office must be filled with many duties, but I felt that I could not see you leave Washington without telling you how I feel about one phase of your administration.

I want to thank you and to convey to you my admiration for your efforts in the civil rights field, for your pronouncements and definitions of policy on racial and religious discrimination and segregation.

You have many accomplishments on record during your tenure of the White House (many more by far than is admitted publicly by the Republicans or the majority of the nation's press) but none more valuable to our nation and its ideals than your outspoken championing of equality of opportunity for all Americans without regard to race, color or national origin.

Mr. President, no Chief Executive in our history has spoken so plainly on this matter as yourself, or acted so forthrightly. We have had in the White House great men—great diplomats, great politicians, great scholars, great humanitarians, great administrators. Some of these have recognized inequality as undesirable, as being at variance with the democratic principles of our country; but none has had the courage, either personal or political, to speak out or act in the Truman manner.

You spoke, Sir, when you knew that many powerful influences in

Roy Wilkins to Harry S. Truman, January 12, 1953, Papers of Harry S. Truman, Official File 596, Harry S. Truman Library. Reprinted by permission of the Harry S. Truman Library and Roy Wilkins.

your own party (and in the party of the opposition) would not heed you. You reiterated your beliefs and restated your demands for legislation when political expediency dictated a compromise course. This is sheer personal courage, so foreign to the usual conduct in political office—high or low—as to be unique in the annals of our government. But it was worthy of the presidency of the United States of America. No little man, no mere politician would have sensed the fitness of such conduct in the nation's leader.

Your great desire was to achieve peace. Your sincere efforts toward this goal have saved us from a Third World War thus far and have laid a foundation on which others, if equally devoted, can bring peace to the world.

In urging that America erase inequality between its citizens, as citizens, you were outlining a component of the complex mosaic for peace in the world: the hope, dignity and freedom that democracies offer mankind in contrast to the offerings of totalitarianism. Your sure realization of the truism that preachment without practice would be powerless as a force for peace is a measure of the quiet greatness you brought to your high office.

As you leave the White House you carry with you the gratitude and affectionate regard of millions of your Negro fellow citizens who in less than a decade of your leadership, inspiration and determination, have seen the old order change right before their eyes.

Their sons are serving their country's armed forces in pride and honor, instead of humiliation and despair.

A whole new world of opportunity in education is opening to their children and young people.

The barriers to employment and promotion on the basis of merit have been breached and will be destroyed.

Some of the obstacles in the way of enjoyment of decent housing have been removed and others are under attack.

Restrictions upon the precious citizenship right of casting a ballot have been reduced and soon this right will be unfettered.

Some of the cruel humiliations and discriminations in travel and accommodation in public places have been eliminated and others are on the way out.

But in addition to these specifics, Mr. President, you have been responsible through the pronouncements from your high office, for a new climate of opinion in this broad area of civil rights. By stating a government policy, by relating that policy to the cherished ideals of our nation, you have recalled for the American people that strength of the spirit, that devotion to human welfare and human liberties, that made our country man's best hope for the things all men hold dear.

In their prayers for your health and long life, Negro Americans are joined, I am sure, by hosts of other citizens who have had their spirits renewed and their convictions strengthened by your espousal of the verities of our way of life.

You have said often that the people will act when they have understanding. The people who have had their faith fanned fresh by you will not fail to press toward the goals you have indicated. No change of personnel or party labels will stay them.

May God's blessing and guidance be with you in your new endeavors.

Respectfully yours,
Roy Wilkins

(Administrator, National Association
for the Advancement of Colored People)

Richard M. Dalfiume

THE ACHIEVEMENT OF
MILITARY DESEGREGATION

By the end of the Truman presidency, the armed forces of the United States, rigidly segregated during World War II, were substantially integrated by executive order. Arguing that this was one of the most important steps in the history of American race relations, Richard M. Dalfiume depicts military desegregation both as important in itself and as a precedent for future progress.

During the years 1939 to 1953 the United States armed forces moved from a policy of restricting and segregating the Negro to one of equal opportunity and integration. This was truly a social revolution, the extent of which was summarized several years ago and remains accurate to this day:

> *Today the national armed forces are the most integrated major segment of American life. Great numbers of Americans, Negro and white, obtain their first contact with nonsegregation after they enter uniform, whether stationed North or South.*

This revolution was not achieved without expenditure of a great deal of time and effort. Throughout American history the black American viewed his military service in the nation's conflicts as proof of his loyalty and as a brief for his claim to full citizenship. White Americans appear to have realized this, and they continually sought to restrict or downgrade the black soldier's military service. In the Dred Scott decision, for example, Chief Justice of the Supreme Court Roger Taney cited the fact that Negroes were excluded from the state militia as part of his argument that they were not to be considered citizens. In the United States it has always been assumed that citizens have the obligation to participate in the armed forces. If a group was denied the opportunity to fulfill this obligation, this restriction could provide a rationale for denying that group its full rights of

From *Desegregation of the U.S. Armed Forces: Fighting on Two Fronts, 1939–1953* by Richard M. Dalfiume, pp. 1–4. Copyright © 1969 by The Curators of the University of Missouri. Reprinted by permission of the University of Missouri Press. (Footnotes omitted.)

citizenship. Aware of this reasoning, the Negro has sought to participate in America's wars in the hope that his sacrifices would bring the reward of increased rights.

With the World War II crisis of 1939–1945, the questions of restriction, discrimination, and segregation in the armed forces became one of two major issues for black Americans. Employment discrimination was the other, and this subject has been investigated by several authors. Although employment discrimination was the main bread-and-butter issue for Negroes in World War II, discrimination and segregation in the armed forces was the more emotionally charged concern. What a hypocritical and paradoxical position for the United States—fighting with a rigidly segregated military force for the four freedoms and against an enemy preaching a master race ideology! This manifest difference between the American creed and practice provided Negroes with a powerful argument in their fight for equality. The psychological impact of the war's democratic rhetoric on the nation's largest minority has heretofore been overlooked. Ignoring these earlier years and the seeds of militancy planted in them, most writers claim that a Negro "revolution" or "revolt" occurred in 1954, 1955, 1960, or 1963.

By World War II the military had developed a racial stereotype of the Negro soldier—a military version of white supremacy—that exerted a strong influence on the use of black manpower. Military planners constantly stated that their racial policies were based upon the requirements of efficiency and that they were not concerned with social problems or social theories. The opposite was in fact the truth. Negro soldiers were restricted to certain kinds of military duty because of a widespread belief in their inherent racial inferiority. Furthermore, black servicemen were rigidly segregated because it was felt that most whites insisted that this be so. Segregation seemed necessary to prevent bloody racial conflict and a reduction of the armed services' effectiveness. This kind of thinking obscured the tremendous waste and inefficiency that were the actual results of segregation. Racism was not peculiar to the military; it was only a reflection of the strong thread of racism running through the general American mind. Charles E. Silberman, one of the most poignant critics of American race relations, has recently reminded us that the United States "is a racist society in a sense and to a degree that we have refused so far to admit, much less face."

Segregation and discrimination in the armed forces continued into the post–World War II period and remained a grievance for black Americans. But the postwar era witnessed the emergence of several forces that made it impossible for the federal government and the American people to ignore the race issue any longer. The United States became, in the eyes of itself and others, the leader of the free world, and its race problem was a handicap in the Cold War battle over the destiny of the nonwhite people of the world. The American Negro came out of World War II with a determination to change his status. Coupled with this determination was a new political power, derived from the strategic location of Negro voting blocs in Northern states with large electoral votes. In addition, numerous white Americans came to the conclusion that the deferred commitment of equal rights must be fulfilled at last. All of these forces converged in the administration of Harry S. Truman.

The Truman administration's legislative proposals and actions in the field of civil rights set the pattern for a continuing involvement on the federal level that is still evident today. No longer was it the federal government's policy to condone or extend segregation. Of the Truman administration's precedent-breaking actions in the civil rights field, desegregation of the armed forces was among the first. The military services were a logical place to begin adjustment of black grievances. Negroes had long been incensed over segregation and discrimination in this part of the government. Furthermore, the president, as commander in chief, could move in this area without the consent of a reluctant Congress. Truman's Executive Order 9981 of 1948, which established the President's Committee on Equality of Treatment and Opportunity in the Armed Services, led to military integration; it was one of the first federal actions against segregation, coming six years before the 1954 school desegregation decision. This example of accomplishing integration by executive authority also provided a precedent for the Eisenhower, Kennedy, and Johnson administrations.

The success of military integration, proven in the Korean War, provided a powerful argument against the conservative position that government cannot legislate mores. Integration actually led to a decrease of racial conflict and prejudice within the military services. There is some evidence that the Supreme Court was interested in this successful experience in the period when it began to nibble away at the "separate but equal" doctrine. In 1950, for example, members of the Court gathered evidence from the President's Committee on Equality of Treatment and Opportunity in the Armed Services prior to some important decisions pointing toward a reversal of the separate but equal position. In 1954, before the epochal decision on school desegregation, members of the Court read in manuscript form journalist Lee Nichols's *Breakthrough on the Color Front* (1954), the first book-length account of military integration. Desegregation of the military was indeed an important precedent for the federal government's new role in race relations.

William C. Berman

CIVIL RIGHTS AND POLITICAL CENTRISM

A revisionist historian, William C. Berman stresses the limitations of Truman's civil rights accomplishments and questions the president's motives. He depicts Truman as a political "centrist" striving to hold the Democratic party together, not a reformer deeply and genuinely committed to civil rights. The results, he believes, were mixed—token actual gains but a humane legacy.

The politics of civil rights became nationally prominent at approximately the time Harry Truman became president of the United States. Both challenged and threatened by this issue, President Truman responded to it in such a way as to obtain maximum political benefit for him and his party. Personal wariness and political canniness characterized his *modus operandi* in handling an issue which could have produced lasting division within the Democratic party.

President Truman had already worked his way through the civil rights maze in the years he served as a senator from Missouri. That is, he gave evidence in his senatorial years that he appreciated the power of the black vote in Kansas City and elsewhere. Like most of his fellow white Missourians, Truman opposed social equality;

From *The Politics of Civil Rights in the Truman Administration* by William C. Berman, pp. 237–240. Copyright © 1970 by the Ohio State University Press. Reprinted by permission of the author and the Ohio State University Press.

but he was also a political realist who acknowledged that the interests of his Negro constituents needed protection. Hence, as a senator he could support civil rights proposals, knowing that they would not clear the Senate and come back to haunt him in his home state.

This ambivalence, a respect for the traditional order combined with a recognition of political realities, Truman carried with him into the White House in April 1945. Operating on a national level, where political hazards were so much greater, Truman employed the same tactics in dealing with the FEPC controversy that had worked so well in Missouri. He raised the art of civil rights advocacy to new heights while shying away from anything that resembled a substantive program, which could have alienated the South, the section that had supported him in the showdown fight with Henry Wallace at the 1944 Democratic national convention. Later, of course, the development of new and more subtle tactics led to the establishment of the President's Committee on Civil Rights and the dispatching of the February 2, 1948, civil rights message to Congress, which, in turn, precipitated a furious Southern reaction.

The evidence adduced in this study would suggest that President Truman's sponsorship and endorsement of a civil rights program from 1948 on was not synonymous with active support for its passage. He, his supporters, and his opponents in Congress were participants in a civil rights drama in which ritualized action characterized the role performances of the players from the White House down. Thus, Southerners who took umbrage at President Truman's *legislative* commitment to civil rights mistook his rhetoric for the real thing. Surely, the leading House Democrat, Sam Rayburn, and even Senator Richard Russell, knew that Truman was not about to smash the Democratic party for the sake of a dubious congressional victory. It must be remembered that the men who controlled the national Democratic party were centrists, whose role was to preserve the party as a viable political organization, come what may, by making concessions to key interest groups only when necessary and by preventing potentially disruptive internal struggles from becoming embarrassingly manifest.

Truman's willingness to make such a concession to Negro voters led him to issue Executive Order 9981 creating the Fahy Committee. It should be noted, then, that this order was not simply an exercise in good will, but rather the product of political pressure applied by A. Philip Randolph, Walter White, and others at a time when a presidential incumbent needed all the support he could muster in states with the greatest votes in the electoral college. Like Executive Order 8802, which President Roosevelt had issued to create an FEPC, 9981 was further recognition of the growing political influence of Northern Negroes and their white allies.

Ironically, then, an authoritarian military establishment, itself no model for theorists of the good society, was altered somewhat to accommodate the ethos of democratic man. Here was the beginning of a controlled experiment that was hardly applicable to civilian society at large, but which for Negroes represented a breakthrough of sorts and a challenge to the stereotypes of many whites who never thought of black Americans except in terms of servitude based upon assumptions of biological and cultural inferiority.

That racial breakthrough was undoubtedly President Truman's greatest civil rights achievement—and it illustrates the intelligent use of executive power to change, within admittedly narrow limits, a racist social structure. This emphasis on executive action, an extension of precedents developed by the Roosevelt administration, included the issuance of executive orders and the drafting of *amicus curiae* briefs which the Justice Department submitted to the Supreme Court, as in the important case of *Brown* v. *Board of Education*. Thus, President Truman recognized his responsibility to hold the country together. But centrist politician that he was, Truman moved only because he had no choice: Negro votes and the demands of the Cold War, not simple humanitarianism—though there may have been some of that—produced whatever token gains Negroes were to make in the years Truman inhabited the White House.

In the 1940s the Truman administration, whose liberal rhetoric was well ahead of the country, at least did not have to worry about a political reality which developed in the mid-1960s: the wrath of the Northern backlash. In the Truman years the economy was still able to provide jobs for most everyone, thereby reducing the psychological tensions and economic fears of lower-middle-class whites. Furthermore, memories of the depression tended to unite Negroes and whites in the North along class lines, preventing division solely along lines of race. Also, the black population in the Northern cities was not as large in the Truman years as it was to become in the 1960s. For these reasons, then, Truman's stance in favor of civil rights did not jeopardize the Northern urban Democratic party coalition.

If the Truman administration failed to resolve America's most tragic and dangerous domestic problem, it was not because of political indifference. The problem was too vast and too complex for even the most politically skilled and popular of presidents, which admittedly Harry Truman was not. Nevertheless, President Truman helped to move the issue of civil rights into the forefront of American life, where it has been ever since. His legacy was humane, his commitment to federal action sound. Because of him and a number of key figures within his administration, the politics of civil rights had become a primary issue of concern for the American people.

V CIVIL LIBERTIES: THE POLITICS OF LOYALTY

Harry S. Truman, March 21, 1947

EXECUTIVE ORDER 9835 ESTABLISHING A FEDERAL LOYALTY PROGRAM

Historians have been nearly unanimous in their condemnation of the federal loyalty program which Truman established during the early stages of the Cold War. Hastily thrown together in early 1947 to forestall legislation by Congress, it failed to provide sufficient protection for individual rights and established a repressive atmosphere throughout the federal bureaucracy; nevertheless, the growing national concern with communism made the program politically unassailable. This executive order, slightly abridged, explains the details of the loyalty program.

EXECUTIVE ORDER 9835

Prescribing Procedures for the Administration of an Employees Loyalty Program in the Executive Branch of the Government

* * *

Part I—Investigation of Applicants

1. There shall be a loyalty investigation of every person entering the civilian employment of any department or agency of the executive branch of the federal government.

a. Investigations of persons entering the competitive service shall be conducted by the Civil Service Commission, except in such cases as are covered by a special agreement between the Commission and any given department or agency.

b. Investigations of persons other than those entering the competitive service shall be conducted by the employing department or agency. Departments and agencies without investigative organizations shall utilize the investigative facilities of the Civil Service Commission.

2. The investigations of persons entering the employ of the executive branch may be conducted after any such person enters upon actual employment therein, but in any such case the appointment of

From 12 *Federal Register* (1947), 1935–38.

such person shall be conditioned upon a favorable determination
with respect to his loyalty.

*   *   *

3. An investigation shall be made of all applicants at all available
pertinent sources of information and shall include reference to:
  a Federal Bureau of Investigation files.
  b. Civil Service Commission files.
  c. Military and naval intelligence files.
  d. The files of any other appropriate government investigative or
intelligence agency.
  e. House Committee on un-American Activities files.
  f. Local law-enforcement files at the place of residence and employment of the applicant, including municipal, county, and state
law-enforcement files.
  g. Schools and colleges attended by applicant.
  h. Former employers of applicant.
  i. References given by applicant.
  j. Any other appropriate source.
4. Whenever derogatory information with respect to loyalty of an
applicant is revealed a full field investigation shall be conducted.
A full field investigation shall also be conducted of those applicants,
or of applicants for particular positions, as may be designated by
the head of the employing department or agency, such designations
to be based on the determination by any such head of the best
interests of national security.

Part II—Investigation of Employees

1. The head of each department and agency in the executive
branch of the government shall be personally responsible for an effective program to assure that disloyal civilian officers or employees
are not retained in employment in his department or agency.

*   *   *

2. The head of each department and agency shall appoint one or
more loyalty boards, each composed of not less than three represen-

tatives of the department or agency concerned, for the purpose of hearing loyalty cases arising within such department or agency and making recommendations with respect to the removal of any officer or employee of such department or agency on grounds relating to loyalty, and he shall prescribe regulations for the conduct of the proceedings before such boards.

a. An officer or employee who is charged with being disloyal shall have a right to an administrative hearing before a loyalty board in the employing department or agency. He may appear before such board personally, accompanied by counsel or representative of his own choosing, and present evidence on his own behalf, through witnesses or by affidavit.

b. The officer or employee shall be served with a written notice of such hearing in sufficient time, and shall be informed therein of the nature of the charges against him in sufficient detail, so that he will be enabled to prepare his defense. The charges shall be stated as specifically and completely as, in the discretion of the employing department or agency, security considerations permit, and the officer or employee shall be informed in the notice (1) of his right to reply to such charges in writing within a specified reasonable period of time, (2) of his right to an administrative hearing on such charges before a loyalty board, and (3) of his right to appear before such board personally, to be accompanied by counsel or representative of his own choosing, and to present evidence on his behalf, through witness or by affidavit.

3. A recommendation of removal by a loyalty board shall be subject to appeal by the officer or employee affected, prior to his removal, to the head of the employing department or agency or to such person or persons as may be designated by such head, under such regulations as may be prescribed by him, and the decision of the department or agency concerned shall be subject to appeal to the Civil Service Commission's Loyalty Review Board, hereinafter provided for, for an advisory recommendation.

4. The rights of hearing, notice thereof, and appeal therefrom shall be accorded to every officer or employee prior to his removal on grounds of disloyalty, irrespective of tenure, or of manner, method, or nature of appointment, but the head of the employing department or agency may suspend any officer or employee at any time pending a determination with respect to loyalty.

5. The loyalty boards of the various departments and agencies shall furnish to the Loyalty Review Board, hereinafter provided for, such reports as may be requested concerning the operation of the loyalty program in any such department or agency.

Part III—Responsibilities of Civil Service Commission

1. There shall be established in the Civil Service Commission a Loyalty Review Board of not less than three impartial persons, the members of which shall be officers or employees of the Commission.

a. The board shall have authority to review cases involving persons recommended for dismissal on grounds relating to loyalty by the loyalty board of any department or agency and to make advisory recommendations thereon to the head of the employing department or agency. Such cases may be referred to the Board either by the employing department or agency, or by the officer or employee concerned.

b. The Board shall make rules and regulations, not inconsistent with the provisions of this order, deemed necessary to implement statutes and Executive orders relating to employee loyalty.

c. The Loyalty Review Board shall also:

(1) Advise all departments and agencies on all problems relating to employee loyalty.

(2) Disseminate information pertinent to employee loyalty programs.

(3) Coordinate the employee loyalty policies and procedures of the several departments and agencies.

(4) Make reports and submit recommendations to the Civil Service Commission for transmission to the president from time to time as may be necessary to the maintenance of the employee loyalty program.

2. There shall also be established and maintained in the Civil Service Commission a central master index covering all persons on whom loyalty investigations have been made by any department or agency since September 1, 1939. Such master index shall contain the name of each person investigated, adequate identifying information concerning each such person, and a reference to each department and agency which has conducted a loyalty investigation concerning the person involved.

*   *   *

3. The Loyalty Review Board shall currently be furnished by the Department of Justice the name of each foreign or domestic organization, association, movement, group or combination of persons which the attorney general, after appropriate investigation and determination, designates as totalitarian, fascist, communist or subversive, or as having adopted a policy of advocating or approving the commission of acts of force or violence to deny others their rights under the Constitution of the United States, or as seeking to alter the form of government of the United States by unconstitutional means.

a. The Loyalty Review Board shall disseminate such information to all departments and agencies.

Part IV—Security Measures in Investigations

1. At the request of the head of any department or agency of the executive branch an investigative agency shall make available to such head, personally, all investigative material and information collected by the investigative agency concerning any employee or prospective employee of the requesting department or agency, or shall make such material and information available to any officer or officers designated by such head and approved by the investigative agency.

2. Notwithstanding the foregoing requirement, however, the investigative agency may refuse to disclose the names of confidential informants, provided it furnishes sufficient information about such informants on the basis of which the requesting department or agency can make an adequate evaluation of the information furnished by them, and provided it advises the requesting department or agency in writing that it is essential to the protection of the informants or to the investigation of other cases that the identity of the informants not be revealed. Investigative agencies shall not use this discretion to decline to reveal sources of information where such action is not essential.

3. Each department and agency of the executive branch should develop and maintain, for the collection and analysis of information relating to loyalty of its employees and prospective employees, a staff specially trained in security techniques, and an effective security

control system for protecting such information generally and for protecting confidential sources of such information particularly.

Part V—Standards

1. The standard for the refusal of employment or the removal from employment in an executive department or agency on grounds relating to loyalty shall be that, on all the evidence, reasonable grounds exist for belief that the person involved is disloyal to the government of the United States.[1]

2. Activities and associations of an applicant or employee which may be considered in connection with the determination of disloyalty may include one or more of the following:

a. Sabotage, espionage, or attempts or preparations therefor, or knowingly associating with spies or saboteurs;

b. Treason or sedition or advocacy thereof;

c. Advocacy of revolution or force or violence to alter the constitutional form of government of the United States;

d. Intentional, unauthorized disclosure to any person, under circumstances which may indicate disloyalty to the United States, of documents or information of a confidential or nonpublic character obtained by the person making the disclosure as a result of his employment by the government of the United States;

e. Performing or attempting to perform his duties, or otherwise acting, so as to serve the interests of another government in preference to the interests of the United States.

f. Membership in, affiliation with or sympathetic association with any foreign or domestic organization, association, movement, group or combination of persons, designated by the attorney general as totalitarian, fascist, communist, or subversive, or as having adopted a policy of advocating or approving the commission of acts of force or violence to deny other persons their rights under the Constitution of the United States, or as seeking to alter the form of government of the United States by unconstitutional means.

---

[1] In 1951, the standard was revised to read "reasonable doubt exists as to the loyalty of the person involved." In practice, the revised standard placed the burden of proof on the accused to a greater degree than ever.—Ed.

Part VI—Miscellaneous

1. Each department and agency of the executive branch, to the extent that it has not already done so, shall submit, to the Federal Bureau of Investigation of the Department of Justice, either directly or through the Civil Service Commission, the names (and such other necessary identifying material as the Federal Bureau of Investigation may require) of all of its incumbent employees.

a. The Federal Bureau of Investigation shall check such names against its records of persons concerning whom there is substantial evidence of being within the purview of paragraph 2 of Part V hereof, and shall notify each department and agency of such information.

b. Upon receipt of the above-mentioned information from the Federal Bureau of Investigation, each department and agency shall make, or cause to be made by the Civil Service Commission, such investigation of those employees as the head of the department or agency shall deem advisable.

2. The Security Advisory Board of the State-War-Navy Coordinating Committee shall draft rules applicable to the handling and transmission of confidential documents and other documents and information which should not be publicly disclosed, and upon approval by the President such rules shall constitute the minimum standards for the handling and transmission of such documents and information, and shall be applicable to all departments and agencies of the executive branch.

*   *   *

The White House   Harry S. Truman

March 21, 1947.

"Say, What Ever Happened To 'Freedom-From-Fear'?"

FIGURE 7. This Herblock cartoon, drawn in August 1951, depicts the state of hysteria and intimidation that characterized the peak years of McCarthyism. In the background, Senator Joseph R. McCarthy wields a smear brush, closely followed by right-wing Democratic Senator Pat McCarran of Nevada. (From *The Herblock Book* (Beacon Press, 1952))

Harry S. Truman, August 14, 1951
"REAL AMERICANISM MEANS FAIR PLAY"

Despite the abuses of his loyalty program, despite his decision to sanction a constitutionally debatable prosecution of the leaders of the U.S. Communist party, Truman resisted the mounting tide of anti-Communist hysteria which accompanied the later years of his administration. In August 1951, he lectured the conservative American Legion on the dangers of character assassination and, by implication, McCarthyism.

In the preamble to the Legion's constitution, its members pledged themselves—among other things—to "uphold and defend the Constitution of the United States . . . to foster and perpetuate a one hundred percent Americanism . . . to safeguard and transmit to posterity the principles of justice, freedom and democracy."

At the present time it is especially important for us to understand what these words mean and to live up to them.

The keystone of our form of government is the liberty of the individual. The Bill of Rights, which protects our individual liberties, is a fundamental part of our Constitution.

When the Legion pledged itself to uphold the Constitution, and to foster 100 percent Americanism, it pledged itself to protect the rights and liberties of all our citizens.

Real Americanism means that we will protect freedom of speech —we will defend the right of people to say what they think, regardless of how much we may disagree with them.

Real Americanism means freedom of religion. It means that we will not discriminate against a man because of his religious faith.

Real Americanism means fair opportunities for all our citizens. It means that none of our citizens should be held back by unfair discrimination and prejudice.

Real Americanism means fair play. It means that a man who is accused of a crime shall be considered innocent until he has been proved guilty. It means that people are not to be penalized and persecuted for exercising their constitutional liberties.

Real Americanism means also that liberty is not license. There is

From *Public Papers of the Presidents of the United States: Harry S. Truman, 1951* (U.S. Government Printing Office, 1965), pp. 462–464.

no freedom to injure others. The Constitution does not protect free speech to the extent of permitting conspiracies to overthrow the government. Neither does the right of free speech authorize slander or character assassination. These limitations are essential to keep us working together in one great community.

Real Americanism includes all these things. And it takes all of them together to make 100 percent Americanism—the kind the Legion is pledged to support.

I'm glad the Legion has made that pledge. For true Americanism is under terrible attack today. True Americanism needs defending— here and now. It needs defending by every decent human being in this country.

Americanism is under attack by communism, at home and abroad. We are defending it against that attack. And we are protecting our country from spies and saboteurs. We are breaking up the Communist conspiracy in the United States. We are building our defenses, and making our country strong, and helping our allies to help themselves.

If we keep on doing these things—if we put our best into the job —we can protect ourselves from the attack of communism.

But Americanism is also under another kind of attack. It is being undermined by some people in this country who are loudly proclaiming that they are its chief defenders. These people claim to be against communism. But they are chipping away at our basic freedoms just as insidiously and far more effectively than the Communists have ever been able to do.

These people have attacked our basic principle of fair play that underlies our Constitution. They are trying to create fear and suspicion among us by the use of slander, unproved accusations, and just plain lies.

They are filling the air with the most irresponsible kinds of accusations against other people. They are trying to get us to believe that our government is riddled with communism and corruption— when the fact is that we have the finest and most loyal body of civil servants in the whole world. These slandermongers are trying to get us so hysterical that no one will stand up to them for fear of being called a Communist.

Now, this is an old Communist trick in reverse. Everybody in Russia lives in terror of being called an *anti*-Communist. For once that charge is made against anybody in Russia—no matter what the facts are—he is on the way out. And what I mean is, he is on the way out!

In a dictatorship everybody lives in fear and terror of being denounced and slandered. Nobody dares stand up for his rights.

We must never let such a condition come to pass in this great country of ours.

Yet this is exactly what the scaremongers and the hatemongers are trying to bring about. Character assassination is their stock in trade. Guilt by association is their motto. They have created such a wave of fear and uncertainty that their attacks upon our liberties go almost unchallenged. Many people are growing frightened—and frightened people don't protest.

Stop and think. Stop and think where this is leading us.

The growing practice of character assassination is already curbing free speech and it is threatening all our other freedoms. I daresay there are people here today who have reached the point where they are afraid to explore a new idea. How many of you are afraid to come right out in public and say what you think about a controversial issue? How many of you feel that you must "play it safe" in all things—and on all occasions?

I hope there are not many, but from all that I have seen and heard, I am afraid of what your answers might be.

For I know you have no way of telling when some unfounded accusation may be hurled at you, perhaps straight from the Halls of Congress.

Some of you have friends or neighbors who have been singled out for the pitiless publicity that follows accusations of this kind—accusations that are made without any regard for the actual guilt or innocence of the victim.

That is not fair play. That is not Americanism. It is not the American way to slur the loyalty and besmirch the character of the innocent and the guilty alike. We have always considered it just as important to protect the innocent as it is to punish the guilty.

We want to protect the country against disloyalty—of course we do. We have been punishing people for disloyal acts, and we are going to keep on punishing the guilty whenever we have a case against them. But we don't want to destroy our whole system of justice in the process. We don't want to injure innocent people. And yet the scurrilous work of the scandalmongers gravely threatens the whole idea of protection for the innocent in our country today.

Perhaps the Americans who live outside of Washington are less aware of this than you and I. If that is so, I want to warn them all. Slander, lies, character assassination—these things are a threat to every single citizen everywhere in this country. And when even one American—who has done nothing wrong—is forced by fear to shut his mind and close his mouth, then all Americans are in peril.

It is the job of all of us—of every American who loves his country and his freedom—to rise up and put a stop to this terrible business. This is one of the greatest challenges we face today. We have got to make a fight for a real 100 percent Americanism.

You legionnaires, living up to your constitution as I know you want to do, can help lead the way. You can set an example of fair play. You can raise your voices against hysteria. You can expose the rotten motives of those people who are trying to divide us and confuse us and tear up the Bill of Rights.

No organization ever had the opportunity to do a greater service for America. No organization was ever better suited or better equipped to do the job.

I know the Legion. I know what a tremendous force for good it can be—and what a tremendous force for good it has been.

Now go to it. The job is up to you.

God bless you.

Athan G. Theoharis

TRUMANISM AND McCARTHYISM

Athan Theoharis, one of Truman's most scathing critics among the revisionists, suggests that the rise of McCarthyism was largely the president's own fault. According to this thesis, Truman's negative anti-Communist foreign policies and his rhetorical justifications for them created an atmosphere in which right-wing demagogues could seize the issue of anticommunism and employ it against the administration which had created it.

Were Truman's failures after 1949 simply the product of an irrational public disaffection? Were his problems simply those caused by a public that, because incapable of understanding and thus accepting the complex, frustrating responsibilities of the Cold War, naively responded to the McCarthyites' simplistic appeals? Historians of the Cold War period have generally represented Truman as a helpless victim of an irrational, emotional public. Popular frustration and discontent were pinpointed as contributing to the conservative congressional leadership's success in assuming the offensive.

The reality was more complex. Indeed, Truman, unwittingly and admittedly unintentionally, had contributed to the development of this intolerant, hysteric climate. In fact, public responses, if apparently irrational, reflected the level of the postwar foreign policy–internal security debate.

The nature of Truman's rhetoric and his administration's various foreign policy–internal security decisions during the 1945–1949 period had served to shift the focus of the national debate to national security questions and to legitimate a conservative anticommunism. From an earlier concern over economic security and domestic issues, by 1950 the political debate centered on international developments and national security arguments; an appeal to anticommunism, without clearly defining what this denoted, had become the norm in post-1950 politics.

The necessity to secure popular support for the adoption of foreign–internal security policies that marked a shift away from

From "The Truman Presidency: Trial and Error," *Wisconsin Magazine of History* 40 (Autumn 1971): 53–58. Copyright © 1971 by the State Historical Society of Wisconsin. Reprinted by permission of the Editor of the *Wisconsin Magazine of History.*

Roosevelt's emphases had led Truman, particularly during 1947–1949, to resort to a distinctly alarmist rhetoric. Truman helped restructure the postwar political debate by defining an interventionist, power-oriented foreign policy as necessary, defensive, and internationalist and claiming that the surveillance of the political associations and beliefs of federal employees was essential to internal security while protective of individual liberties. Further, his emphasis on United States omnipotence and altruism helped create a climate of over-bearing innocence. In addition, when responding to the McCarthyites' criticisms, Truman did not substantively refute their arguments but dismissed them either as partisan, without justification, or unpatriotic. Truman's overt partisanship, combined with his oversimplification of international and national security issues, in the long run contributed to the undermining of his administration's credibility.

In the national security realm—military defense, foreign relations, foreign intelligence, internal security—a modern president has considerably greater political leverage vis-à-vis the Congress than he does in strictly domestic matters. Executive powers which enable a president to focus discussions on particular issues or to define priorities maximize presidential influence. The Congress could repudiate or support a particular policy course, but the manner of its restraint would be responsive not initiatory. When dealing with executive national security decisions, moreover, the Congress confronted actions justified as essential to the national interest. The Cold War, owing to the more sophisticated techniques of subversion and the unprecedented power of nuclear weapons, added a new dimension to this relationship. Intelligence and time acquired new significance; speed, flexibility, and secrecy became imperative and further served to increase the power of the executive branch.

A new situation had been created during the postwar years which subverted traditional checks-and-balances types of restrictions. The real restraint on presidential authority came to rest on the administration's credibility. Able leadership of public opinion, thus, acquired especial importance. Because President Truman had the opportunity to make unilateral decisions, by so doing he made possible partisan, even if irresponsible, attacks on his policies. The opposition could simply debunk and suggest the need for restraints on the executive, emphasizing its lack of identification with, and the unilateral character of, these presidential decisions. This situation, moreover, precluded the necessity of simultaneously proposing viable alternatives.

Moreover, many Americans, because national security matters were not a direct or conscious experience, responded more uncritically to foreign policy appeals than they would to domestic ones. The ability of a president to define policy responses in patriotic terms or to justify policy as responsive to alleged threats to the national interest enabled him to shape popular understanding and acquiescence. How a president defined the national interest could structure significantly the political debate. For this reason, Truman's anti-Communist rhetoric, by delimiting the debate and the public climate, ultimately legitimated attacks from the right.

In 1950 Truman faced a different public than he had in 1945. This popular suspicion of the executive had not been foreordained: indeed, in 1945 Truman had commanded uncritical popular support for executive foreign policy initiatives, partly because of popular antipathy toward Congress and the Republican leadership. In 1945 the public's prevalent fear had been that the Congress might, for either partisan or isolationist reasons (as it had in 1919), frustrate a negotiated settlement or preclude an active United States internationalist role. In addition, in 1945 Roosevelt's foreign policy leadership enhanced popular sympathy and support for executive authority.

After 1945 Truman lost this support and confronted a public concerned over success in the Cold War. In part, this change derived from Truman's decisions and leadership. After 1945 Truman had adopted a less conciliatory approach toward the Soviet Union than Roosevelt followed, relying on military strength, not the development of mutual trust or a policy based on accommodation. This shift away from Roosevelt's emphasis and procedures was gradual, though steady, and thereby tended to blur the distinctiveness. Moreover, although Truman's rhetorical emphasis centered on the United Nations, his actions represented a nationalistic and militaristic course. Beginning with the Truman Doctrine and extending to economic aid to South Korea or Yugoslavia, Truman evolved a domino-theory analysis of international developments and also described his policy proposals in emotional, crisis-oriented terms. Even this shift from Roosevelt's policies was marked by major differences in policy objectives. Initially, Truman attributed international problems to economic chaos and underdevelopment, and

his proposals centered on economic aid. Gradually, his policy statements stressed military aid; he presented policy in confrontation and
subversive terms and in the context of a bipolar international model.
After 1949 the orientation was power-political and the administration's main commitment was to order and stability.

This analysis provided an essentially conservative anti-Communist
direction to the administration's foreign policy. Each decision carried
new commitments, served to redefine the international situation, and
accordingly reduced Truman's subsequent alternatives. Truman's
November 1950 request of Congress for economic aid to Yugoslavia
indicates this domino theory, alarmist emphasis. Truman then observed:

> *The drought, the consequent crop failure, and the imminence of famine
> in Yugoslavia is* [sic] *a development which seriously affects the security
> of the North Atlantic area. These events dangerously weaken the ability
> of Yugoslavia to defend itself against aggression, for, among other cir-
> cumstances, it* [sic] *imperils the combat effectiveness of the Yugoslav
> armed forces.*
>
> *Yugoslavia, moreover, is a nation whose strategic location makes it of
> direct importance to the defense of the North Atlantic area. . . .*
>
> *As a result of these factors, an immediate increase in Yugoslavia's
> ability to defend itself over that which would exist if no assistance were
> supplied will contribute to the peace and security of the North Atlantic
> area [and] is vital to the security of the United States.*

In addition, the administration's foreign policy decisions were
increasingly unilateral. Thus, Truman either bypassed the United
Nations or relied upon that organization as a forum for acquiescence
to U.S. policy. A nationalist, if in a different sense from Robert Taft,
Truman suggested that the United States could impose its values
on the postwar world and presented United States intervention in
noble, altruistic terms. Rejecting preventive war and overt liberation,
Truman's statements, nonetheless, exuded confidence. Truman did
not aver that international problems of change or disruption, or the
attainment of stability, were impossible of solution; nor did he counsel the public that the United States might fail to create a postwar
world in its image. In this same vein, he represented revolutionary
developments as evidence of Soviet subversion. Presumably cog-
nizant of the realities of power, Truman never publicly defined the
limits to American power posed by the conflicting objectives between

the United States and an equally powerful and nationalistic Soviet Union. Instead, the president identified international conflicts and threats to the peace in moralistic terms verging almost on a crusade; in addition, his rhetorical references to the Soviet Union depicted it as the Antichrist. Because American ideals were laudable and the Soviet Union's aggressive and sustained through terror, Truman affirmed that U.S. policy would in the long run prove successful.

This conspiratorial depiction of revolution as manufactured by a small cabal in Moscow was reflected in Truman's characterization of Chinese Communist intervention in the Korean War. In a November 30, 1950, press conference, Truman asserted:

> Recent developments in Korea confront the world with a serious crisis. . . . If the United Nations yields to the forces of aggression, no nation will be safe or secure. If aggression is successful in Korea, we can expect it to spread throughout Asia and Europe to this hemisphere. We are fighting in Korea for our own national security and survival. . . . We hope that the Chinese people will not continue to be forced or deceived into serving the ends of Russian colonial policy in Asia.
>
> I am certain that, if the Chinese people now under the control of the Communists were free to speak for themselves, they would denounce this aggression against the United Nations.

This implied that revolutions, because Soviet-inspired aggression, must be resisted lest inaction, i.e., appeasement, lead to further aggression and to a future world war. This analysis further implied that revolutionary movements, because alien and not indigenous, could be defeated or averted by the appropriate use of power. It tended to fortify popular expectations that intervention was both altruistic and, owing to American technological and material superiority, inevitably successful. By this confident, crisis-oriented presentment of policy, that the United States must, and, should it so will, could avert disruptive change, Truman misled the public. Options were not that clear-cut and the containment of Soviet revolutionary influence neither easy nor attainable.

Truman's responses to loyalty-security matters reflected a similar confident, moralistic tone. Initially, when establishing the Federal Employee Loyalty Program, Truman presumably intended to prevent Soviet espionage or intelligence. As this program subsequently evolved, it exceeded these legitimate, limited bounds. Thus, in 1951, the standard for dismissal of an employee on "loyalty" grounds changed from overt actions confirming disloyalty to implications about the individual's loyalty.

The program's success inevitably lent itself to a statistical assessment of the number of employees dismissed. By suggesting that the employment of "even one person of doubtful loyalty" constituted a "serious threat" to the national security and by failing to establish the subjective nature, indeed inaccuracy, of much of the information contained in the FBI loyalty reports, Truman had created the unrealistic standards by which his loyalty program was subsequently judged.

The establishment of the loyalty program also had legitimated investigations into the political associations and beliefs of individual citizens, and the attorney general's list became a litmus test for judging personal loyalty. Moreover, the assumption underlying the loyalty program was that a real threat, formerly ignored, existed. Truman's post-1947 denial that this program needed improvement and his refusal to cooperate with congressional committees were seemingly contradicted by his own subsequent revisions of the program's procedures and the uncovering of the Alger Hiss, Judith Coplon, and Julius and Ethel Rosenberg "spy" cases.

Lastly, Truman's reaction to criticism and his attempts to discredit McCarthyite attacks by implying that they undermined the national security reduced his own credibility. Rather than substantively confronting the McCarthyites' criticisms of his loyalty program or foreign policies, he questioned their motives, implying that they sought partisan advantage or harmed the national interest, and he sought to appear "more anti-Communist than thou." Thus, in the 1948 campaign, Truman sought to link Wallace with the Communists and contended that his Republican opponents were playing into the (Soviet) Communists' hands by encouraging the Wallace candidacy. In 1950 Truman described Senator McCarthy as "the best asset the Kremlin has," termed the McCarran Internal Security Act a measure that aided the Communists, and identified congressional defeat of the South Korean Aid Act as benefiting the Soviet Union.

This approach, highlighting Truman's partisanship, made it easier for conservative Republicans to accuse Truman of seeking to "cover up" for political reasons. The anti-Communist nature of the postwar debate also ensured that Truman would come off second-best; Truman's conservative critics had far better anti-Communist credentials. Moreover, seeking to undercut the impact of the McCarthyites, Truman often eventually changed his position to conform more closely with their demands. The timing of Truman's more important loyalty-security decisions reflected this political submission. Thus, he established the Temporary Commission on Employee Loyalty in November 1946, after the Republican congressional victory and not when the institution of a loyalty program had been first proposed in July 1946. He established the President's Commission on Internal Security and Individual Rights in January 1951, after the 1950 congressional elections confirmed the political impact of McCarthyism and not in June 1950, when the idea of the commission had been proposed by members of the White House staff. In 1947 he sought to prevent abuses of individual employee's rights when establishing the Loyalty Program, but in 1951 when confronted by McCarthyite attacks he changed the procedures and standards of that program. He vacillated, first wholly opposing, then allowing the Tydings Committee limited access to State Department loyalty records when it became obvious that the committee could not successfully rebut McCarthy's "Communists-in-Government" charges. These reversals indirectly credited Truman's critics; they implied that the president's original stance had been inadequate, that further surveillance had been needed.

Truman's resort to censorship in internal security–defense–foreign policy matters further contributed to undermining his credibility. His restriction on the release of the Wedemeyer Report, his initial failure to publish the Yalta Far Eastern agreements or to inform the Congress and the public about the administration's China policy, and the March 1948 Executive Order preventing congressional access to FBI loyalty reports caused deep public doubts about administration priorities. These restrictions, justified on national security grounds, appeared to be efforts to cover up mistakes either in policy or loyalty. Moreover, the administration's contention that the FBI's effectiveness required preserving the confidentiality of the loyalty reports was discounted by the fact that much of the information presented by Senator McCarthy and the McCarthyites had been derived from these reports. After 1948 the House Committee on Un-American Activities could also effectively point out that the Truman administration, despite its unlimited access to these reports, had not dismissed disloyal employees—Alger Hiss, William Remington, John Stewart Service—until the committee had publicly exposed their disloyalty.

An assessment of the postwar presidency of Harry S. Truman highlights Truman's failure as a presidential leader. Even conceding the overwhelming problems confronting a post–World War II executive, Truman failed to deal effectively or imaginatively with them. These problems transcended Truman's limited vision and abilities. At a critical time in American history when a great president possessing sensitivity and understanding was needed, a man of moderate abilities exercised power.

The nature of Truman's foreign policy–internal security decisions and their underlying rationale, by narrowly restricting the domestic political debate to national security and anti-Communist themes, helped to legitimate conservatism and to undermine reform. In one sense, Truman became a victim of his rhetoric, elitism, and partisanship and not simply of war-created hysteria or a frustrated public seeking scapegoats and easy solutions.

Truman's comments at an April 17, 1952, press conference best summarize the Truman presidency:

> *I have tried my best to give the Nation everything I had in me. There are a great many people—I expect a million in the country—who could have done the job better than I did it. But, I had the job, and I had to do it. . . . When he [a person] gives everything that is in him to the job that he has before him, that's all you can ask of him. And that's what I have tried to do.*

Contrary to Truman's rejoinder, trying was not enough. Unfortunately for the nation, at a critical juncture in history an average man held the office of the presidency. While his intentions were noble, his vision was narrow and parochial. In the absence of effective presidential leadership, a reactionary Congress regained the initiative. More importantly, the resolution of basic problems and consideration of other options were thereby precluded.

Alan D. Harper

THE WHITE HOUSE AND THE COMMUNIST ISSUE

As Alan Harper sees it, the growth of McCarthyism was less a consequence of Truman's mistakes than of situations not amenable to presidential control. Harper's analysis stresses the independence and hypercaution of the federal bureaucracy, the nature of the presidency during the Truman era, the undisciplined character of the American party system, and the irresponsibility of the Republican opposition.

The Truman administration cannot be held entirely blameless for its own predicament. The institution of the loyalty program was accompanied by rather too much stress on protection against subversion and rather too little on protection of traditional rights. Probably not enough time was allowed to devise the program; certainly it was done under pressure. Despite the president's genuine concern with how the program was administered, concerted efforts at reform were not launched before second-line (or third-line) administrators within the executive departments had yielded their judgment to what must have seemed the greater power outside. The appointment of persons sympathetic—in some cases, far too sympathetic—to the opposition to key positions of administration in the loyalty and security programs was surely a mistake. It was too great a concession, even in the search for broad public support, and the event proved it largely futile.

There can be no question, however, of the president's own devotion to the principles of civil liberty. His commitment to traditional values of personal freedom was complete. But, although not truly a simple man, he shared some of the small-town simplicities of outlook characteristic of so much of his opposition; the complexities, both philosophical and practical, of the loyalty issue at least partly eluded him. To him, loyalty could not be defined: "You're either loyal to the United States, or you're not!" The change in the loyalty standard, for example, apparently struck him as a useful administrative adjust-

From *The Politics of Loyalty: The White House and the Communist Issue, 1946–1952*, pp. 232–252. Copyright © 1969 by Alan D. Harper. Reprinted by permission of Alan D. Harper and Greenwood Press, Inc.

ment—the strong legal and philosophical objections of several members of his staff not convincing him otherwise—while the dangers inherent in confounding the requirements of security with the demand for loyalty never seemed evident to him. Mr. Truman, of course, was more than sincere in attempting to correct abuses by loyalty boards, although he was surprised as well as indignant at the frequency of their occurrence. Because of the strength and clarity of his own convictions, the president must have found it difficult to believe that others would deliberately trifle with individual liberties either out of prejudice or partisan purpose.

Some of the difficulties faced by the administration, along with some of the errors it made in dealing with them, were inherent in the president's institutional situation. An examination of certain aspects of that situation might repay us.

The president faced problems, to begin with, in imposing his will on the federal bureaucracy. That bureaucracy had expanded fairly rapidly with the New Deal's creation of many new executive and independent agencies, but it blossomed mightily during the Second World War. With the postwar economic boom and the advent of the Cold War, it continued to grow at a regular, impressive pace. Its annual growth rate, indeed, was quite as imposing as that of the gross national product in the postwar period. Since the process has continued, the present structure dwarfs that of twenty years ago, but the youthful outlines of the exuberant monstrosity were fully apparent during the Truman years.

It is, of course, extremely difficult, if not impossible, for the president—any president—to keep tabs on how all his programs and directives are being carried out by this sprawling bureaucracy. Mr. Truman and his immediate aides, for instance, learned of peculiarities in the administration of the loyalty program through complaints by persons who had to be considered reliable. In most cases, subsequent checks confirmed the complaints.

The interests of federal employees are just not those of their ultimate superior. Nearly all want security, which means retention of employment. Most hope for promotion. Some aim at advancement to the highest ranks of the civil service. A few dream of achieving political place. All, from the most restlessly ambitious to the most stolidly content, are in some sense dependent upon being able to ride the shifting tides of opinion. The higher echelons of the permanent civil service, at least, not only follow the election returns, as the Supreme Court is reputed to do, but try to anticipate them. In serving today's master, it is advisable to avoid giving serious offense to tomorrow's.

The anxiety is greatest—and, frequently, the vulnerability, as well —at the level of the assistant secretaries and division heads in the cabinet departments and the assistants to the director, and whatnot, in the agencies. These men, either higher-ranking civil servants or lesser political appointees, play a constant guessing game trying to determine where the actual power to reward lies—or, what is often more important, may lie in the near future. The civil servants in this class are better off than the others, since any political appointee, no matter how unobtrusive he has tried to make himself, is apt to disappear with the administration that has placed him—unless he has the rare luck, and lack of conviction, properly to stage-manage a judicious biting of the hand that has fed him. The climbing civil servant with an eye to the future, however, must be slow to identify himself with the brisk forwarding of any program that is clearly novel or controversial. Observing the administration and party in power, he knows, with King Solomon, that this, too, shall pass away. His problem is to make sure that its passing does nothing to interfere with his ascent to the next higher rung of the bureaucratic ladder. His tools are numerous. The order whose execution is delayed to the brink of oblivion by the difficulty of preparing to execute it, the division and subdivision of a program into sections, in the process of making assignments for execution, until the parts become hopelessly separated from one another and the whole is swallowed up in confusion, the interpretation of a policy in a rather different way from that intended by its framers (since the prose of government directives and instruction sheets is in no way outstanding for forthrightness and clarity)—all these will recommend themselves to the hopeful placeman.

The task of the lower-ranking civil servant, possessed of no more than routine ambition, so to speak, is less intricate but quite as exacting in its way. His job is to work hard, in terms of time and even of effort, without accomplishing anything his superiors seem not to want accomplished.

The nature of the bureaucracy could not fail to influence the administration of the loyalty and security programs. Testimony before the Civil Rights Committee made it clear that common practice was for the chief executive officer of a department or agency to delegate supervision of the programs to a subordinate, who would, in turn, delegate them to a subordinate, or subordinates, of *his*. The poor devil who had the actual management of the business might feel (and with some justification) that his career depended upon his success in this job, or at least the avoidance of error. The loyalty and security programs were designed to keep the government free of subversives. A reading of the headlines—certainly after Joe McCarthy burst upon the scene—would make it obvious that the strictest vigilance against communism was the straight path to advancement. In bringing charges or—what was safer, much safer— forcing a resignation, it was better to chance wronging an innocent man (certainly if the case was unclear) than to risk letting a subversive escape the net. The responsible officer, himself normally junior, would of course give the benefit of any doubt to the government—and himself.

No wonder the president looked at the government apparatus with wry humor, and a tinge of bitterness.

> *In the early summer of 1952, before the heat of the campaign, President Truman used to contemplate the problems of the General-become-President should Eisenhower win the forthcoming election. "He'll sit here," Truman would remark (tapping his desk for emphasis), "and he'll say 'Do this! Do that!' And nothing will happen. Poor Ike—it won't be a bit like the Army. He'll find it very frustrating."*

It needs to be said that all the obstacles to achievement erected by a bureaucracy are not the consequence of self-serving intrigue. Many, probably most, are raised up by honest misunderstanding, inertia, and incompetence. Timely stupidity has assisted more than one career. And McCarthy's heyday introduced simple fear as a widespread motive for inaction—or unjust action.

*   *   *

The President was quite probably in error when he gave the commission [which developed the loyalty program] its head. If he had indicated in advance, at least in broad terms, what sort of program he wanted, the commission would have produced a more acceptable result. It is unlikely, to be sure, that Mr. Truman, personally, knew what a proper program might be like—almost no one did, the problem being unprecedented—but he could have asked his staff to prepare an outline, or at worst a catalogue of limits, for the commission's use. He did not do this, and the White House staff of the time took no independent interest in the problem.

The worst features of the program, of course, were the consequence of the way in which it was administered, rather than with the way it was drawn up; but the administrators were left too much leeway by the drafters. In effect, many departmental and regional loyalty boards adopted the viewpoint of antiadministration elements in Congress as the norm for patriotism, and translated suspicion into reasonable doubt. The quality of the appointments to these boards was responsible for this result, but in this respect the departments and agencies simply followed the example set by presidential appointments to the Loyalty Review Board. It was a bad example; appeasement once again produced the historically predictable consequence. It seems certain, too, that the hasty institution of a fairly drastic loyalty program, run by identifiable nonliberals, excited rather than reassured public opinion.

None of the weaknesses of the loyalty program, administrative, structural, or psychological, were beyond correction. Procedures could have been revised, administrative personnel replaced or brought under better discipline, and an administrative court of review established outside the Civil Service Commission (however it might have objected), with a membership sufficiently prominent and an operation sufficiently public to promote popular confidence. These, or other reforms similar in effect, would have been adequate for all purposes at any time prior to the eruption of the debate over China, the climax of the Hiss case, and Senator McCarthy's serendipitous discovery of communism. No reform was attempted, however, until it was, at least politically, too late.

That this was the case derived from Mr. Truman's rather traditional approach to his office. He believed that a president should govern through his cabinet; like many of his Southern and Border state colleagues in the Senate, he had been suspicious of Roosevelt's reliance on unofficial advisers and the nascent White House staff. "I propose to get Cabinet officers I can depend on and have them run their affairs, and when I can't depend on them I'll keep on firing

Cabinet Members until I can get that kind." The president, at least
in the beginning, was thus committed to reliance on the Justice
Department in loyalty and security matters. But, as one first-hand
observer noted, "in the Truman Administration, the Justice Department tended to be evasive, sometimes downright unresponsive, in
providing the Executive Office with forthright legal guidance on
legislative or operational issues."

*   *   *

The White House staff, as such, could not undertake any positive
action in the loyalty field because it was too closely identified with
the president. It could discreetly investigate complaints against
loyalty boards; it could bring under-the-table pressure to bear on
erring agencies; it could propose, and plan for, what became the
Nimitz Commission.[1] It could not, so to speak, show its face. To do
so would have invited a flood of abusive, irrational criticism of the
president for meddling with the loyalty program to save "Reds."

It is at least possible that things would have been different if the
president had assigned some member of the staff to special over-
sight of the loyalty program. It could not have hurt to have had the
departments and their loyalty boards regularly reminded of the intent
of the program, as understood at the White House. It might have
helped to have had permanent staff liaison with the Justice Department, to make sure that it executed the president's desires; yet at
the same time to reassure the FBI and the Internal Security Division
of all necessary cooperation. It would have made sense to designate
staff members to help prepare and direct the Tydings Subcommittee
investigation of the McCarthy charges. And so on. But Mr. Truman
simply did not use his staff that way. Neither Clark Clifford nor
Charles Murphy, despite real executive ability and political "feel,"
ever had the extensive control over legislative planning or the broad
right to speak authoritatively for the president, within the government, that characterized Theodore Sorenson's tenure as Kennedy's
special counsel. Neither man possessed anything approaching the

[1] In 1951, Truman appointed a special commission headed by Admiral Chester
Nimitz to review the loyalty program and the entire range of internal security
problems. The president hoped that the commission would be a moderating force,
but McCarthyite congressmen blocked enabling legislation which would have
allowed it to begin work and it was unable to fulfill its mission.—Ed.

real power over domestic policy that Bill Moyers and Joseph Califano had during the Johnson administration. There was nothing in the Truman White House that remotely resembled the elaborate congressional liaison operations that General Wilton B. ("Slick") Persons created for the Eisenhower administration or that Lawrence F. O'Brien maintained for Presidents Kennedy and Johnson.

It is nevertheless unfair to criticize Mr. Truman for not having used his staff in a more audacious manner. The retrospective consideration of his experience was in good part responsible for the recent elaboration of the White House office and the delegation to it of substantial authority once delegated only to cabinet secretaries. It took a little time to see what was happening to the federal bureaucracy and to invent remedies for the inhibitions it laid upon a president. It was indeed a credit to President Truman that he organized and utilized the staff as well as he did, and that, in time, he put together so good a one. It has not had a good press, for being made up largely of government career men, it was short on what is now meretriciously called style; and lacking real power, it had no political glamor. What influence it could exert depended wholly on the president's power (as is still true), and in the political (as opposed to the institutional, executive, or personal) sense, Mr. Truman has been our most embattled president since Hoover.

Any advertence to Mr. Truman's political weakness must refer to his position in Congress. At almost no time in his tenure of the White House—despite the miracle of 1948—could he have been regarded as a good bet politically. This fact made a strong impression on the leaders of both parties in both houses of Congress, as it certainly influenced some cabinet members and top-level civil servants. His weakness on the Hill was made up of roughly equal parts of his own lack of prior political distinction, the incredible flabbiness and ineptitude of the Democratic leadership in the Senate, and the peculiar character of the congressional opposition.

Mr. Truman, to begin with, was an "accidental" president to a degree that has been true of no other Chief Executive since Chester A. Arthur. Although he had a good reputation in the Senate, he had no personal following in it, and he was not a member of the fabled "club." His record and his personal qualifications, as understood in 1944, added up to availability, not authority. Senator Truman owed his nomination as vice-president more to the party leaders' distaste for Mr. Wallace and their doubts about Mr. Byrnes's vote-getting abilities than to any recognized merits of his own. His succession to the presidency caused as much shock in Congress as elsewhere in the country, and it required a long time for the panjandrums of the powerful congressional committees to take him seriously. Some, indeed, never learned. Without strong leadership in Congress, the president had little hope of securing passage of most of his programs.

*   *   *

It is clear enough that the weakening of party discipline in both houses of Congress and the incompetence or cowardice of the Senate Democratic leadership undermined the president's efforts to control the bureaucratic leadership of the executive departments and agencies. The bureaucrats were naturally anxious to keep in the good graces of an opposition that showed every sign of coming to power in the near future.

Nothing more damaged the administration's efforts to offer coherent guidance in the loyalty and security fields than to be faced with a Republican opposition that refused to play the game. The game simply requires taking the patriotism and good faith in matters involving national security of one's opponent for granted, while belittling his intelligence and judgment, or even questioning his common honesty in ordinary domestic matters. Senator Goldwater, who was frequently accused of running an extreme campaign in 1964, never violated this rule of minimal civility.

One can only speculate why the congressional leadership of a whole party—and much of its state and local leadership as well—gave itself over to a demagogy that might, if unchecked, have subverted the structure of the state. Agitation of the idea that the president and the secretary of state would deliberately nourish communism within the government of the United States produced a degree of popular excitement that came close, in some places, to ending ordinary political discourse. By support of McCarthy, the Republican leaders of Congress foreclosed any possibility of a bipartisan examination of the genuine problems raised by the need for adequate security within the government. They raised a barrier against any rationalization of foreign policy. Where they would have ended, had not General Eisenhower been elected president in 1952, is not at all sure. McCarthy's supporters set out to prove that they held a monopoly of patriotism, and in the long run demonstrated only that fanaticism is inimical to the democratic process and consistently threatens the constriction, if not the paralysis, of democratic government.

Senator Taft, like the president, was an intense partisan. His partisanship, however, unlike the president's, frequently seemed irrelevant to the real world of politics and government. Taft apparently never understood the mediating function of the party system and its consequent crucial role in giving life to the constitutional structure he professed to revere. In using McCarthy, he adopted an argument that would have been entirely discredited (and the party with it) by any appearance of compromise, or even cooperation, with the administration. The Republican position was, in more recent jargon, "nonnegotiable." Mr. Truman may have been impolitic, but he was not inaccurate, in pinning the "red herring" label on his opponents' investigative activities. For many Republicans, the possibility of Communist infiltration of the government was not a problem, but an opportunity. A terrible sense of frustration, born of an unusually prolonged period of electoral defeat, seems to have liberated a very substantial number of them from the restraints imposed by the historic consensus of the American party system. After the trauma of 1948, several of their most important leaders broke loose, too. They were able to go so far, in 1952, as to force upon General Eisenhower the public appearance of acquiescing in their fanciful attacks on his friend and mentor, General Marshall.

The Truman administration, nevertheless, was never overwhelmed. Because, as his staff aides were inclined to believe, the president "could think better with his guts than [they] could with [their] heads," he was successful in fighting off the most dangerous efforts to ravage the executive branch.

*   *   *

The crisis was ended by time. The termination of the misunderstood Korean War, the passive resistance of a largely invulnerable Republican administration, and a revived public conscience (freed by relief to be pricked by shame) eventually checked most of the excesses symbolized by Senator McCarthy. When his censure finally came, it was in some part a belated vindication of the Truman administration, above all of the former president himself.

Suggestions for Additional Reading

Primary Sources

For the most thorough compilation of Truman's public pronouncements, see *Public Papers of the Presidents of the United States:
Harry S. Truman, 1945–1953,* 8 vols. (Washington, D.C., 1961–66).
Truman's *Memoirs,* 2 vols. (Garden City, N.Y., 1955–56) are not overly
useful as a historical account but are valuable for their insights into
the author's character. William Hillman, ed., *Mr. President* (New
York, 1952) is a highly selective compilation of excerpts from
Truman's private papers. Barton J. Bernstein and Allen J. Matusow,
eds., *The Truman Administration: A Documentary History* (New York,
1966) is a good collection of contemporary materials. Robert S.
Allen and William V. Shannon, *The Truman Merry-Go-Round* (New
York, 1950), an acerbic and entertaining survey of the Washington
scene during Truman's second term, is worth reading if its biases
are kept in mind.

Secondary Works

Jonathan Daniels, *Man of Independence* (Philadelphia, 1950), is the
best account of Truman's prepresidential career. See also the articles
on Truman's Missouri years by Lyle W. Dorsett and Franklin D.
Mitchell in *Mid-Continent American Studies Journal* 7 (Fall, 1966),
and Eugene F. Schmidtlein, "Truman the Senator" (Ph.D. Dissertation, University of Missouri, 1962). Richard S. Kirkendall's "Truman's
Path to Power" is a by-product of research for what promises to be a
major biography.

Alfred E. Steinberg, *The Man from Missouri: The Life and Times of
Harry S. Truman* (New York, 1962) and Cabell Phillips, *The Truman
Presidency: The History of a Triumphant Succession* (New York,
1966) are competent journalistic surveys. Bert Cochran, *Harry
Truman and the Crisis Presidency* (New York, 1973), is shallow in
research and conceptualization. Margaret Truman, *Harry S. Truman*
(New York, 1972), is part memoir, part biography, and perhaps best
characterized as the official family history. To date, the most com-
plete scholarly account of the administration is Alonzo L. Hamby,
Beyond the New Deal: Harry S. Truman and American Liberalism
(New York, 1973). Richard S. Kirkendall, ed., *The Truman Period as*

a Research Field (Columbia, Mo., 1967), contains four essays touching upon aspects of domestic politics; a second edition (Columbia, Mo., 1974) contains new essays, commentaries by the first-edition authors, and an up-to-date comprehensive bibliography.

Voting analysts and political scientists have done valuable work on the Truman era. Among historians the most influential interpretation is Samuel Lubell, *The Future of American Politics* (New York, 1951; 3d ed., rev., 1965). V. O. Key, *The Responsible Electorate: Rationality in Presidential Voting, 1936–1960* (Cambridge, Mass., 1966) relies heavily upon public opinion data. For specific campaigns, see Bernard R. Berelson et al., *Voting: A Study of Opinion Formation in a Presidential Campaign* (Chicago, 1954); Angus Campbell and Robert L. Kahn, *The People Elect a President* (Ann Arbor, 1952); Cambell et al., *The Voter Decides* (Evanston, 1954). Paul T. David et al., *Presidential Nominating Politics in 1952,* 5 vols. (Baltimore, 1954), is a massive study. V. O. Key, *Southern Politics in State and Nation* (New York, 1949), is a classic. On Congress, see especially David R. Mayhew, *Party Loyalty among Congressmen* (Cambridge, Mass., 1966); David B. Truman, *The Congressional Party* (New York, 1959), analyzes the Eighty-first Congress. Richard E. Neustadt's notable *Presidential Power: The Politics of Leadership* (New York, 1960) draws heavily upon its author's experience in the Truman administration. See also Elmer E. Cornwell, Jr., *Presidential Leadership of Public Opinion* (Bloomington, Ind., 1965). Historians should be especially interested in James MacGregor Burns's work on American politics: *Congress on Trial* (New York, 1949), *The Deadlock of Democracy* (Englewood Cliffs, N.J., 1963), and *Presidential Government* (Boston, 1965). The political science journals and the *Public Opinion Quarterly* contain many useful articles.

In addition to Irwin Ross, *The Loneliest Campaign* (New York, 1968), one should also consult Richard S. Kirkendall's essay on the 1948 election and for 1952 see Barton J. Bernstein's interpretation, both in Fred R. Israel and Arthur M. Schlesinger, Jr., eds., *A History of American Presidential Elections, 1789–1968,* vol. 4 (New York, 1971). Susan M. Hartmann, *Truman and the 80th Congress* (Columbia, Mo., 1971) provides excellent coverage of the prelude to 1948. The Dixiecrat insurgency has received little attention, but see Emile B. Adler, "Why the Dixiecrats Failed," *Journal of Politics* 15 (August, 1953): 356–369; Numan V. Bartley, *From Thurmond to Wallace: Political*

Tendencies in Georgia, 1948–1968 (Baltimore, 1970); and, of course, Key, *Southern Politics.* Coverage of the radical opposition has been more thorough: Karl M. Schmidt, *Henry A. Wallace: Quixotic Crusade, 1948* (Syracuse, 1960); Curtis MacDougall, *Gideon's Army,* 3 vols. (New York, 1965); Edward L. and Frederick H. Schapsmeier, *Prophet in Politics: Henry A. Wallace and the War Years* (Ames, Iowa, 1970); Norman D. Markowitz, *The Rise and Fall of the People's Century: Henry A. Wallace and American Liberalism, 1941–1948* (New York, 1973); David A. Shannon, *The Decline of American Communism* (New York, 1959); Joseph R. Starobin, *American Communism in Crisis, 1943–1957* (Cambridge, Mass., 1972). For the conservative Republican opposition to Truman, see especially James T. Patterson, *Mr. Republican: A Biography of Robert A. Taft* (New York, 1972), and Athan G. Theoharis, *The Yalta Myths* (Columbia, Mo., 1970).

Specific issues receive coverage in Richard O. Davies, *Housing Reform during the Truman Administration* (Columbia, Mo., 1966); Davis R. B. Ross, *Preparing for Ulysses* (New York, 1969); Stephen K. Bailey, *Congress Makes a Law: The Story behind the Employment Act of 1946* (New York, 1950); Allen F. Matusow, *Farm Policies and Politics in the Truman Administration* (Cambridge, Mass., 1967); Reo Christenson, *The Brannan Plan: Farm Politics and Policy* (Ann Arbor, 1959); R. Alton Lee, *Truman and Taft-Hartley* (Lexington, 1966); Arthur F. McClure, *The Truman Administration and the Problems of Postwar Labor* (Rutherford, N.J., 1969); Grant McConnell, *The Steel Seizure of 1952* (University, Ala., 1960). Barton J. Bernstein has written several significant articles on reconversion; especially noteworthy is "The Truman Administration and Its Reconversion Wage Policy," *Labor History* 6 (Fall, 1965): 214–231, and consult either edition of *The Truman Period as a Research Field* for a full listing. On economic problems and policies, see A. E. Holmans, *United States Fiscal Policy, 1945–1959* (London, 1961); Bert G. Hickman, *Growth and Stability of the Postwar Economy* (Washington, 1960); Herbert Stein, *The Fiscal Revolution in America* (Chicago, 1969); Edward S. Flash, Jr., *Economic Advice and Presidential Leadership: The Council of Economic Advisers* (New York, 1965); C. A. Blyth, *American Business Cycles, 1945–1950* (New York, 1969).

The best and most comprehensive study of civil rights and minority problems during the Truman years is Donald R. McCoy and Richard

T. Ruetten, *Quest and Response* (Lawrence, Kan., 1973). Other significant works are William C. Berman, *The Politics of Civil Rights in the Truman Administration* (Columbus, O., 1970); Richard M. Dalfiume, *Desegregation of the U.S. Armed Forces* (Columbia, Mo., 1969); Barton J. Bernstein, "The Ambiguous Legacy: The Truman Administration and Civil Rights" in Bernstein, ed., *Politics and Policies of the Truman Administration* (Chicago, 1970); Harvard Sitkoff, "Harry Truman and the Election of 1948: The Coming of Age of Civil Rights in American Politics," *Journal of Southern History* 37 (November 1971): 597–616.

The problems of civil liberties have received extensive coverage. On loyalty-security matters and the rise of McCarthyism, see, in addition to Alan Harper, *The Politics of Loyalty* (Westport, Conn., 1969), Eleanor Bontecou, *The Federal Loyalty-Security Program* (Ithaca, 1953); Richard P. Longaker, *The President and Individual Liberties* (Ithaca, 1961); Athan G. Theoharis, *Seeds of Repression: Harry S. Truman and the Origins of McCarthyism* (Chicago, 1971); two articles by Theoharis, "The Rhetoric of Politics" and "The Escalation of the Loyalty Program," both in Bernstein, ed., *Politics and Policies of the Truman Administration;* Richard M. Freeland, *The Truman Doctrine and the Origins of McCarthyism* (New York, 1972); Earl Latham, *The Communist Controversy in Washington: From the New Deal to McCarthy* (Cambridge, Mass., 1966). Focusing more specifically on McCarthy and McCarthyism are Richard Rovere, *Senator Joe McCarthy* (New York, 1959); Robert Griffith, *The Politics of Fear* (Lexington, Ky., 1970); Daniel Bell, ed., *The Radical Right* (Garden City, N.Y., 1963); and Michael Paul Rogin, *The Intellectuals and McCarthy: The Radical Specter* (Cambridge, Mass., 1967).